ACCESS YOUR ONLINE RESOURCES

Creating an Anti-Racist Curriculum for Children with Special Educational Needs is accompanied by a printable audit, designed to ensure this resource best supports your professional needs

Go to https://resourcecentre.routledge.com/speechmark and click on the cover of this book

Answer the question prompt using your copy of the book to gain access to the online content.

"In modern Britain, the importance of being an anti-racist school is paramount. Priya is at the forefront of this mission, embedding anti-racist values that challenge biases and celebrate the contributions of Black, Asian and other ethnic minority communities."

– **Sheetal Smith-Batish**, School Senior Leader

"This book is a compelling call to action for educators and school leaders committed to transforming their curriculum into one that reflects and celebrates the diversity of today's classrooms. Bhagrath skilfully unpacks topics such as cultural competency, intersectionality, and the critical role of leadership, making it an essential guide for all SEN schools seeking to build an educational environment where students, regardless of race or ability, feel noticed and valued. This is not just a book – it's a timely roadmap for meaningful change in our schools."

– **Dr Mike Baldwin**, SEND teacher and author

"Priya's powerful narrative not only highlights the pressing issues but also inspires hope and action, fuelling our collective efforts towards a more inclusive and equitable educational landscape [...] offers invaluable insights and practical strategies for schools, making it a must-read for educators, parents, and individuals interested in this field [...]. An indispensable resource."

– **Frances Akinde, Education Advisor**, SEND consultant and author of *Be an Ally, not a Bystander*

CREATING AN ANTI-RACIST CURRICULUM FOR CHILDREN WITH SPECIAL EDUCATIONAL NEEDS

This thought-provoking and experience-led book guides teachers and leaders to create anti-racist practices and to develop a curriculum for children with SEND, promoting cultural representation and giving all pupils a voice and a sense of belonging.

Informative and practical chapters challenge the reader to review their whole school system and policies, taking them on a step-by-step journey through three main parts. The book enables educators to understand how this work can be meaningfully applied when working with SEND pupils and families in all settings, with topics covered including:

- exploring what an anti-racist curriculum is and why it's needed for pupils with SEND
- establishing buy-in from school staff and meaningful support from key stakeholders
- creating an action plan and establishing accountability
- providing opportunities for high-quality CPD for all stakeholders
- how to create a cultural calendar and curriculum offer of representation
- developing whole school practices to link to home and the community
- preparing pupils for life beyond school.

Pupils with SEND can access complicated topics if the subject matter is presented in a way that makes sense to them, with purpose, clarity and relevance to their lives. This book provides essential content and guidance for professionals to follow and implement for the benefit of SEND pupils and will be key reading for educators working in mainstream education, additional resource provisions, SMEH provisions and special schools.

Priya Bhagrath is the Headteacher at Bishopswood Special School in Oxfordshire, UK. She has over 20 years of experience as a teacher and senior leader in mainstream and SEND schools. She has also worked as a Specialist Leader in Education and set up an Outstanding Additional Resource Provision. Priya is a co-founder and co-national leader of the BAME Education SEND hub, launched in 2023, and a South-East regional lead for Women's Education.

CREATING AN ANTI-RACIST CURRICULUM FOR CHILDREN WITH SPECIAL EDUCATIONAL NEEDS

Moving Beyond Saris, Samosas and Steel Drums

Priya Bhagrath

LONDON AND NEW YORK

Designed cover image: Getty Images

First published 2025
by Routledge
4 Park Square, Milton Park, Abingdon, Oxon OX14 4RN

and by Routledge
605 Third Avenue, New York, NY 10158

Routledge is an imprint of the Taylor & Francis Group, an informa business

© 2025 Priya Bhagrath

The right of Priya Bhagrath to be identified as author of this work has been asserted in accordance with sections 77 and 78 of the Copyright, Designs and Patents Act 1988.

All rights reserved. The purchase of this copyright material confers the right on the purchasing institution to photocopy or download pages which bear the support material icon and a copyright line at the bottom of the page. No other parts of this book may be reprinted or reproduced or utilised in any form or by any electronic, mechanical, or other means, now known or hereafter invented, including photocopying and recording, or in any information storage or retrieval system, without permission in writing from the publishers.

Trademark notice: Product or corporate names may be trademarks or registered trademarks, and are used only for identification and explanation without intent to infringe.

British Library Cataloguing-in-Publication Data
A catalogue record for this book is available from the British Library

ISBN: 9781032542768 (hbk)
ISBN: 9781032542751 (pbk)
ISBN: 9781003416081 (ebk)

DOI: 10.4324/9781003416081

Typeset in Interstate
by codeMantra

Access the Support Material: https://resourcecentre.routledge.com/speechmark

Dedicated to
Saffron Zuri and Mahi Ellara
May you always have the courage to fight and speak your truth,
and the wisdom to know when to lay down your bow.
I hope you always know your worth.

Amarjit, my partner and greatest inspiration.
Thank you for your unwavering encouragement, support,
and belief in me throughout the years.
This wouldn't have been possible without you.
Thank you for always being my safest place.

Mum, Dad, Nanna and Arjun
For teaching me the value and importance of education, and the doors it opens.
You instilled in me a fight, and a right, to earn a seat at the table.
Our family table continues to be a place of debate, challenge, and growth.

And finally, to all of the children and parents,
"Your children are not your children.
They are the sons and daughters of Life's longing for itself.
They come through you but not from you,
And though they are with you yet they belong not to you.
You may give them your love but not your thoughts,
For they have their own thoughts.
You may house their bodies but not their souls,
For their souls dwell in the house of tomorrow, which you cannot visit, not even in your dreams.
You may strive to be like them, but seek not to make them like you.
For life goes not backward nor tarries with yesterday.
You are the bows from which your children as living arrows are sent forth.
The archer sees the mark upon the path of the infinite, and He bends you with His might that His arrows may go swift and far.
Let your bending in the archer's hand be for gladness;
For even as He loves the arrow that flies, He also loves the bow that is stable."

Khalil Gibran

CONTENTS

Acknowledgements   *xiii*
Foreword   *xiv*

Part I
Roots of inequity: Systemic barriers and cultural perspectives   1

    Introduction: Racism, disability and the unspoken struggles in education   3

1   What is an anti-racist curriculum, and why is it needed in a SEND school?   24

2   How can leaders start this work by ensuring it is purposeful?   40

3   How do you establish buy-in and support from the teachers and support staff?   53

4   What does an anti-racist curriculum mean to parents of SEND children?   61

Part II
Collaborative action: Empowering communities and schools   79

5   Ensuring your community is informed to resist racism, empower change and shape an inclusive society   81

6   How to create allyship with colleagues   99

Part III
Shaping futures: Transforming the curriculum and preparing students for lifelong success   111

7   A window and mirror: How to create a curriculum offer of multicultural representation   113

8   How to create a cultural calendar to reflect your school community   136

9   Knowing the difference between multicultural experiences and anti-racist practices   145

10   How to review recruitment and retention and ensure representation within the staff community   151

11   How to review and improve the representation of all nine protected characteristics within policies and practice in SEND settings   161

xii Contents

12 How can young ethnic minority people with SEND be prepared for an intersectional life in Modern Britain post-schooling? 167

13 How to collaborate with stakeholders and the community to prepare for life beyond the school 190

14 Conclusion 201

   Index 209

ACKNOWLEDGEMENTS

A special thank you to the editors, Clare and Molly, for attending my talk at Wellington College and spotting a story. Thank you to Taylor and Francis for giving me a platform to share my work, and my story.

Dr Donna Marie Holder - Thank you for your support with this work. This one is for you, and Dace. We did it!

Some other important people who championed me along my journey, without even realising - Barbara McIntosh, Barbara Smith, Shirley Drummond and Paula Keen. And Jan Martin - the wisest person I know.

Thank you to BAME education - Penny Rabiger and Frances Akinde, for mentioning my name wherever possible, and creating opportunities.

Finally, to Mike Baldwin, for always being in my corner. Through the toughest moments, as well as celebrating the triumphs with me.

FOREWORD

It is an absolute honour to be asked to pen the foreword to this book. Priya's book delves deeply into key issues around race and special educational needs with lived as well as professional experience. Drawing from her own journey as a school leader and the racism she has endured, she offers invaluable insights and practical strategies for schools, making it a must-read for educators, parents and individuals interested in this field.

Through her lived experiences, Priya speaks candidly about the racism, isolation, systemic barriers and trauma that many face. Although at times painful to read, her openness and willingness to share her story underscores the pressing need for immediate and comprehensive systemic change to address racism and inequity. This change is crucial to ensure that young people from ethnic minority backgrounds and with SEND have improved outcomes beyond school.

As a school improvement consultant and former headteacher specialising in supporting special and mainstream schools to become more inclusive, I found this book to be an indispensable resource. Priya eloquently illuminates the challenges faced by ethnic minority educators, families and students as they navigate the UK education system in a way that is accessible to parents, carers, educators and individuals with lived experience of the SEND system in UK schools.

Her emphasis on an anti-racist curriculum, increased cultural competence and inclusive strategies is timely and essential.

This book is a must-read for everyone involved in education and those caring for children and young people with additional needs. Priya's powerful narrative not only highlights the pressing issues but also inspires hope and action, fuelling our collective efforts towards a more inclusive and equitable educational landscape.

Frances Akinde
Education Advisor, SEND consultant and
author of *Be an Ally not a Bystander*

Part I
Roots of inequity
Systemic barriers and cultural perspectives

Introduction
Racism, disability and the unspoken struggles in education

"We're not racist here ..."

The scent of prejudice

"You have to do something about these children coming into school smelling of curry… it makes you sick first thing in the morning… don't these people wash the uniforms? Who is cooking that food first thing in the morning? The smell is everywhere – it's disgusting!"

Toxic leadership and the silence of complicity

This comment was made in a leadership meeting I attended by one of the most senior staff members. They entered the room and sat around the table looking for corroboration, wafting their hand in front of their face and breaking into laughter. Another senior leader laughed and nodded along. Around the leadership table were both White and ethnic minority leaders. They all sat silent and found something more interesting to fixate their gaze upon. It took me a few minutes to comprehend what had just been said. I could not believe it. I searched the faces, thinking, "Did you hear what they just said?!"

No one met my gaze.

No one said anything.

I did not say anything.

These comments were not the last, and I strongly felt that there was a high degree of toxicity and probable racism amongst some of the senior leaders. Their attitudes towards children with additional needs and the diverse community were even worse. My experience at the school rapidly progressed into persistent verbal abuse, including being told my "face doesn't fit" and I "don't belong here". On one occasion, when I was being shouted at in an office, I tried to leave the room. I was followed, and the door slammed with my fingers still in the frame.

I gathered the courage to speak up and followed the process to governors. There was no interest, follow-up, or action. I was distraught, as I had such high hopes for the role and the work I was doing with the children and families. I left the school and thought I would leave the experience behind and move on. But like an oil spill, there were severe, messy, lasting effects in my shorter- and longer-term life. I felt punished for speaking up.

The struggles for leadership and career progression

My career aspirations were set early on in my career. I pivoted away from pursuing a career as an educational psychologist towards wanting to pursue headship, as I genuinely love working with children and their families. I am so committed to seeing a child make progress from their starting points, and I am so aspirational for them to be successful in whatever that means for an individual child. I am motivated by being involved in the journeys of their parents and families as we all grow in our understanding of their children, celebrate their successes and join together to troubleshoot when things aren't going too well. It really is a joy and privilege to work in Special Educational Needs and Disability (SEND) settings.

However, I saw ethnic minority role models and colleagues apply for senior positions throughout the years but fail. Or there would be some "issue" in their workplace, bullying, capability or some other kind of barrier that would force them to sidestep or, sometimes, leave education instead of advance and flourish. I had chased a more senior leadership position for years but was always "pipped to the post" or "needed more experience". I thought if I had just gained another qualification, if I was the best in the room, maybe that might secure the roles for me. I was almost always the most qualified candidate with an MA in Special Needs, SENCO qualification, experience in SEN schools, and a specialist leader of resource provisions. Yet others surpassed me.

The feedback from leadership interviews was always re-packaged but, in a similar vein, only something tangible or substantial. Feedback such as "smile more" resulted in attending interviews and ensuring I punctuated every sentence with a beaming smile, usually at a panel of middle-aged White men.

I wanted to scream that I was not smiling because I was filled with anxiety and stress from the horrendous racist experience that I had. I was on high alert – preparing myself for any untoward comment while trying desperately hard to prove my worth.

Speaking up in this school and flagging the prejudiced comments made by the leaders caused me to develop a reputation of being a "live wire". Miller and Lashley (2022) found that there are several factors affecting leaders of colour exiting the profession, including "bullying from peers and supervisors, toxic school cultures, racism, lack of support and the creation of a disabling environment for school leaders of colour".

While I remained confident in my knowledge and skills of teaching pupils with SEND, I lost confidence in my contributions and interactions with others. I retreated, became paranoid and scared to use my voice. Still, the residue of fear remaining with me was somehow being perceived as overconfidence, or perhaps an air of being unapproachable. I feared the label attributed to me by people who were not even working in that school or did not know the scope of the awfulness. The experience stayed with me for a long time and left a scar that has taken a long time to heal and fade. Only when you are in a place of safety and security can you look back with the lens of hindsight and realise that it all was not "just in your head".

It was only recently, and leading the work that led to this book, that I could process and fully make sense of the experience at this school. Through attending various equality and diversity workshops, creating an "anti-racist curriculum" or listening to the experiences of fellow Black and Minority Ethnic (BAME) educators in the UK, I finally felt a colossal weight lifted from my shoulders that it was not "just me" being "difficult". I felt a sense of belonging. A sense of alignment, and clarity - a completely different lens to view my experience. The jigsaw pieces effortlessly slot together.

As my career progressed, I initially felt immense gratitude for being appointed to the position. I was grateful that someone had offered me the opportunity when I had seen so many other colleagues not promoted. I did not want to rock the boat while internally scared in case anything was to go wrong. I invested in a coach to help me identify these lingering feelings and to help me work through feelings of inadequacy. Her coaching has provided a secure foundation from which my leadership abilities and confidence have flourished – and she has helped me immeasurably to gain clarity, perspective and belief in myself.

Before the coaching, I kept my head low for years after the experience. I was anxious that if I continued to raise awareness, I would never be presented with other opportunities. Early in my career, it was already so evident that doors did not open easily for ethnic minority teachers. I did not want my career to stagnate.

When I was younger, and I watched films centred around the British Raj such as "Lagaan", internally I would struggle with the lack of loyalty by the Indian soldiers, in cahoots with the English soldiers as the country was stripped of the tapestry of riches, spice and fabrics. I recall not understanding that mentality – how could you not look out for your own? My paternal grandad fought for India's independence; my father fought for equality in the Southall Youth Movement in the late 1970s and early 1980s. Yet, I gained some semblance of empathy and understanding through my experience and viewing these soldiers' positions differently. Where social and economic opportunities and standing are unevenly distributed, you take opportunities where you can or where you are able, "allowed" even, to succeed and advance.

Current education research demonstrates similar aspects of "gatekeeping" and barriers to progression. There are opportunities in education to advance into leadership, opportunities that allow sharing your philosophies, but also allow for social and economic mobility. However, research shows that White teachers are consistently over-represented across all stages of the teaching roles, including leadership and headship. Ethnic minority teachers

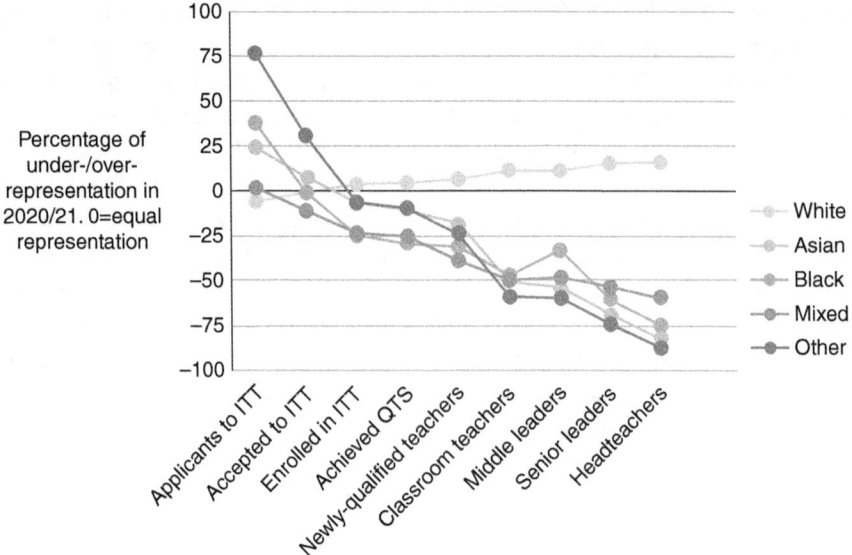

Figure 0.1 Career progression of teachers, per ethnicity

Adapted from Worth, McLean and Sharp (2022)

fail to follow the same upward trajectory of success. They are under-represented in all categories, with an observable and widening gap between progressive opportunities into leadership, senior leadership and headship, a stark disparity observable from their Initial Teacher Training applications.

Worth, McLean and Sharp (2022) reported that "In 2020/21, 60% of schools in England had an all-White teaching staff and 86% had an all-White senior leadership team". UCL (2020) found this applicable, even in ethnically diverse communities. The diversity gaps in areas with high ethnic populations are striking, as although the pupil population is more diverse, the teacher workforce, despite also being more ethnically diverse in these areas, remains predominantly and overwhelmingly White.

In research published by Sharp and Aston (2024), the reasons for this disparity are unpacked. Reasons include underlying sources of bias in favour of White applicants, negative experiences of ethnic minority teachers in Initial Teacher Training and classroom teachers, as well as a lack of retention. The main reasons identified tend to fall within these three parts:

1. Covert racism
   Ethnic minority teachers have a higher workload and face overt and covert racial discrimination from staff, pupils, and parents
2. Disillusionment
   Ethnic minority teachers feel disillusionment with their ability to make a difference for pupils from ethnic minority backgrounds and

3. Lack of recognition and opportunity
   Ethnic minority teachers need better talent management and more progression opportunities.

Worth, McLean and Sharp (2022) found that teachers, middle leaders and senior leaders are "significantly less likely to be promoted to middle, senior leadership and headship positions than their White counterparts". Miller (2019) in Sharp and Aston (2024) identifies three ways in which ethnic minority teachers respond to this lack of progression:

1. assimilation,
2. appeasement, and
3. group membership, including adjusting their behaviour to fit in.

Ethnic minority teachers may downplay part of their culture and experiences that are different to the majority or keep quiet for fear of expressing views that might not be well received. As a result, teachers from minority groups experience more symptoms of stress and poor mental health.

Therefore, it is not difficult to understand that securing one of my earlier senior leadership positions was genuinely thrilling. I was excited to work alongside teachers and develop the knowledge, understanding and skills required to promote inclusion in their classes. I was not fazed by some of the teachers' lack of experience or their lack of sense of responsibility or accountability for the children with special education needs in their classes. I felt privileged to have been afforded the opportunity.

The school was a mainstream school in a predominantly ethnic minority community. I could make a difference here.

One of my earliest teaching experiences had been working in a SEND school, supporting Autistic children with Severe Learning Disabilities (SLD). Due to the complexity of needs, these children's needs were identified early on, either at birth or shortly after, within their first few years. We would receive the families that had been through the identification process. They understood their child had additional needs and would require additional support from a particular school. They had experienced the initial shock, possibly grieving and sorrow for the loss of the "normal child" they had expected, but on route to developing their understanding of how to meet their child's needs (Kearney and Griffin, 2001).

Bronfenbrenner (1994, in Akbar, 2019) and the ecological model is a framework for understanding multiple levels of influence on an individual's development. The framework comprises five nested systems: microsystem, mesosystem, exosystem, macrosystem and chronosystem. Akbar (2019), in her work on "Understanding the Experiences of minority ethnic heritage parents who have a child with Special Educational Needs and Disability (SEND)", adopts the framework and applies it to reflect the experiences of the ethnic minority parent of a SEND child and the barriers they may face within each strand of the framework.

8 Creating an Anti-Racist Curriculum for Children with Special Educational Needs

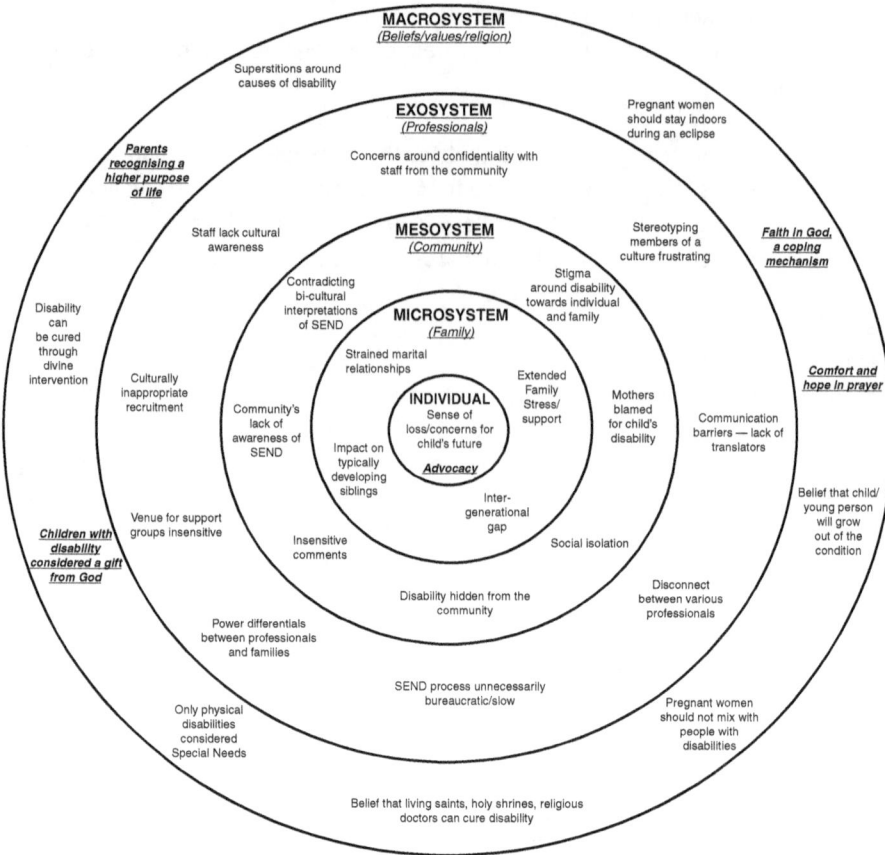

Figure 0.2 Ecological framework: Levels of influence on SEND development

Adapted from Akbar (2019)

Exosystem: Professionals

In reviewing Akbar's interpretation of Bronfenbrenner's framework, I reflect that I considered I could provide some level of impact in this mainstream school within the "exosystem" on two levels. The exosystem encompasses relationships between the school and home, levels of interaction and engagement. First, I was bringing a unique set of skills to a mainstream school, having worked in a SLD SEND school. Parents of children with SEND in mainstream schools often report a lack of support and signposting from mainstream staff, sometimes including their SENDCOs (Special Educational Needs and Disability Co-ordinators).

Nasen (2019), in their "Whole School SEND: Review Guide", identifies that "schools and SENCOs often lack training in cultural competence", which can result in misunderstandings and inadequate support for ethnic minority families. This is supported by previous research conducted by Contact a Family (2014); they identified that many parents feel SENCOs do not provide sufficient information or guidance on the support available for their children. Parents can, therefore, feel isolated and unsure about how to advocate for their child's needs.

Second, numerous research indicate that many ethnic minority parents face additional barriers in accessing and navigating not only the education system but also the SEND processes due to cultural and language barriers. This can lead to reduced engagement and, perhaps, the child receiving less adequate support than could be available. As these families cannot access information easily, they begin to withdraw. These families, in turn, become labelled as "hard to reach" by schools, and very few schools consider their responses to increasing engagement from these parents. I felt that by working in a diverse community, I could offer a semblance of support and information and use my additional language skills (however basic!) to help parents.

SEND schools are established with solid and positive practices and processes to support the parents in this "exosystem". These may include substantial support for the child transitioning to a SEND school, workshops and information provided to parents on developing communication, support behaviour, toilet training, and so on. Information on the bespoke curriculum is offered to meet the child's every need, from communication to independence. Parents are encouraged to support one another through coffee mornings, forming contacts and connections. For some, these form a lifeline of support for one another.

Leaders and teachers are trained and experienced to support parents on their emotional journeys, and together they quickly establish a way to understand and support each child through collaboration. In the best schools, it is understood that those with English as an additional language may need further support in accessing and applying the information, so specific groups are established, for example, Somali parents groups and Pakistani Parents groups, as they can provide safe spaces for shared experiences, providing spaces to address unique cultural and educational needs and provide empowerment and advocacy, especially if language is the main barrier.

The early identification, assessment and diagnosis process can be exceptionally challenging for parents to navigate, comprehend or ask the right questions. While most schools and SENDCOs try to be supportive and implement effective strategies to support children with identified additional needs, adequate signposting and support for families from local authorities through the identification and assessment process is limited. It is evident that there is a great deal of work to do within the "exosystem" at school levels and where we can effect change through policy and curriculum innovation. We will explore this further as the book progresses.

There are also broader issues within the "exosystem", which highlight broader social systems that affect the individuals' experiences, such as accessing resources or information. For all parents, navigating these systems is incredibly challenging. For ethnic minority parents with language barriers, it can be impossible. The Children's Commissioner, on 26 June 2023, identified that there is an increase of initial Education Health Care Plans (EHCP) applications by 23% between 2021 and 2023, and the total number of children with EHCP has risen by 9.5%. However, only 51% of EHCPs were issued within the 20-week legal deadline, and this rate varies according to where you are in the UK, with East Midlands at 32% and London at 63%. It is essential to consider that there are frustrated parents on the other side of this process who are usually attempting to navigate this process, desperately seeking information, and navigating delays, usually entirely alone.

There is a need for further work to bridge the gap and restore feelings of trust and support, as well as the belief that the support children receive in schools meets their individual needs and allows for success. A recent article, "Children with special needs are being failed. Parents have a right to be furious", in *The Independent* (May 2023), clearly recognises parents' challenges in accessing and interpreting the SEND systems. It also stated that those parents who persistently navigate the stormy waters of the SEND world are labelled as "difficult" or "angry" for their consistent efforts in forcing responses from the local authorities and advocating for their children. These parents are in danger of becoming stigmatised and isolated, which could be a factor in the high rates of pupil absenteeism.

Throughout my 20-year career spanning various educational settings, including mainstream schools, Additional Resource Provisions, and special schools, I have repeatedly encountered parents from all racial backgrounds who struggle to navigate the "exosystem". From initial calls for assessment, there is a lack of knowledge and awareness of the potential diagnosis and what this means regarding schooling and their child's life outcome. Parents often feel overwhelmed by a colossal lack of timely information and updates, coupled with an inability to secure the outcomes they want for their children due to underfunding. They also tend to experience ineffective communication due to a severely high staff turnover within local authority SEND departments and SEND officers. Parents often feel overwhelmed by a lack of communication, support and understanding from local authorities, which schools try to bridge. These barriers may then contribute towards a lack of engagement within the mesosystems provided within schools.

But what about parents and carers from ethnic minority communities, with English as a second language, or those new to the country? How do they navigate these complex and multi-layered processes and systems?

Mir (2008) identifies ethnic minority communities as having "poor knowledge of available services, poor standards of communication, experience delays in diagnosis and treatment, isolation, poor access to services and benefits, high levels of stress amongst parents and have significant unmet needs which contribute to mental health challenges". Burke and Cole, in "Reaching out to people with learning disabilities and their families from Black and Minority Ethnic communities" (2012), also confirm that ethnic minority families struggle with accessing the correct information, and those with the most limited English continue to be the most vulnerable. Ethnic minority families are unaware of available services or how to access and navigate them. When they access some support, they assume the services "talk" to one another and automatically share information, "as a result, people wait for support to come to them, which does not materialise".

Miller (2022) identifies prolonged, historical and multi-layered inadequacies in the UK education system's persistent failure to address the significant disparity between the intersectional groups of race and disability. In her 2023 article "Double jeopardy: When race meets special educational needs", Akinde states that "parents of children from marginalised backgrounds often report that schools are dismissive or unsupportive of their requests for information and help. Their requests are often ignored unless they understand how to push for support. Concerns minimalised." This echoes the work of Akbar (2019), who found that minority groups "showed a predominantly negative experience of professional services, due to cultural dissonance, perceived stereotyping and perceived power imbalances between the ethnic heritage families and professionals who are most likely to be from, or to be perceived as representing the majority culture".

Slade (2014), in The National Autistic Society's report titled "Diverse perspectives: The challenges for families affected by Autism from Black, Asian and Minority Ethnic communities", supports these series of challenges faced by the community, including "challenges getting a diagnosis, barriers in accessing support services, communication problems with professionals, awareness and understanding of autism within communities and denial and isolation".

A 2022 survey conducted by "The Special Needs Jungle" indicated that "racial discrimination and unconscious bias are everyday experiences for disabled children and their families from ethnic and marginalised communities. Parents say they, and their children, are visibly less well-treated, and schools disregard their needs and culture…" The study also highlights that "there is a lack of representation of non-white staff and leaders".

Ethnic minority families, especially those with English as an additional language, can sometimes be lost entirely, wading through complicated processes, hugely reliant on professionals working efficiently and ongoing communication to speed through deadlines. Parents can lack awareness of the processes without apparent attempts to communicate to the families through translators or translated material. Due to the challenges in collaborating with parents, it has become a longstanding aim to provide as many school tours for parents as possible, as this usually serves as the first port of call for families. Parents can freely ask questions, seek information, and receive signposting. However, this has sometimes resulted in some genuinely challenging situations, especially if they needed somewhere else to turn to for advice.

For families in the early stages of SEND identification, whose children are unable to continue at nursery or Reception due to challenging behaviours, the situation can be deeply frustrating. Their child may be placed on a reduced timetable as the school struggles to meet their needs, and the local authority may take too long to find an alternative setting. Many families attend school tours, desperate for help or any information. It is common for parents to repeatedly call the school and seek advice on the process or schools as they struggle to contact their SEND officer within the local authority.

On one occasion, a mother from an ethnic minority community with limited English and unknown to the school, arrived at the gates of a school I was working in, holding her young daughter's hand, pleading with the school to offer a place to her child. She did not know "how it worked" or who to contact for help. In her 2022 article for SEN magazine, titled "Navigating the EHCP labyrinth", Fitzgibbons (2022) identifies that the EHCP process "contains a plethora of documents to read and sign. Most... are time-consuming, complicated, and even intimidating". Is it any wonder why some ethnic minority communities and parents feel so alienated from this process? Families from ethnic minority communities are less likely to receive support, signposting, and guidance on a truly complex system.

Taking on one of my earlier senior leader roles within a diverse community felt meaningful, and I wanted to make an impact. I stayed on for as long as I did, despite the behaviour I experienced, partly out of fear of sabotaging my career but mostly because I loved serving this community.

Mesosystem: Community

Not long after I started at the school, parents would speak to me in the playground or meetings in Punjabi or Hindi, communicating that they had yet to feel heard or supported. They were excited to see "one of their own in a leadership position", and they championed me. It became apparent that those parents with the most limited English formed their cliques, congregating together and forming their sub-groups in the playground depending on their first language. This is where they shared information about the school, asked questions and sought clarity. The community was desperate for leaders from a minority background or a leader who demonstrated empathy and allyship.

The school served as one of the largest estates in West London, comprised of prefabricated and concrete buildings. In the 1980s, the population was made up of new residents from the homeless person units and those recently released from the local psychiatric hospital. Many residents were from ethnic minority backgrounds, as the borough was close to an airport and had a well-established Indian and Caribbean community. The broader backdrop of the community saw historic, large-scale divides between the ethnic minority community and the National Front, with racist riots, attacks and violence being every day and commonplace in the late 1970s and early to mid-1980s. Racial tension and crime were rife. Over 70% of residents surveyed at the time were afraid to go out due to racial harassment; local pubs, youth centres and clubs excluded those from minority backgrounds.

I was born into this community. A child of two star-crossed lovers of different religions who eloped and married at a young age, at that time much to the shame of their respective families. My parents, at 19 and 21, found themselves disowned and, for a brief period, homeless. I was born into this estate. They frequently recount stories of their time in school, running home as soon as the bells sounded, as they were sure to be targeted, and physically and verbally assaulted on their journey home. They spoke of the infamous Southall race riots, the formation of the Southall Youth Movement and my dad's involvement in fighting for the community's rights and equality.

We were not there for long, though. My parents' affluent families extended "forgiveness" and helped them move towards a more middle-class lifestyle, crossing the bridge out of the area to the Whiter, intensely racist, outer-London boroughs.

I have worked in some of the most picturesque and affluent areas across the country – streets lined with Farrow and Ball-painted front doors, curated with wreaths that hang year-round, and where crime feels like a distant rumour. I will never forget the sense of belonging, warmth and acceptance that I felt working in this rough corner of London. The people who wore their lives on their faces, etched deep into their lines from hard days. A melting pot of humanity, the rawness of some of their stories, the shock of life circumstances, and realness, moving together in a desperate rhythm that cannot be explained.

They were on my side and championed me to succeed – one of their own had "made it", they would tell me. I came back to the place I had been born and felt I was giving back to this community, which had homed so many of my family, created their identities and given them the struggles and wings to grow and move on. I loved working there.

Navigating the dual stigma: Ethnic minority families and special educational needs

I was fervently discouraged from becoming a SEND teacher. Even more bewildering was my desire to work in a community my family had moved away from so long ago. A family intervention from my mother, aunts and cousins tried to convince me to pursue law, as they were sure that my opinionated and strong-willed attitude would lend itself well to this career. Not to mention the status, title and potential earnings. As is typical in most Indian families, money and status are second to none, but on equal footing with milky complexions, being tall and blessed with good looks. There was no having one without the other. And do not dare eat that second samosa at an Indian wedding if you are packing a few extra pounds…

It is, in general, a hugely judgemental culture. Think *Bend it like Beckham*: "You've become so dark playing in the sun!"

When I insisted on pursuing my route into SEND, the resounding statements eventually surmised: "Ah well, at least you'll do good in this life and get lots of god's blessings".

I remember my grandmother telling me how children with SEND are disregarded in India and how only the most fortunate, and those from wealthy families, will access any form of educational experience. The others would "not see the light of day". She spoke of how having a child with SEND, in some families in India, was regarded as "bad fortune" and that it was seen that the parents must have done something terrible in their previous lives to have a child with additional needs. I was horrified. How could the thinking across cultures be so vastly different? As my career progressed and my experiences from working in both predominantly ethnic minority communities or majority White, I realised that in most cases, this was the thinking demonstrated amongst ethnic minority families, and with some consistency.

Since the start of my career in SEND, it has been a common occurrence when I have met with parents from ethnic minority communities as a SENDco to either initially indicate that their child may have additional needs or to communicate during admissions meetings and welcoming them to a new school that further assessments were required or SEND schools; I am almost always met with parents clarifying their child's potential. A pure demonstration of hope that their child will, someday, "grow out of it". Their child might attend university, attend a mainstream secondary school or get married and have children. The hope is always palpable.

I have yet to experience a non-ethnic minority family asking these same questions.

However, there does seem to be an emerging disparity between these parents and more educated, informed, or younger minority parents. There is emerging knowledge, acceptance and desire for home and school to work together towards shared aspirations. Sometimes, parents demonstrate more awareness and acceptance of their child's needs but may be influenced by the opinions of grandparents or older relatives who may live with the family.

Macrosystem: Beliefs, values and religion

Fatmilehin and Nadirshaw (1994) identify a range of essential distinctions in the perception, attitudes and actions of families from Asian and White British backgrounds related to disability. Asian families were more likely to "have had contact with a holy person, were less aware of what their child's 'problem' is called, believed in spiritual causes for their child's disability, believed religion provided explanation for disability and wanted care for child to be provided by a relative when they were no longer able to provide it themselves". White British families however, "received a medical explanation for their child's disability, knew the cause of their child's disability and what it was called. Their religion offered social support, but they wanted their child to be cared for in a community home provided by statutory services." It could, therefore, be considered that minority parents can lack access to the same levels of information both at diagnosis and after compared to White families. They seek to make up this knowledge wherever they can, and usually rely on other families for this information.

However, O'Hara (2014) states that there *is* a difference in the interpretation of disability between the Western and Eastern cultures; for example, "Many Chinese people believe in fate and… seek supernatural power and praying to their ancestors" when a child is diagnosed with a disability (Cheng and Tang, 1995 in O'Hara, 2013). Middle Eastern cultures also believe that "disability is a punishment from heaven… caused by an evil eye". Ingstad and Whyte (1995) identify similar trends in the traditional beliefs within African communities, whereby "disabilities can be perceived as a curse, punishment, or a result of witchcraft".

In some instances, there is a failure to accept disability and a sense of perhaps "fixing" the diagnosed need or some form of treatment to allow reversal is offered by community members. As identified by Hatton and colleagues (2004), upon diagnosis, some South Asian families receive reassurance from their wider community that "they will be perfectly fine when they are older" or "they will be normal, don't worry". However, this is juxtaposed with the other traditional viewpoints, in that parents are blamed for the disability, with comments such as "There are no other children like this in the family, so why has this happened to you?" or "You didn't look after yourself properly when you were pregnant, and this is why you have a child with a disability".

There are similarities between the traditional views of South Asian and African communities in that faith-based healing and cures can be sought. Hatton et al. (2004) identify that religion is vital in South Asian families, and they "pray to god to accept the burden". Desperate parents can be encouraged by their community to see traditional healers in private, who may tell them: "You should have come sooner, as now, it's too late, and nothing can be done". Cochrane (2011) identifies similar trends in the South African community; however, there is more "faith-based healing" and hope that "divine intervention, through community healing prayers, will cure disability". As religious leaders hold prominent roles within the community, they promote "miraculous healing and encourage congregations to seek spiritual cures".

South Asian communities can shun children with disabilities as if they can be transmitted to other children. Some parents report being told that new babies were knowingly kept away from a child with additional needs in case the "bad luck was transmitted" and that "you must have done something in a previous life for this to happen to you" or "my friend thought it was a jinn (evil spirit)" (Hatton et al., 2004).

"Curing" autism

Throughout my career, I have encountered many desperate parents contemplating a range of measures to "fix" their child, from changing their diet and following Ayurvedic meals with the aim to negate any challenging behaviour to considering "corrective surgery" on tongues and mouths to promote speaking and cure autism. A more recent "fix" became mainstream after appearing on the BBC news on 17 April 2024 with headlines that "Met police investigates 'stem-cell autism cure' claim".

The "cures" can range from every day (e.g., drinking holy water) to being quite intrusive and extreme. O'Hara (2018) identifies that in some Asian cultures, there is "an important misconception about learning disability held by Asian parents is the notion of curability and that the marriage of the person with a learning disability may alleviate the condition". She argues that a degree of "cultural competence" is essential for staff in bridging the divide between ethnic minority communities and providing a level of education on SEND, which informs and empowers families.

As we have explored, some families share that they initially refuse to acknowledge their child's additional needs in the hope that "they will grow out of it". Ethnic minority communities can feel that they must not share their family information externally or outside of the family home. Parents can feel a sense of shame or blame themselves, which can result in a lack of accessing services which could help, leaving them further isolated.

Microsystem: Family

Sullivan and Knutson (2000) identify that families of children with additional needs and disabilities experience stress and higher divorce rates, with minority families facing exacerbated marital tensions. This is confirmed by Hartley and colleagues (2010) who found that parents of children with special needs and disabilities are more likely to experience increased stress levels and marital strain, which can lead to higher divorce rates. The cultural stigmas compound the stresses families experience, described by the lack of support from the community and additional strain caused by ongoing systemic inequalities, such as the poverty of minority parents.

The Joseph Rowntree Foundation (2016) identifies a range of alarming statistics, highlighting structural racism and the severe impact this can have at the cellular level within individual families: 49% of Pakistani families live in poverty, 53% of Bangladeshi families, 42% of African families and 28% of British Caribbean families, compared with 19% of British White families. In addition to the identified issues, ethnic minority families are, therefore, more likely to experience economic hardship, which can exacerbate the challenges of raising a child with additional needs.

It is common to hear stories of families struggling with their living conditions. The 2021 census found that Black people in England and Wales are more likely to live in social housing compared to any other group (44% of Black people living in social housing compared with 16% of White people). The National Housing Federation (2023) found that "one in every six children are living in overcrowded homes with no personal space and that households from ethnic minority backgrounds are three times more likely to be affected". Government figures indicate that 1.7% of White British households were overcrowded, compared with 22.5% of Bangladeshi, 17% Arab and 16% Black African families. The research also highlights that "Black people are more than three times more likely than White people to experience homelessness in England" and that "Pakistani and Bangladeshi households face greater risks of homelessness than Indian and other Asian groups".

Furthermore, the Institute of Race Relations (2024) has identified that ethnic minority workers are 2.2 times more likely to face unemployment than White workers. In 2023, ethnic minority unemployment rates were 7%, compared with 3.2% for White workers. These figures increase when intersectional factors are added; for example, unemployment in ethnic minority women was 7.8% compared with 2.8% for White workers.

The impact of this structural inequality is visible through analysis of comparative statistics reviewing mental health and stress per racial group. Bains and Gutman (2021) state that Pakistani, Bangladeshi and Black Caribbean children experience more internalised problems than White children. Bignall and colleagues (2019) found that Black men are "ten times more likely than White men to experience a psychotic disorder".

Additionally, ethnic minority families are less likely to seek external respite care in caring for their child with additional needs, relying on extended families, such as grandparents, aunts and uncles, to support with caregiving. Hatton and colleagues (2004) identify that although family and friends could provide essential emotional, practical and financial support and mitigate some of the stresses and challenges in caring for a child with SEND, in some cultures, due to perceptions of special needs and disability, this support is not always forthcoming. Mir and colleagues (2001) suggest that ethnic minority parents face ongoing "stigma within their communities, which limits the extent of the support they receive". Mir continues the argument by stating that reliance on the extended network can delay parents in seeking further external support to which they are entitled.

Working with children with SEND means supporting their families. All the staff I have met while working in schools have wanted to be there with a united passion to make a difference in the young people they teach. Supporting parents in their various stages of acquiring knowledge and developing their understanding and trust in the school can be more challenging. For some parents, it is apparent they are in the various stages of acceptance, or there are other dynamics at play, including a lack of respite, exhaustion from the sheer persistence of advocating for their child, to masking issues within their relationships and marriages, as the data indicates. In my experience, in ethnic minority communities, staff can also be fielding "when will they get better?" questions for quite some time, and, at times, well into secondary school age.

I have experienced children returning from unauthorised holidays wearing necklaces with lockets or vials to encourage healing from their identified need or to minimise any issues that could arise, such as lack of communication or reducing incidents of challenging behaviour. Some parents can become overwhelmed as their journey towards understanding and acceptance commences.

As a parent of two young daughters myself, I can only imagine the desperate grief and hope many parents must feel. In my limited experience, having suffered from severe pre-eclampsia in both of my pregnancies, with my first being in the special baby care unit as she came almost seven weeks early. I know that when it comes to the health of your loved ones, there is no greater pull to bring you to your knees and clasp your hands in prayer. Fear and hope that it will all be OK. I also know the pressure that being from the Indian community can bring, in that despite having almost fatal pre-eclampsia twice and receiving medical advice that I should not have any more children, my community has still asked me, "Oh, you must carry on trying for a boy!"

As a parent and educator, I wish that my own children and the children in my care are always happy and can fulfil their truest potential by communicating, self-regulating and becoming as functionally independent as possible.

There is no intention of judgement in this book.

There is no intent to stereotype or generalise parents of ethnic minority children with SEND. The book is intended to bring together data, research and experiences and provide a window to a community to inform and educate. This book promotes an anti-racist curriculum in SEND schools and settings but aims to dissect what the anti-racist curriculum should comprise and prioritise, unpicking why each of the identified components of the curriculum are important and describing what it would look like in this community. It is not, and should not, be about box-ticking. With the rise of courses and awards for creating anti-racist curriculums, many schools are riding the trend but only scratching the surface of this work.

A recent article in *The Guardian* (20 May 2024) by Malik entitled "The Black Lives Matter era is over: It taught us the limits of diversity for diversity's sake" unpicks the mass global movement attempts to increase "representation" in workplaces and schools and argues these may have been a surface-level response which has dwindled away, rather than a much-needed "roots and branch reform".

Leading for change: Building inclusive, anti-racist school communities

This book aims to promote and ensure that cultural representation in SEND schools and the curriculum is not tokenistic but meaningful and embedded as part of daily life. To do so, we must unpick the many layers and challenges that the intersection of ethnic minorities and SEND communities encounter within Bronfenbrenner's five spheres.

To do this, we must understand what race, religion and culture mean to any family and collective group. We need to support the isolation which can be felt by parents due to the potential and perceived cultural stigma of having a child with additional needs. We need to understand schools' power and position within the exosystem in providing a safe space for parents to celebrate their religion, culture and identities, and their children.

For some parents, supporting them to move from the shadows of pain, shame and blame into the light, where individuals are empowered with knowledge of how to help their child and, through raised aspirations, restore hope. As parents, to feel safe and have a sense of belonging, which can be restored through the school community, and through their support of one another.

We will explore the significant role schools can play for minority community groups, acting as a bridge towards inspiring collaboration and support. We will review the ways in which festivals and celebrations can be supported and adapted into meaningful learning opportunities for pupils with special needs. We will review how to celebrate the ethnic minority community and, indeed, the whole community, but with authenticity and meaning.

Along with social isolation and the lack of support that ethnic minority families can experience, either from friends and family or from accessed services, over 80% of parents report that their child experiences difficulties with eating, sleeping, bedtime, behaviour and communication. Families have little time to consider celebrating their own culture, traditions and festivals. Most of the time our families are in survival mode. So, while the book intends to unpick how to deliver an anti-racist curriculum for SEND pupils, it is important to understand some of the challenges for the ethnic minority community and identify the significant role schools can play.

We will continue reviewing research, studies, experiences and action plans. When you think about organising steel pans for Black History Month, scheduling a rotation of the dusty Diwali box with the tired, old saree being passed around as part of a sensory story or making the clay diva pots, you will have more context and cultural interpretation. You will review the teaching and learning opportunities you offer through a lens of understanding that the core of creating an anti-racist curriculum is not box-ticking, but a profound response to historical and cultural experiences, socio-economic factors, data and research spanning decades.

Each chapter has a main title heading, outlining the content of the chapters and navigating the project sequentially. At the start of each chapter and under the chapter heading is an additional epigraph, taking the form of a question. These are based on the questions, comments and concerns, which were made by the staff, as we started and progressed through leading the anti-racist work in schools. They are included to signpost the potential challenges and barriers that you can face when leading anti-racist work in schools, and support you in pre-empting your responses, as well as in action planning. The epigraphs are intended to act as signposts and alerts, or to consider alternative perspectives, as you navigate this potentially contentious work in your settings.

You are signing up not just to "jazz things up" with this book but to make deep, meaningful and lasting changes in schools - to provide support and establish a sense of belonging, pride and togetherness in fragmented, isolated and disaffected community groups.

You are signing up to be an ally.

We need to go "roots and branch" to reform our offer, reviewing historical literature on the intersectional lens of race and disability and review current data and literature to ensure we get it right for our children and families.

Note

The terms "ethnic minority" and "SEND - Special Educational Needs and Disability" are used throughout this book to explore the intersection of race and SEND. The term "SEND" is well-established in educational and legal frameworks, including the Children and Families Act 2014 and the SEND Code of Practice, to describe children and young people who require additional support in school. It is an inclusive term that encompasses all such children, including those who may be described as "neurodivergent", a category that often includes conditions like autism, dyslexia, dyspraxia and ADHD. These neurodivergent conditions represent a subset of SEND.

The terminology used to describe ethnic groups has evolved, and there are various terms in use, such as "people of colour", "racialised communities", "minority ethnic groups" and "global majority groups." The term "BAME" (Black, Asian and Minority Ethnic) has become less common due to its broadness and tendency to generalise the diverse experiences of different communities. While acknowledging that "ethnic minority" can feel reductive, as it describes groups not in the majority in the UK, it remains a commonly understood term and is used in this book for clarity and consistency.

Chapter summary

We have explored the experiences of systemic racism within educational leadership, specifically around Special Educational Needs and Disability (SEND) settings, posing pertinent questions, such as considering how your leadership team addresses racism, not just through policies, but through everyday actions and interactions. We have focused on the deeply embedded biases and challenges faced by ethnic minority educators, the cultural stigmas surrounding disability within the minority community, and the profound effects of silence in the face of racism. Through personal narrative and research, the chapter highlights the urgent need for leadership that actively challenges racism and champions the representation and inclusion of all pupils and staff.

TIFFIN TAKE-AWAY

1. **Cultural competency**
   Schools should provide targeted support that considers the cultural beliefs, values and challenges families face in navigating both the educational system and the stigma around disabilities.

   - You could consider how well your school understands and addresses the unique challenges faced by minority families with children with SEND.

2. **Representation and progression for ethnic minority staff**
   Leaders must ensure that ethnic minority staff have equal professional development and growth opportunities.

   - What structures are in place to support the progression of minority educators in your school, and how do you manage potential systemic biases?

3. **Challenging silence and complicity**
   Leaders must model courage in addressing prejudice and discrimination in their schools. Silence or complicity reinforces toxic behaviour, and school leaders must ensure the community feels safe speaking out against injustice.

   - How are you actively creating a culture where racism is reported and addressed?

References

Akbar, S. (2019) "The experiences of minority ethnic heritage parents having a child with SEND: a systematic literature review". *British Journal of Special Education*, 46(3).

Akinde, F. (2023) "Double jeopardy: When race meets special educational needs". *Teaching Times*, np.

Bains, S. and Gutman, L. (2021) "Mental health in ethnic minority populations in the UK: Developmental trajectories from early childhood to mid adolescence". *Journal of Youth and Adolescence*, 50. https://link.springer.com/article/10.1007/s10964-021-01481-5

BBC News (2024) "Met investigates 'stem-cell autism cure' claim". www.bbc.co.uk/news/uk-england-london-68759263

Bignall, T., Jeraj, S., Helsby, E. and Butt, J. (2019) "Racial disparities in mental health: Literature and evidence review". Race Equality Foundation. VCSE health and well-being alliance. https://raceequalityfoundation.org.uk/wp-content/uploads/2022/10/mental-health-report-v5-2.pdf

Cochrane, J. (2011) *When religion and health align: Mobilising religious health assets for transformation*. African Religious Health Assets Program Cluster Publications. www.academia.edu/1475490/When_Religion_and_Health_Align_Mobilising_Religious_Health_Assets_for_Transformation

Cole, A. and Burke, C. (2012) "Reaching out to people with learning disabilities and their families from Black and Minority Ethnic communities: Guidance for practitioners from social care and health services in developing culturally competent practice". Foundation for people with learning disabilities. https://carers.ripfa.org.uk/wp-content/uploads/Case_Study_5_Tool_7.pdf

Contact a family (2014) "Forgotten families: The impact of isolation on families with disabled children across the UK". https://contact.org.uk/wp-content/uploads/2021/03/forgotten_isolation_report.pdf

Fatimilehin, A. and Nadirshaw, Z. (1994) "A cross-cultural study of parental attitudes and beliefs about learning disability". *Mental Handicap Research*, 7(3): 202-227.

Fitzgibbons, S. (2022) "Navigating the EHCP labyrinth". *SEN Magazine*. https://senmagazine.co.uk/featured-articles/17520/navigating-the-ehcp-labyrinth/

Hartley, S., Barker, E., Seltzer, M., Floyd, F., Greenberg. J., Orsmond, G. and Bolt, D. (2010) "The relative risk and timing of divorce in families of children with an autism spectrum disorder". *Journal of Family Psychology*, 24(4): 449-457.

Hatton, C., Akram, Y., Shah, R., Robertson, J. and Emerson, E. (2004) *Supporting South Asian families with a child with severe learning disabilities*. Jessica Kingsley Publishers.

Ingstad, B. and Whyte, S. (1995) *Disability and culture*. University of California Press.

Institute of Race Relations (2024) "BME statistics on poverty and deprivation". https://irr.org.uk/research/statistics/poverty/

Joseph Rowntree Foundation. (2024) "Race and ethnicity". www.jrf.org.uk/race-and-ethnicity

The Independent (2023) "Children with special needs are being failed: Parents have a right to be furious". www.independent.co.uk/voices/parent-blaming-send-senco-disability-b2341278.html

Kearney, P. and Griffin, T. (2001) "Between joy and sorrow: Being a parent of a child with developmental delay". *Journal of Advanced Nursing*, 34(5): 582-592.

Malik, N., (2024) "The Black Lives Matter era is over: It taught us the limits of diversity for diversity's sake". *The Guardian*. www.theguardian.com/commentisfree/article/2024/may/20/black-lives-matter-diversity-racial-equality

Miller, P. and Lashley, R. (2022) "A report on factors responsible for and / or contribute to BAME school leaders exiting the profession or accepting a junior role". Education and Social Equity and Fig Tree International.

Mir, G. (2008) "Ethnicity and inequalities in health and social care: A race equality Foundation". *Ethnicity and Inequalities in Health and Social Care*, 1(1): 71-78.

Mir, G., Nocon, A., Ahmad, W. and Jones, L. (2001) *Learning difficulties and ethnicity*. Department of Health.

Mirza, H. and Warwick, R. (2022) "Race and ethnicity". Institute for Fiscal Studies. Nuffield Foundation. https://ifs.org.uk/sites/default/files/2022-11/Race-and-ethnicity-IFS-Deaton-Review-of-Inequalities.pdf

Miller, D. (2022) "Race, higher education and special educational needs and disabilities". British Educational Research Association. www.bera.ac.uk/publication/race-higher-education-and-special-educational-needs-and-disabilities

Nasen (2019) Whole School SEND 2018/2019 report. Department for Education. Nasen. https://asset.nasen.org.uk/wss_report_2018_2019%20%281%29_0.pdf

National Housing Federation (2023) "How diverse is England's housing association workforce in 2023?" Equality, diversity, and inclusion in housing. www.housing.org.uk/globalassets/files/edi/edi-national-data-report-a4-2023-v8-accessible–final-oct-20232.pdf

O'Hara, J. (2014) "Culture, spirituality and psychotherapy: Personal reflections from clinical practice in intellectual disability psychiatry". World Cultural Psychiatry Review. www.worldculturalpsychiatry.org/wp-content/uploads/2019/08/04-Culture-V09N2.pdf

O'Hara, J. (2018) "Learning disabilities and ethnicity: Achieving cultural competence". *Advances in Psychiatric Treatment*, 9: 166-176.

Office for National Statistics – Census 2021. www.ons.gov.uk/census

Sharp, C. and Aston, K. (2024) "Ethnic diversity in the teaching workforce: evidence review". National foundation for educational research. www.nfer.ac.uk/publications/ethnic-diversity-in-the-teaching-workforce-evidence-review/

Slade, G. (2014) "Diverse perspectives: The challenges for families affected by autism from Black, Asian and Minority ethnic communities". The National Autistic

Society. https://positiveaboutautism.co.uk/uploads/9/7/4/5/97454370/nas-diverse-perspectives-report-1.pdf

Special Needs Jungle (2022) "The casual bias and daily discrimination faced by disabled children and their families from ethnic and marginalised communities". www.specialneedsjungle.com/casual-bias-discrimination-children-families-send-ethnic-marginalised-communities/

Sullivan, P. and Knutson, J. (2000) "Maltreatment and disabilities: A population-based epidemiological study". *Child Abuse Neglect*, 24(10): 1257–1273.

UCL (2020) "46% of all schools in England have no ETHNIC MINORITY teachers". www.ucl.ac.uk/ioe/news/2020/dec/46-all-schools-england-have-no-Ethnic minority -teachers

Worth, J. McLean, D. and Sharp, C. (2022) "Racial equality in the teacher workforce: An analysis of representation and progression opportunities from initial teacher training to headship". National foundation for educational research. Teach First. Ambition Institute. www.nfer.ac.uk/media/hxpdemc4/racial_equality_in_the_teacher_workforce_full_report.pdf

1

What is an anti-racist curriculum, and why is it needed in a SEND school?

"Why are you creating more problems for the children?"

We're an outstanding school – we don't need to do this work – everything is fine here. None of this means anything to the children… they don't know what's going on with all of that…"

Unpacking resistance: The comfort of complacency

This is how the anti-racist work was met when we first started it – with hostility, indifference, scepticism and, sometimes, anger and tears. For some, bringing these issues to the table was causing "issues" between co-workers and friends – as, suddenly, people were being questioned on their views, and the conversation turned contentious very quickly.

COVID-19: Unmasking vulnerabilities in SEND schools

The world was burning.

At the height of the COVID-19 pandemic, with little information or direction, we were told that under the Coronavirus Act 2020, SEND schools and all those with Education, Health and Care Plans (EHCPs) should continue to attend school as normal by providing critical support to one of our most vulnerable groups. With a caveat, we needed to prioritise the most vulnerable of needs, as well as the children of key workers.

Suddenly, everyone became a key worker, and we had parents demanding that we take their children. Parents presented various bits of evidence and letters instructing us that we absolutely must take their children into school. This was an exceptionally challenging time for special schools, as our duty and passion are to serve this community – the children, their parents and families. We knew that providing this support to parents and offering places served as an essential and desperate respite in extremely challenging situations. However, there were also staff shortages to manage, scared and panicked staff, the constant risk assessments, creating "bubbles" and maintaining staff ratios to ensure the needs of the children could be safely met and high levels of personal care and support could be maintained.

Race, risk, and Inequity: Navigating fear and responsibility

In the daily COVID briefings, the public were also informed that rising evidence indicated that ethnic minority groups were being significantly more affected by COVID than White groups. We watched deserted global landscapes and tuned into the daily toll of doom, totalling lives lost to date, and tried to make sense of when and if we should have vaccinations. We speculated when it would all end, but we ploughed on, planning for school openings, organising rotas and schedules, bubbles, online meetings and lessons, recording virtual stories and songs, and trying to alleviate staff concerns who feared for their own safety and wellbeing.

Some staff were terrified to come into school for their shifts, as they had underlying health conditions or vulnerable family members. With little guidance or support, leaders in SEND schools were wading through, completing risk assessments and making ill-informed judgements on who was fit to work. There became a very visible divide between those staff who were happy to come into school and "just get on with it" and those who were genuinely frightened or unable to manage the pressures of the situation, such as juggling their childcare, wider dynamics of the situation and increasing anxiety. There were also those who were worried by the media sharing that ethnic minority communities were more affected by COVID-19, especially if they had underlying health issues such as Type 2 diabetes, high blood pressure, high cholesterol, and so on, and this caused an air of panic in some ethnic minority communities, including school staff.

As the only ethnic minority in the leadership team, I had my own health conditions and felt in a panic myself. Having spent time in the ICU only 12-18 months prior, I felt I had to repress these concerns. I did not vocalise these concerns, as I didn't want it to be perceived as avoiding my turn on the rota, as other staff with similar concerns had been accused. I found that the data suggesting the virus was affecting minority groups more severely was completely disregarded. We now know the disproportionate rates in how much and how severely the minority communities were affected by COVID-19 to be true.

Cook, Kursumovic and Lennane (2020) identified that ethnic minority people make up 14% of the UK population, yet they accounted for a disproportionate percentage of overall deaths: 63% of NHS staff deaths were from minority backgrounds, despite minority staff making up only 21% of the workforce. Leadership discussions resulted in "we all know someone who has had it bad"; the debate was reduced to luck, as opposed to systemic racism through underlying health inequalities, access to health care, culturally appropriate support, socio-economic conditions or lack of community support mechanisms. To appease the concerns of the ethnic minority staff, I, specifically, was identified and asked to lead on and complete "ethnic minority at-risk assessments" with staff. No adjusted actions were taken, and it was entirely a tick-box exercise to appease any potential union involvement.

From George Floyd to Stephen Lawrence: A legacy of injustice

Amid this once-in-a-lifetime, life-altering event and lockdown came the news from the USA of the brutal murder of George Floyd by a police officer. Chaos ensued. A global thumping ground, in unison, was created with a sound reverberating - a demand for change. The movement affected a semblance of change. While the death of George Floyd in the US sparked widespread UK protests, bringing to light systematic racism within the UK, there have been similar historic cases on our doorstep which has brought attention to the issue.

The racially motivated murder of Stephen Lawrence in 1993 led to all five individuals suspected of his murder walking away free due to "insufficient evidence" despite there being multiple witnesses and substantial evidence on the identification of suspects. The case collapsed due to a continual lack of professionalism and incompetence by the police, including failure to make timely arrests, failure to follow basic protocol and procedures, procedural errors and an overall lack of urgency. Additionally, the Macpherson Report (1999), which concluded that the Metropolitan Police were also "institutionally racist", is defined as "the collective failure of an organisation to provide an appropriate and professional service to people because of their colour, culture, or ethnic origin".

Nineteen years after Stephen's murder, two of the five suspects were arrested for his murder. The other three were not brought to justice.

The House of Commons: The Macpherson Report: Twenty-two years on (2021) suggested that the report led to the implementation of cultural awareness training for police officers and introduced the requirement that officers record stop and searches, which, it felt, would lead to reduced racial profiling. However, more recent research and data suggest that this is not the case, and the Black community is still significantly more likely to be stopped and searched than White racial groups.

In December 2020, a 15-year-old Black schoolgirl was strip-searched by two female Metropolitan Police officers at her secondary school in Hackney, London. She was suspected of carrying cannabis. The police officers broke UK law and procedures by searching her without permission or an appropriate adult present. No drugs were found. An independent safeguarding review found that the search should not have gone ahead and that it was likely that racism was an influencing factor in the decision to proceed with the search. The case was yet another example that 20 years after the murder of Stephen Lawrence, there is ongoing institutional racism and broader discrimination against the Black community.

The legislative and policy changes remain similar to those of the Stephen Lawrence case - further police training, policy revisions, and "increased accountability". It is more of the same, demonstrating no lessons learned or changes. Despite an increase in ethnic minority police officers from 2% in 1999 to 6.3% in 2020, there remains ongoing racial discrimination and unfair treatment within the police and broader communities (Institute of Race Relations, 2021).

In 1979, Gurdip Singh Chaggar was stabbed and left to bleed to death in the street by a group of young White people. Police were slow to respond, and the investigation was regarded as inadequate, with a lack of robustness, due to the victim being an ethnic minority.

The community became awakened to the institutional racism of the police. However, the Scarman report (commissioned by the UK Government in 1981), which was an investigation commissioned after the 1981 Brixton race riots due to excessive stops and searches conducted on the Black community, denied that there was any form of racism in the police. And so the community were left to fend for themselves.

There are numerous names similar to George Floyd, Stephen Lawrence, and Child Q; Ricky Reel, Mark Duggan, Christopher Alder, Sean Rigg, and Dalian Atkinson, all highlight racial bias, misconduct and institutional racism and have influenced public perception of ongoing racist attitudes and behaviour by the police. The persistence of these issues spanning decades highlights that any semblance of legislative efforts or reform is not demonstrating rapid enough progress.

A moment of reckoning: BLM, Britain, and the Pandemic Intersection

So, the story was not new. But, at a moment in time, COVID-19 intersected with the murder of George Floyd as a catalyst, and the global movement of Black Lives Matter took hold like wildfire, demonstrating global solidarity through organised marches and protests in major cities around the world. Alongside the calls to end police brutality, the Grenfell fire, the Windrush scandal and the disparity of ethnic minorities losing their lives to COVID-19 compared with White communities, there came an increasing glare on Britain's colonial past and its substantial wealth built on the foundations of slavery and theft.

A report from Hope Not Hate, entitled State of Hate (2021), suggests that the pandemic created a unique moment in time where global attention could focus intensely on issues raised by the BLM movement. Due to lockdowns, people were at home, which led to higher engagement with the news and social media. The widespread video of Derek Chauvin murdering George Floyd led to rapid and widespread attention, galvanising support for the BLM movement. The report also highlighted through retrospection that while ethnic minorities felt they had not seen any change over the years since this time or that the events did not highlight anything new to them, they did note and observe "BLM's messages taken up by white friends and colleagues".

There was a sense of allyship.

There was also a divide between the tech-savvy population manipulating a changing digital landscape and the far-right, mostly older population, who found this difficult to contend with. Although they were heavily focused on "getting Brexit done", anti-immigrant policies and keeping up the media portrayal of Britain being "invaded" by immigrants, this gave rise to "White Lives Matter", countering the BLM movements led by Tommy Robinson and Nigel Farage.

This was the time for the world to stop and review that there was a colossal failure of those meant to protect and serve our community. A global movement. Black Lives Matter gave rise to a range of phrases that took hold, and suddenly, there was interest, discussion and debate in the meaning of the terms "white privilege", "systemic racism" and "systemic bias". You were expected to know these terms and understand what an "ally" was and how to be one. The counterargument - "Everyone has become too 'woke'".

Sledgehammer to the system: Disrupting "harmonious" schools

The school population in some areas of London predominantly comprises ethnic minority communities. In his art installation "Steve McQueen Year 3" (2019-2021), McQueen aimed to create a visual portrait of an entire age group in London: 76,000 photographs of Year 3 pupils from more than 1,500 primary schools across London were collated and exhibited at the Tate Britain, London. The installation highlighted the immense diversity in London's population, highlighting various ethnicities, cultures and socio-economic backgrounds. *The Guardian* called the exhibition "a racist's nightmare… there are kids in wheelchairs, kids with topknots, kids with headscarves". The project emphasised themes of unity, community and shared childhood experiences. It presented a vision of a generation growing up in a diverse and inclusive city and visualised the future demographics of London's diverse landscape.

Therefore, the photographs should also provide foresight into the changing educational landscape of London. To be inclusive of an increasing melting pot of different cultures and ethnicities, how can we review and ensure the curriculum offered is meaningfully progressive, futureproofing itself and truly reflective of the community it serves? And outside of London, in predominantly White areas, how does the curriculum prepare young people for life outside of their "bubble"?

Decolonising education: Superficial gestures or meaningful change?

In response to the BLM movement, the government devised the "Inclusive Britain" strategy, published in March 2022, outlining 74 actions to promote "equality of opportunity, nurturing agency, greater inclusion" to "level up ethnic disparities". Action 69 of the plan is "committed to Inclusion in the workplace: disseminate resources that can help employers achieve fairness and inclusion in the workplace". After the BLM movement, there was a notable increase in opportunities for working in the diversity and inclusion sector, with dedicated roles to ensure the implementation of policies to address systemic racism and promote equity. Companies and organisations made public commitments to improve workplace equality and increase the representation of minority employees at all levels.

Another of the actions from the "Inclusive Britain" strategy was to "introduce significant changes to the History curriculum". The Department for Education (DfE) states that this curriculum reform aims to "help students to understand the complex history of modern Britain, including the significant contributions of the BAME communities" and that this reform will "support teaching all year around on Black history in readiness for Black History Month" ("Inclusive Britain", 2022). Therefore, the curriculum reform is intended to reflect the diversity of Britain's population better, develop critical thinking and analysis of Britain's history. There is an attempt to promote the understanding and analysis of the interconnectedness of global events and their impact on our modern-day society.

Schools soon joined the cause in response to the focus on corporates. There was a mass springing and bombardment of continuing professional development (CPD), courses and consultants offering to support schools to create an "anti-racist curriculum". Training and coaching packages delivered to staff, parents and governors on how to "decolonise the curriculum". Moncrieffe (2022) notes that while there are increased efforts to "include teaching about the Windrush Generation and colonialism", teachers are completely clueless on how to get started with this and expected to use their knowledge, or lack of, to begin teaching these concepts in history lessons.

In some of the schools I have worked in with extremely high ethnic minority pupil populations and a White majority staff, staff report feeling "scared" to lead on "Black History Month" or "Windrush Day" as they lacked knowledge of the events. They also stated they were worried about getting it wrong or offending anyone. So, they did nothing. They not only failed to celebrate events that reflected their pupil and school community but also failed to prioritise gaining knowledge. Hence, they missed opportunities to gain the required knowledge and appropriately plan and deliver these opportunities in school.

Building an anti-racist framework: The four pillars

Creating a genuinely anti-racist curriculum requires a deliberate approach beyond tokenistic gestures and surface-level celebrations. Based on both practical experience and extensive research, four core strands have emerged as essential pillars for building a robust and meaningful anti-racist curriculum:

1. Providing multicultural education in the curriculum
2. Increased representation in the curriculum
3. Decolonising the curriculum
4. Anti-racist practice

This book explores these pillars in summary below and in further detail throughout. The book's structure is also laid out in three sections: (Part A) providing historical context and identifying barriers; (Part B) demonstrating collaborative action; and (Part C) reviewing the curriculum and beyond. Completing the curriculum audit, found later in the book, will identify areas of focus for School Improvement Planning and, as a school, priority areas for development.

1. Providing multicultural education in the curriculum

Many schools consider their practice to be "inclusive" and "representing their community"; for example, on Diwali, teachers may pass around their old saris, photocopy hand outlines for children to create henna patterns and a bag of clay, paint and sequins, to make diva lamps. The planning usually involves celebrating Diwali as a bolt-on to "Festivals and Lights", Guy Fawkes, Hannukah and Christmas – hitting all those birds with one stone. Many schools tend to make reasonable attempts at surface-level nods to "multicultural education" due to the National Curriculum expectations.

In the past four years, schools have embraced increasing multicultural education opportunities and increasing representation. My LinkedIn, Facebook and Instagram pages are flooded with photographs from schools and Multi Academy Trusts photographs, celebrating "International Day" or "Culture Day – we all belong".

However, although these events allow all cultures "to be seen", which supports a sense of belonging, we must question whether these tokenistic nods to multiculturalism are enough and whether there are further opportunities to develop knowledge and understanding of the country's colonial past. We will explore how this work is applicable in special schools, and how relevant it is.

Troyna (1987) criticises the "food and festivals" approach to increasing cultural diversity, arguing that this approach trivialises the work needed to deepen understanding of the challenges that the ethnic minority community faces. He argues that focusing only on "multicultural education" can reinforce stereotypes rather than challenge them. Therefore, schools need to do more than surface-level celebrations.

The challenge is even more significant for SEND settings. They must move beyond sensory-based celebrations of cultural differences and focus on creating learning experiences that foster genuine understanding, empathy and respect. This requires sustained efforts to educate pupils, staff, parents, families and the broader community on the challenges marginalised communities face. Multicultural education is not just a one-off but a continuous thread throughout the learning experience.

2. Increased representation in the curriculum

Representation matters, especially for pupils who rarely see themselves in the curriculum. Schools are beginning to review representation in teaching materials, books, and visuals, including symbols and images.

Neuroscience shows that children, especially those with identified SEND, benefit from the repetition of familiar sensory experiences, such as hearing the same language, music, food and smells. These experiences lead to feelings of security and belonging and strengthen neural pathways. When schools incorporate these cultural elements into the curriculum, they reinforce a child's identity and support their development by linking their home with school experiences.

Representation means ensuring pupils from ethnic minority groups feel seen and understood in every aspect of school life. This includes weaving their experiences, strengths, and contributions to society into the curriculum. Schools should review their materials, including language use, music, food and smells, to ensure diverse voices are not tokenistic but embedded into the learning process.

3. Decolonising the curriculum

Decolonising the curriculum goes beyond adding diverse perspectives for children with special educational needs. Some pupils may be able to access content that questions histories, voices and perspectives from marginalised or omitted groups. Pupils can be exposed to different cultures and individuals, from music, smells and sensory experiences to accessing and interpreting alternative stories and viewpoints to those they have been exposed to. For children with SEND and from ethnic minority backgrounds, this is even more critical, as their curriculum opportunities must address their intersectionality, ensuring their unique experiences and identities are represented and valued in education.

Decolonising the curriculum means providing content that questions and challenges historical narratives and actively involves and includes the voices, perspectives and input from diverse racial and ability backgrounds. This is important for SEND ethnic minority learners and their families, as when stories, cultural attitudes and barriers are identified and communicated, the communities are more likely to feel seen, understood and empowered to engage fully with their education.

4. Anti-racist practice

While multicultural education, increased representation and decolonising the curriculum are necessary, they are not enough alone. Schools must actively embrace multi-layered and numerous anti-racist practices that challenge and dismantle systemic racism within the institution and beyond. This requires critical reflection on policies, practices and everyday interactions.

Schools must ask themselves difficult questions about all school policies and practice strands: Are their recruitment processes biased? Are their probation or disciplinary practices fair across different ethnic groups? Do teachers consider socio-economic factors that may influence the engagement or attainment of ethnic minority pupils with SEND? Are there systemic biases in how certain ethnic groups are assessed, labelled or diagnosed with SEND?

For example, research shows that Black pupils with SEND are often misdiagnosed, or their behaviour is viewed through a biased lens, resulting in exclusions, and missed opportunities for proper support. The intersectional challenges these pupils face, being both Black and having SEND, require educators to have a deep understanding of the complexities of race, disability and socio-economic status.

Ethnic minority communities are often disproportionately affected by SEND labelling and misdiagnosis. Bernard Coard's *How the West Indian Child is Made Educationally Subnormal in the British School System* initially highlighted this systemic bias and racial prejudice in the 1970s, and the work stands true and reflective of even the most recent data. The University of Oxford (2019) found that Black Caribbean and Mixed White and Black Caribbean pupils are more than twice as likely to be identified with Social, Emotional and Mental Health needs

(SEMH) compared with White British peers and that this overidentification is expected to lead to exclusion from school, which is a significant risk factor for later criminal activity.

A review by Demie in BERA (2022) confirms that Black pupils, especially those with SEMH needs, are the most excluded groups in British schools. DfE statistics confirm that young people from the Black community who have also been identified with behavioural needs, special needs and SEMH or have been excluded are disproportionately represented in the criminal justice system. Although we know there are multi-faceted and complex socio-economic issues, these factors do not fully explain the disparity. The Hechinger Report (2020) highlights that Black pupils are viewed through a biased lens, which can lead to higher rates of misdiagnosis. As a result, they are placed in inappropriate educational settings, indicating that little progress has been made over the past 50 years since Coard's initial work in this field.

Additionally, the National Autistic Society identify that autistic individuals and those with other learning disabilities are at

> increased risk of police interactions, often due to a lack of understanding and appropriate response strategies from law enforcement officers.
>
> People with disabilities, including those with learning disabilities and mental health conditions, are more likely to experience police interactions that may not always be appropriately managed.
>
> (Sims, 2017)

We also know that the stop and search rates continue to be the highest in the Black community. In March 2023, these were 25 per 1000 people, compared with 18 per 1000 in the Mixed-race community and 11 per 1000 in the Asian community. The rates in the White community are 4 per 1000 (Home Office, 2024). These rates continue to cause significant concern around continual systematic biases, as when these two strands of Race and SEND intersect and are factored into these statistics; there is reasonable concern regarding our young autistic Black community.

Schools and educators should review this data and consider how their policies, practices and curriculum offer may better prepare young people with SEND from ethnic minority groups for the wider world. Booking steel drums or playing Bob Marley in the lunch hall to celebrate Black History Month does not develop this more comprehensive knowledge, nor does it equip staff with the skills or abilities to ask pertinent questions on current trends in education and society. We must understand the intersectional landscape, the systemic and structural racism and how this affects the young people in our schools. It is our responsibility to ensure parental engagement with our "hard to reach" groups are successful and maintained so that we can co-create a curriculum that promotes advocacy, self-esteem and identity.

A study by the Centre of Mental Health by McHayle, Obateru and Woodhead (2020) identifies that ethnic minority parents are disproportionately affected by mental health issues exacerbated by social isolation and systemic discrimination. Many ethnic minority children experience social isolation and lack of interactions, leading to loneliness and exclusion, which is magnified in special schools. Therefore, a curriculum offer should centre around parental involvement and include elements of cultural competence training and community outreach programmes. A curriculum should be underpinned by a focus on communication, independence and interaction with policymakers to continue to raise awareness and make a stand to make a change.

A focus on working with the parents, from those isolated from their cultural communities and in the infancy of their journey of acceptance, supporting them to best engage with and support their child, to recognising the fears of other parents, those parents who stay awake at night questioning, what if their child were to experience a "stop and search?"

Would they be OK? Would they know what was happening?

An anti-racist curriculum in a special school must do more.

There is a responsibility, a duty, and therefore, a call to action that we must respond to-that we and our staff are aware of, respond to and act on the multi-layered, intersectional issues between race and disability at all four levels.

Moving from cultural tokens to systemic change

A commitment to developing an "anti-racist curriculum" is beyond the nods to "multicultural" – the samosas in the staff room are not enough. True anti-racist work requires a commitment to systemic change through these four strands. Schools must move beyond cultural tokens and focus on dismantling the biases that shape educational experiences for minority pupils, families and staff. This involves creating policies that ensure fair treatment, building a diverse leadership team that understands the process and journey to change, and who can lead in fostering an inclusive school culture that welcomes all voices.

An anti-racist curriculum cannot be limited to sporadic isolated events like assemblies or themed days. It must be an ongoing effort to engage with and respond to the complex realities of race and disability in education. A framework based on these four pillars can be built:

1. multicultural education
2. representation
3. decolonisation and
4. anti-racist practice

Schools can move beyond surface-level diversity initiatives and create lasting and meaningful change. The journey to achieving this requires critical reflection, professional development and a willingness to confront difficult truths about systemic inequities. Schools can only create an environment where all pupils, regardless of race or ability, can thrive through sustained commitment and action.

Figure 1.1 The four pillars of an anti-racist curriculum

Leading the change: My journey into anti-racism work

Hope Not Hate (2021) identified trends, with 62% of British ethnic minority people feeling that the protests either made no difference or that the government was taking racism less seriously than before the protests. They "felt disillusioned with the movement and that it had not triggered the societal changes they'd hoped for"; however, 50% felt there was "a shift in how seriously white friends and colleagues take racism".

I was in this 50%.

I was asked to lead on this "anti-racist" work by the White headteacher I was working with, who decided the work was essential – and I was thrilled to. I had just become involved in BAME education and started exploring the value I could add to this field. I was elated to be working alongside a headteacher whose attitudes and beliefs were supportive and even progressive, and this felt so refreshing from my previous experience. I did not know how this work would translate into a SEND school or understand its relevance or applicability. The strategies did not seem as transferrable, and I wrestled with ensuring the work was committed to remaining meaningful and with intent.

I felt the work would be purposeful at a critical time and that my experiences, my ethnic minority colleagues and the families I had worked with would bring authenticity and credibility to the work. However, I was unprepared for the nuances leading the project would create, which felt like a sledgehammer to the school community. Some of my other minority colleagues supported the work in school, and we were disillusioned and saddened by some of the feedback we received. I had not anticipated that embarking on this work would open a Pandora's box or that the work would take me down a path of self-discovery, reflection and, in some respects, great frustration. However, I knew I had to open that Pandora's box, start the work through self-reflection and unpick my journey.

Data from the academic year 2022/23 exposes significant racial disparities within the UK education system, particularly in leadership roles. Although 34.4% of the pupil population identifies as belonging to an ethnic minority group, representation in school leadership is alarmingly low: only 4.5% of headteachers come from ethnic minority backgrounds, while 92.5% are White.

When considering these figures, the disparity becomes even more evident. For every 1,000 ethnic minority pupils, there are only about 13 ethnic minority headteachers, compared to approximately 141 White headteachers for every 1,000 White pupils. This stark contrast illustrates the systemic barriers and unequal opportunities that ethnic minority educators face in advancing to leadership positions. Despite the diversity of the pupil population, leadership does not reflect this diversity, demonstrating a clear and pressing need for systemic change to ensure equal representation and opportunities for ethnic minority professionals (GOV.UK, 2023).

Of the 4.5% ethnic minority headteachers, 0.9% of the headteacher workforce are Indian (DfE, GOV.UK, 2023). I am part of this 0.9%. I have struggled and fought my way to this position, and it rested on "give me a chance to prove myself – give me a year..."

In starting the anti-racist work reviewing how to decolonise a SEND curriculum, I learned two main shocking facts which I was not prepared for:

1. The ongoing, restricted opportunities ethnic minority staff face in accessing career progression opportunities in education, and
2. The response of my colleagues of all ethnicities to the anti-racist work we were doing.

This also led to a two-part journey of self-development for me. One was leading the school through the challenges of COVID-19, the response to COVID-19 expectations and immediately after, developing within my leadership capacity to lead a contentious topic in school and bring everyone along with me.

Second, the work on developing and implementing an anti-racist curriculum led to deep personal reflection. It has been a journey of understanding my own struggles through understanding those of a wider group of ethnic minority leaders and educators.

In attending several anti-racist CPD courses, I was exposed to the stark reality of the lack of opportunity for ethnic minority staff in education and found these shocking and inexcusable. I was not prepared for the facts on systematic and widespread racism in education, the limited career development opportunities and the barriers to progression that were shared. It was as if all my hurdles and experiences were being laid out in front of me; dealing with this uncovering and the sense of injustice I felt while navigating the project of creating an anti-racist curriculum felt enormous and desperately challenging.

Upon reflection, I am surprised by my naivety. I had not considered racism as a possible factor in my career history, especially as I had such intense experiences growing up and in one of the schools where I had worked. I had only ever experienced obvious, overt racism. I was unprepared for the nuances of covert racism and systemic biases.

Reviewing how our school would "decolonise the curriculum" while processing these experiences seemed inapplicable, superficial and even surface-level. It felt too systemic and deep-rooted to feel like I could make a difference in ensuring more diversity and equity in education. I was very much navigating and making sense of my own journey and experiences.

Research also shows that even when we make it to those most senior positions, ethnic minority staff often take on the positions, roles, and schools that require the most work. They are the most "difficult". I was the only ethnic minority leader and also the only leader spearheading this work on anti-racism. No other leader was tasked with this project and did not take an interest or participate in the work. The information, statistics and research all felt so familiar.

How could I lead this project when, it seems, according to factors outside of my control, I can barely help myself? When research shows that many ethnic minority leaders work in schools that require the most work, in the most challenging areas, with the fewest resources, with the most obstacles to overcome, serving communities which require the most support and have the most needs (Miller and Lashley, 2022).

Ethnic minority teachers experience "concrete ceilings" and do not make it to leadership positions compared to their White counterparts; what made me think I was the one to make a difference? I struggled with these thoughts for the duration of the project, and then I did not, and I dug deep and ploughed on through.

This book aims to review the existing barriers and disparities while fostering a deep sense of responsibility, resilience and perseverance. By deepening our understanding of the intersection between race and disability and how it affects individuals, families and communities, we can cultivate more meaningful and culturally responsive approaches to support.

I hope this book illuminates the unique challenges faced by different community groups in supporting children and young people with special educational needs and disabilities. As educators and advocates, it is imperative that we stand united with our communities, armed with awareness, knowledge and genuine allyship.

As adults, we bear the responsibility of being role models and leading this vital work to create an inclusive and equitable environment where every child, regardless of race or ability, can not only survive but thrive. I hope this book inspires this responsibility.

Chapter summary

This chapter reflects on the challenges of implementing anti-racist work in SEND schools, particularly when faced with resistance, scepticism and indifference. Drawing on my experiences and research, it explores the intersectionality of race and disability, emphasising the importance of culturally responsive practices. It also highlights the complexities of addressing systemic racism while managing the heightened vulnerability of ethnic minority communities, especially during the COVID-19 pandemic.

The chapter calls for intentional leadership, allyship, a focus on intersectionality, and a long-term commitment to developing an anti-racist curriculum deeply embedded in the fabric of SEN schools.

TIFFIN TAKE-AWAY

1. **Tackling resistance and a lack of commitment to the cause**
   Leaders must proactively address resistance and ensure staff understand the relevance and importance of this work. Consistent and open dialogue is essential to breaking down barriers.

   - What strategies can you implement to engage staff resistant or indifferent to anti-racist initiatives?

2. **Understanding intersectionality**
   Schools must embrace an intersectional approach, recognising the compounded vulnerabilities of race, disability and socio-economic factors.

   - How does your school aim to understand, question and address the unique challenges faced by ethnic minority pupils with SEND and their families?

3. **Ensuring parental engagement and support**
   Building trust and fostering solid home-school partnerships are crucial to providing culturally competent support. Leaders should focus on outreach, community building and offering spaces for parents to share their experiences and concerns, using translators where helpful.

   - What actions can your school take to better engage and support ethnic minority families of children with SEN?

References

Barshay, J. (2022) "Rethinking claims of racial bias in special education". https://hechingerreport.org/proof-points-rethinking-claims-of-racial-bias-in-special-education/

Coard, B. (1971) *How the West Indian child is made educationally sub-normal in the British school system.* McDermott Publishing.

Cook, T., Kursumovic, E. and Lennane, S. (2020) "Deaths of NHS staff from COVID-19 analysed". *Health Science Journal.* www.hsj.co.uk/exclusive-deaths-of-nhs-staff-from-covid-19-analysed/7027471.article

Demie, F. (2022) "School exclusions: What does research tell us about the scale of the problem and challenges?" BERA. www.bera.ac.uk/blog/school-exclusions-what-does-research-tell-us-about-the-scale-of-the-problem-and-challenges

House of Commons (2022) "The Macpherson Report: Twenty-two years on". https://committees.parliament.uk/publications/22402/documents/165350/default/

Home Office (2024) "Stop and search and arrests". www.gov.uk/government/statistics/stop-and-search-and-arrests-year-ending-march-2023/police-powers-and-procedures-stop-and-search-and-arrests-england-and-wales-year-ending-31-march-2023

Institute of Race Relations (2021) Annual Report. https://irr.org.uk/

GOV.UK (2022) "Inclusive Britain: Publications and updates". www.gov.uk/government/collections/inclusive-britain-publications-and-updates

GOV.UK (2023) School teacher workforce. www.ethnicity-facts-figures.service.gov.uk/workforce-and-business/workforce-diversity/school-teacher-workforce/latest/

Hope not hate (2021) "State of Hate 2021: Backlash, conspiracies and confrontation". https://hopenothate.org.uk/2021/02/20/state-of-hate-2021-backlash-conspiracies-and-confrontation/

Macpherson, W. (1999) "The Stephen Lawrence Inquiry". https://assets.publishing.service.gov.uk/media/5a7c2af540f0b645ba3c7202/4262.pdf

McHayle, Z., Obateru, A. and Woodhead, D. (2024) "Pursuing racial justice in mental health". www.centreformentalhealth.org.uk/wp-content/uploads/2024/01/CentreforMH_PursuingRacialJusticeInMH.pdf

Miller, P. and Lashley, R. (2022) "A report on factors responsible for and / or contribute to BAME school leaders exiting the profession or accepting a junior role". Education and Social Equity and Fig Tree International.

Moncrieffe, M. (2022) "Challenging, decolonising and transforming primary school history curriculum knowledge". The Chartered College of Teaching. https://my.chartered.college/impact_article/challenging-decolonising-and-transforming-primary-school-history-curriculum-knowledge/

The Hechinger Report (2020) https://hechingerreport.org/

Sims, P. (26 June 2017) "Supporting autistic people in police custody". National Autistic Society. www.autism.org.uk/advice-and-guidance/professional-practice/police-custody

The University of Oxford (2019) "Ethnic minority children not equally identified with Special Education Needs". www.ox.ac.uk/news/2019-02-13-ethnic-minority-children-not-equally-identified-special-education-needs

Troyna, B. (1987) "Beyond multiculturalism: Towards the enactment of anti-racist education in policy, provision and pedagogy". *Oxford Review of Education*. 13(3): 307-320.

2
How can leaders start this work by ensuring it is purposeful?

"It's a great tick box for us – Ofsted will love it!"

Gatekeepers of change: The role of leadership

Leadership plays a critical role in successfully implementing anti-racist work. Leaders can be key "gatekeepers" who control the work's narrative, direction, priority and implementation.

As most leaders in educational settings are White, and research suggests those leading in anti-racist work in schools are ethnic minorities, gatekeepers can lack lived experience, and this can appear to dismiss or downplay the experiences of those leading the work.

Tokenism v transformational: A superficial commitment

The suggestion that the project would be "great for Ofsted" indicated a lack of regard, knowledge and ignorance of my own lived experiences. This communicated to me that the work was superficial although well-intentioned. It is appreciated that one's own experiences differ greatly when a school "buys into" and commits to taking a stand and pledging to embed anti-racist practices. As there is a lack of lived experiences of racism in most leadership teams, it is crucial that there is an element of curiosity as to why a commitment to developing an anti-racist curriculum is essential. When curiosity and true allyship are lacking, the work is compromised and appears tokenistic and superficial.

School leaders must be committed to these principles and willing to lead by example; this involves setting the vision and actively engaging in professional development, supporting staff and holding the school accountable for progress. Leaders should foster a culture of openness and continuous improvement, encouraging feedback and being responsive to the school community's needs. There should be a commitment to all four strands of creating and embedding an "anti-racist curriculum", from multicultural education, increasing representation, decolonising the curriculum and developing and embedding anti-racist practice.

Intersectionality in practice: When race meets SEND

BAME pupils with SEND tend to encounter distinct socio-economic and cultural barriers that intersect with their educational experiences. These can include differences in language, cultural misunderstandings between schools and families and socio-economic disadvantages, such as poverty. The concept of intersectionality, coined by Kimberlé Crenshaw, is essential in understanding and addressing the multi-layered challenges faced by BAME children with SEND. This perspective shows how race, class, gender and other personal characteristics combine and overlap, impacting pupils' educational experiences. For example, a Black autistic child from a low-income family might encounter obstacles that are very different from those faced by a White child with the same conditions but from a more affluent background. These might include access to services, information, support, healthcare and academic expectations; they may also experience racism, lack of support, signposting or explanation when they do access relevant services.

School leaders are crucial in setting the school's vision and direction. The IOE (UCL-IOE, 2020) suggests that developing a school ethos that values diversity and promotes anti-racist principles is critical to starting this work. This ethos helps leaders articulate a clear and compelling vision of equity and inclusion, which guides the entire community.

School leaders and governors are pivotal in shaping the schools' vision and direction. Their active support and commitment to an anti-racist curriculum are essential for driving systemic change and ensuring that anti-racist principles permeate every aspect of the school's operations. A proactive stance, championed by the governing board, is not merely beneficial but imperative to foster an environment where all pupils, regardless of their background, can thrive.

Crafting an anti-racist vision: Aligning mission with values

Ensuring that a school's vision and mission statement reflect a commitment to anti-racism is a fundamental step, as alignment provides a clear framework for decision-making and sets the tone for the entire school community. A school's vision and mission statement form the foundation upon which its culture, policies and practices are built and developed. When these explicitly commit to an anti-racist stance, they create a beacon that influences everything from curriculum development to staff recruitment and pupil engagement.

According to a report by the National Governors Association (2020), aligning a school's vision and mission with anti-racist principles, is crucial in fostering an inclusive school culture. This alignment ensures that anti-racism is not an add-on or an afterthought but a central focus of the school's ethos and culture; it helps to embed anti-racist practices into the tapestry of the school, ensuring that all stakeholders understand and commit to these principles.

Ensuring a school's vision and mission statement are explicitly anti-racist serves multiple purposes:

1. Guide decision-making
   An anti-racist vision and mission provide a lens through which all decisions are made, including decisions related to curriculum design or recruitment, retention and staff

career progression. For example, a school with a mission to promote equity will prioritise hiring diverse staff members and developing a curriculum that reflects diverse perspectives.

2. Create accountability

A clear, anti-racist mission statement holds the school accountable. It provides benchmarks against which the school's progress can be measured. This accountability extends to all members of the school community.

3. Building trust

When schools publicly commit to anti-racism, they build trust with pupils, families and the wider community. This trust is crucial for creating a supportive and inclusive environment where all pupils feel valued and understood.

4. Encouraging engagement

An anti-racist mission encourages active engagement from all school community members. It invites all, including families and the wider community, to participate in the ongoing work of creating an equitable and inclusive school.

Embedding anti-racism and equity into school improvement plans

Ensuring that anti-racist work is consistently prioritised and effectively implemented within a school requires integration into the School Improvement Plan (SIP). In taking this action, strategic inclusion ensures that the commitment to diversity, inclusion and equity is actionable and measurable.

There should be clear indicators of progress, serving as a roadmap for the anti-racist work. These indicators should outline who is responsible for leading the work at various levels of the school structure, from governors to teachers. Establishing specific timelines and identifying inspirational, relevant CPD required at each level ensures that everyone in the school is equipped to contribute meaningfully to this goal. Embedding commitment within the SIP also ensures that the governors are committed to and responsible for holding the leadership team accountable for progress in these areas.

Allen, Riley and Coates (2020) highlight the importance of developing a school-wide ethos of inclusion and respect; a "safe, dynamic and equitable school environment" is essential not only for the overall school culture but also for the social and emotional wellbeing of pupils from ethnic minority backgrounds, and/or from deprived backgrounds. Creating such an ethos involves a commitment to understanding and addressing the unique challenges these pupils face, fostering an environment where every pupil and staff member feels valued and respected.

Research by the British Educational Research Association (Demie, 2019) indicates that schools focusing on diversity, inclusion and equity in their improvement plans see significant progress in pupil outcomes and overall school performance. The studies highlight that when schools embed these principles into their strategic goals, the benefits are widespread, positively impacting progress and school culture.

Measuring progress: Accountability through appraisals

One effective way to ensure a sustained focus on anti-racist work is to disseminate targets from the School Improvement Plan and incorporate related targets into teachers' appraisal processes. For example, teachers could be required to demonstrate how their Medium-Term Planning promotes diversity and representation. This approach would ensure that anti-racist principles are integrated into everyday teaching practices and are not seen as an additional or separate task.

Commitment to continuous growth: Training and professional development

Providing training and development opportunities for school leaders and governors on anti-racism and inclusive leadership is essential. Professional development should include training on institutional and systemic racism, unconscious bias, privilege and allyship. Training should also reference key anti-racist literature over the past 50 years, data and research demonstrating current issues around identifying underachieving groups, reviewing our biases and how these may affect our engagement with the wider community. Leaders and governors should consider how to embed equity in education and lead inclusive schools effectively.

As school leaders are predominantly White, this work tends to be led by ethnic minority staff who feel compelled to do so because of their lived and first-hand experiences. We know there are not enough ethnic minority leaders and teachers in school to lead this work, which means there requires a level of commitment to allyship. It is essential that they access CPD and training on systemic biases to develop the knowledge and information for the promotion of equity and to create inclusive learning environments for pupils, their families and staff in a manner that is not tokenistic and surface level.

Joseph-Salisbury (2020) identified that school leaders must access racial literacy and anti-racist training, as this helps them to promote a commitment to equity, as well as an understanding of the historical and current context of racism. They should understand how this affects their pupils and explore proactive steps to ensure that all pupils have equal opportunities to succeed. Additionally, a focus on anti-racist perspectives should be embedded in the curriculum, offering alternative viewpoints on core issues and promoting race-conscious critical thinking.

Some school leaders and governors may lack a deep understanding of anti-racism and its implications for education. As it is not a lived experience, it may not appear as high on the agenda for the 92.6% of White headteachers. While they may be supportive of the focus on establishing an "anti-racist curriculum", they may lack the willingness to lead the work themselves.

White privilege: A barrier to anti-racist progress

> White privilege is an absence of the consequences of racism. An absence of structural discrimination, an absence of your race being viewed as a problem first and foremost...
>
> (Eddo-Lodge, 2017)

As Eddo-Lodge presents, with invisible advantages to being White, the negative impacts of racism and structural barriers to progress in education, employment, housing or criminal justice are just not felt. Race will not be seen as an issue because it has not been an issue or defining characteristic for some. Although White privilege is not about individual actions or intentions, it is about the White community recognising and addressing the systematic racial inequalities in schools for pupils, families and staff.

White privilege manifests in educational settings as systemic advantages that are often unrecognised by White staff and pupils, such as seeing their racial identity positively reflected in the curriculum, leadership and promotion opportunities. School leaders need to acknowledge White privilege to address systemic inequalities within their schools. In considering the significant racial disparity within the UK's educational staff, the 92.6% of White headteachers compared with 4.5% ethnic minority headteachers representing the 34.5% ethnic minority pupil population, it should be noted that the imbalance could perpetuate misunderstanding, misrepresentation and a lack of positive representation. There could be a lack of consideration on how policies and curricula are developed and executed to support ethnic minority pupils. How are predominantly White leadership teams and headteachers addressing the significant barriers faced by the ethnic minority community? How are these barriers actively identified, planned for and removed, where possible, by schools?

> Structural racism is dozens, or hundreds, or thousands of people with the same biases joining together to make up one organisation and acting accordingly. If you think it's just about personal prejudice, you're missing the point.
>
> (Eddo-Lodge, 2017)

Leaders need to understand "why" the work is important, how to understand the community better, how to know and understand the investment in preparing young people for adulthood and how to create and align with a wider vision. They need to be honest and reflective to review their own gaps in knowledge to better equip themselves with the skills required to support this work across the school. Providing training and development opportunities for school leaders, governors, teachers and support staff on anti-racism and inclusive leadership is essential.

In developing their understanding, knowledge and skill set, leaders can be more equipped to demonstrate allyship with their BAME colleagues so that a shared and distributed approach can be adopted. They may also be able to offer emotional support, a listening ear and empathy to their colleagues and the wider school community.

Implementing an anti-racist curriculum in schools for children with special educational needs involves a fundamental shift in mindset across all educational stakeholders and a commitment to being an ally. Deeply rooted issues intensify the task. Before there can be any review of the curriculum or implementation of any educational policy change, staff will undoubtedly require training and opportunities to unpick terms such as "white privilege" and "unconscious bias". They will need to understand the statistics presented thus far and why the underrepresentation of ethnic minority teachers and leaders is such a disadvantage.

For meaningful work, they should understand the systemic challenges faced by the ethnic minority community, the barriers the community faces, the intersectional aspects of these barriers and how the curriculum, policy and school practice can profoundly affect the daily lives of the ethnic minority community of pupils, their families and staff.

Sense of belonging

> White fragility is a state in which even a minimum amount of racial stress becomes intolerable, triggering a range of defensive moves.
>
> *(DiAngelo, 2018)*

When leading the initial stages of this work in a school, as discussed in previous chapters, the topic was met with initial uproar. "We are not racist here!" "Why are you making problems?!" or "These things do not matter in a special school – the work is irrelevant!" The rest of the team remained silent. The implications of this silence and failure to display a united front were that the project was perceived as a personal interest and mission. We failed to display a collective, united front, communicating that this is a strategic goal implemented through the School Improvement Plan. The inaction led to several other ethnic minority staff, who were participating in leading the project along with me, feeling marginalised and isolated.

As discussed in DiAngelo's *White fragility: Why it's so hard for White people to talk about racism*, when White colleagues react defensively to conversations about race, it can create a hostile working environment, making ethnic minority staff feel unsupported and undervalued, as we saw in the initial stages of this project. Additionally, as many staff have their own lived experiences to share, their first-hand experiences, such as obstacles and experiences in their personal or professional lives, questioning the relevance of the commitment to becoming "anti-racist" also questions the validity of one's own experiences, leading to these experiences being trivialised. It also creates the opposite stance of allyship.

As an ethnic minority leader leading this project, the constant need to navigate and address White fragility placed an emotional burden on me and my feelings of responsibility on those minority colleagues who had supported the work. When one colleague decided to leave the working party due to significant emotional distress caused by the ongoing opinions and beliefs of other colleagues in the school, there were high levels of stress and feeling undervalued in a wider sense, even though I was a senior leader in the school. In this case, White fragility inhibited the initial progress of the anti-racist initiative. Frustratingly, as the White staff members resisted discussions about race, and Black Lives Matter in particular, it stalled meaningful work and changes, including the implementation of inclusive practice, perpetuating systemic inequities.

Therefore, if I were to start this project in a school again, and if you find yourselves in a similar position, I advise ensuring the leadership team is constantly aligned through discussions on buy-in, allyship and discussion opportunities to discuss and troubleshoot the responses of the wider staff community, for example, how are the staff behaving? Is this behaviour in line with the school code of conduct? Does it demonstrate inclusivity and equality? It requires courageous conversations, holding your colleagues to account, asking for a call to action and requesting their allyship. Has something been missing in the communication, discussion or implementation stages? I would also expect leaders to demonstrate confidence, interest and active buy-in into the work, as well as to recognise and manage their reactions to and interest in discussions about race and how these can lead to promoting anti-racist initiatives.

While we did "buy-in" anti-racist training and coaching, especially for the start of the project, who led on whole school training and worked with leaders, there was a lack of understanding that racism is not just about overt acts – hence the statements of "We're not racist here!" – but is related to both unconscious biases and systematic issues, which leaders need to identify and create comprehensive anti-racist strategies to counteract.

> The simplistic idea that racism is limited to individual acts committed by unkind people allows us to maintain a positive self-image while we work to deny minimise and dismiss the issues…
>
> (DiAngelo, 2018)

Leaders themselves need to understand systemic racism and its effects on the ethnic minority community so that they are better placed to challenge beliefs that "the work is not needed" or is of "no relevance" in special schools. There needs to be clear buy-in and awareness that through School Improvement Plans, policies, appraisals and school operations, anti-racist practices can and should be disseminated throughout the school using a top-down approach. For this to happen, the "top" need to have confidence in their knowledge, understanding and demonstrate commitment, and united, "buy-in".

Cultural competence: Understanding the school's community

To begin integrating anti-racist principles within your school, focusing on SEND settings, it is crucial first to understand your community and its unique challenges. As previously discussed, 92.6% of headteachers in the UK are White, a statistic that, as we know, highlights the racial disparity in educational leadership. The disparity is significant when leading anti-racist work in SEND schools or with SEND pupils in other settings, where intersectional factors of race and SEND converge to create complex educational experiences for ethnic minority pupils.

School leaders are responsible for developing cultural competence and a deep understanding of the complexities that various ethnic groups bring to the school. Cultural competence involves recognising and respecting the diverse cultural backgrounds of pupils and their families and adapting practices to effectively meet their unique needs. For instance, leaders must be aware of how different cultures might perceive and accept a child's diagnosis of SEND and review whether their longer-term aspirations for their child are realistic or more ambitious.

Developing this understanding and relationship with parents is critical in fostering a supportive and inclusive environment for ethnic minority pupils with SEND. It also enables staff to understand better cultural variance in how the child's needs are understood, any barriers the parents face from the wider community and what they may need from the school in relation to workshops on key areas, for example, enhancing communication or transferring communication strategies from school to home.

While it is essential to recognise general trends, research and information within ethnic minority communities, such as a reported lower tolerance and acceptance of special needs, it is equally important to avoid stereotyping or making assumptions about individual families. Stereotyping can lead to miscommunication, misunderstanding and a lack of trust between the school and the families it serves. Each family is unique, and their experiences, perceptions and their own family cultures can vary greatly. Therefore, despite the research indicating certain trends, educators must approach each family with an open mind and a willingness to understand their specific context and needs.

While understanding broader cultural trends is helpful, school leaders must tailor their support to meet the individual needs of each family. The personalised approach requires active listening and a genuine effort to understand the unique circumstances of each pupil and their family. While it is recognised that teachers do not have the capacity within their workload to manage this level of interaction, it is worth considering a home-school liaison worker who may be able to lead some of this work for the teachers and leaders. Some families may be concerned about their child's communication abilities, whereas others may want to discuss toilet training or sensory-seeking behaviours. By recognising and respecting these priorities, leaders can plan for and provide families more effective and meaningful support.

CASE STUDY: HOME-SCHOOL LIAISON WORKER

When parents and schools interact closely together, they share information among themselves, and this information sharing helps families to understand better the schools and schools to understand the families.

(Bojuwoye, 2009 in Campbell, 2011)

Parental engagement with schools is widely researched as highly effective in supporting pupils' progress and sustainability. However, ethnic minority parents are typically regarded as "hard to reach". They usually consist of parents who do not engage with the school, attend meetings or reviews, have low levels of daily engagement and are unavailable or respond to discussions on progress and target setting.

This can usually be due to cultural barriers, including language barriers and the school's geographical location. It can also include parental low self-esteem, their own experiences with school and additional needs.

However, considering research by Epstein (2001, in Campbell, 2011) and the "Three contexts for children's learning", schools must embrace strategies to support parents in becoming involved in their children's education, including parenting strategies, communication, volunteering, learning at home, decision-making and collaborating with the community.

Our school borders two counties, Oxfordshire and Reading, with over half of our families coming from Reading, who tend to be predominantly ethnic minority families. These families struggled to attend parent forum meetings, parent coffee mornings and workshops supporting parents better to understand the school's vision, objectives and curriculum. Due to distance, lack of transport and the school's location, we noticed that attendance at school events tended to be the same 5-10 families.

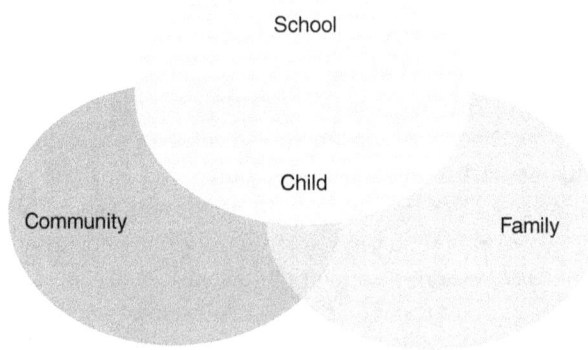

Figure 2.1 Three contexts for children's learning

Source: Adapted from Epstein (2001)

> To develop our response to promoting engagement with these "hard to reach" families, we appointed a home-school liaison worker, who has formed excellent relationships with parents over the past two years. As families join the school for the first time, she attends the headteacher's "Welcome" meeting, introducing herself and her role. She supports all new families with their child's transition to school, ensuring she is available to answer questions and offer support.
>
> She has created a parents WhatsApp group and provided the number to all new parents, showing them how to join the group. All school notifications, reminders and key information are shared through the group.
>
> She has also organised "remote coffee mornings", where we host coffee mornings in more central town centre locations, which resulted in attendance from families we have not managed to engage previously. We speak about what is going well in the school and their ideas and suggestions for improvement. We discuss the school curriculum and how to support their children in developing specific skills, including communication, behaviour and independence. This in-person attendance also allowed us to support parents in navigating some of the digital skills required to use a new school app.

Governance and accountability: A shared responsibility

Leaders should ensure there is a link governor designated for Equality, Diversity and Inclusion (EDI), who is responsible for monitoring the school's adherence to its diversity policies. This includes ensuring that these policies are not only in place but are actively being followed and adapted as necessary to meet the needs of the school community. Regular reviews and assessments of these policies, through SIP monitoring and quality assurance planning, would help identify areas for improvement and ensure that the school environment remains inclusive and supportive to all pupils, particularly those from ethnic minority backgrounds.

Effective implementation of diversity policies requires collaboration between governors and school leaders. They must focus on their personal and professional commitments to establishing and embedding anti-racial approaches in all school policies and processes. A collaborative effort ensures that the school's commitment to diversity is not "surface-level" but translates into tangible actions and outcomes for which the leaders are held accountable. School leaders must proactively support the designated governor's efforts and ensure all staff are engaged in these initiatives (National Governance Association, 2022).

A designated governor plays a crucial role in ensuring that the achievement and wellbeing of ethnic minority pupils, families and staff are prioritised. This includes tracking pupils' academic progress and engagement levels, being a critical friend and providing support to address any barriers to their success. Additionally, by focusing on strategies to promote engagement in otherwise regarded "hard to reach" families, thus supporting the wellbeing of ethnic minority families, schools can foster a more inclusive and supportive environment that recognises and celebrates diversity.

Schools must also clearly understand racism and embed strategies for managing and recording racist incidents. This involves developing comprehensive policies that outline the procedures for reporting and addressing racism within the school. The designated governor ensures these policies are effectively communicated and implemented operationally, creating a safe environment where pupils and staff feel empowered to report incidents without fear.

In my headship, reporting on racist incidents forms a part of the ongoing headteacher report to governors. Governors can then hold leaders accountable for any negative trends related to diversity and inclusion and discuss any identified actions, next steps and CPD. Governors could also regularly review pupil attainment of ethnic minority pupils, compared with White pupils, and drill down into the achievement of specific minority groups, including data on behavioural incidents and any suspensions and exclusions, and challenge school leaders on their knowledge of risk factors for certain groups of pupils and whether any mitigation measures have been implemented. Ofsted (2024) supports the idea that by holding leaders accountable, governors ensure continuous improvement in how the school addresses and promotes diversity and inclusion.

Governors and school leaders should continue to access CPD to keep up with practices in diversity and inclusion, especially training programmes and workshops to help leaders develop a deeper understanding of anti-racist practices and equip them with the tools needed to implement these strategies effectively. An ongoing learning process is crucial for maintaining a school culture that values and promotes diversity. Governors and school leaders can take a thorough approach to ensure the school environment allows all pupils to thrive.

Embedding anti-racist principles into the School Improvement Plan is crucial in creating an inclusive and equitable school environment. Setting clear indicators and providing ongoing professional development to ensure that all aspects of school operations reflect these principles can drive meaningful change. The evidence shows that this approach not only supports the social and emotional wellbeing of ethnic minority pupils but also significantly improves academic and personal targets. Through sustained commitment and strategic action, schools can ensure that anti-racist work remains at the forefront of their practice, creating a supportive and inclusive environment for all pupils.

Chapter summary

This chapter emphasises the crucial role of leadership in implementing and sustaining anti-racist work in schools. School leaders, often acting as gatekeepers, control the direction and effectiveness of these initiatives. A genuine commitment from leadership, driven by curiosity and allyship, is essential to avoid superficial engagement and ensure that anti-racist practices are deeply embedded in the school's ethos, curriculum and policies.

The chapter also discusses the unique challenges faced by ethnic minority pupils with special needs, highlighting the need for intersectional understanding and proactive governance in fostering a truly inclusive environment.

> ### TIFFIN TAKE-AWAY
>
> 1. **Foster allyship**
>   Anti-racist work can be uncomfortable, but leadership is key to making a real impact.
>   - How are you fostering open discussions, addressing biases and building a supportive environment for ethnic minority staff, students and families? How can your leadership team better model allyship and inclusivity in daily practices? Additionally, what actions can your school take to better engage and support ethnic minority families of children with SEND?
>
> 2. **Align vision and mission statements with anti-racism**
>   Ensure your school's vision and mission statements explicitly commit to anti-racist principles, guiding decision-making, fostering accountability and setting a clear tone for the entire school community.
>   - You could consider whether your school's values, vision, and mission statements actively reflect a commitment to anti-racism and how you could further strengthen that alignment.
>
> 3. **Embed anti-racist principles in professional development, including governors**
>   Prioritise ongoing racial literacy and inclusive leadership training for all staff, equipping them with the tools to recognise systemic racism and implement meaningful change in the school environment. Engaging governors and all staff in developing and overseeing diversity policies is crucial. Anti-racist practices should be embedded in the school's structure and operations.
>   - How is your governing board involved in understanding, promoting and monitoring anti-racist initiatives, and how do they know what improvements could be made? How might you enhance CPD to ensure all staff are equipped to lead and support anti-racist work in your school?

References

Allen, T., Riley, K. and Coates, M. (2020) "Belonging, behaviour and inclusion in schools: What does the research tell us?" National Education Union. Institute of Education. https://neu.org.uk/latest/library/belonging-behaviour-and-inclusion-schools-what-does-research-tell-us

Campbell, C. (2011) "How to involve hard-to-reach parents: encouraging meaningful parental involvement with schools". National College for School Leadership.

Demie, F. (2019) *Educational inequality: closing the gap*. UCL IOE press.

DiAngelo, R. (2018) *White fragility: Why it's so hard for White people to talk about racism*. Beacon Press.

Eddo-Lodge, R. (2017) *Why I'm no longer talking to white people about race*. Bloomsbury Publishing.

Joseph-Salisbury, R. (2020) "Race and racism in English secondary schools". Runnymede perspectives. The Runnymede Trust.

National Governors Association (2020) "Tackling racial inequality in schools". www.nga.org.uk/knowledge-centre/tackling-racial-inequity-in-schools/

National Governance Association (2022) "What governing boards and school leaders should expect from each other". www.nga.org.uk/knowledge-centre/what-boards-and-leaders-should-expect/

Ofsted (2024) School Inspection Handbook. www.gov.uk/government/publications/school-inspection-handbook-eif/school-inspection-handbook-for-september-2023

UCL-IOE (2020) "46% of all schools in England have no BAME teachers". www.ucl.ac.uk/ioe/news/2020/dec/46-all-schools-england-have-no-bame-teachers

3
How do you establish buy-in and support from the teachers and support staff?

"Why are we doing this work? We're not racist here..."

Engaging all voices: The collective role of staff

Staff engagement is crucial for successfully creating and implementing a whole-school approach to anti-racism, as it ensures that every aspect of school life reflects and upholds anti-racist values. Leaders, teachers, support staff and other school roles, such as those of the office and admin team, every role within a school contributes to shaping the culture, environment and curriculum, making it imperative that all voices are actively involved and creating an inclusive environment.

Leaders must set the tone for anti-racism work, from shaping school policies and practices, providing clear direction and embedding values in the school's mission to curriculum design and staff recruitment. Leaders who create the spaces for dialogue, offer professional development and set measurable goals can ensure the success of the curriculum review. It is the teachers who implement anti-racist pedagogy. They plan and deliver the curriculum, and their role in implementing anti-racist pedagogy is imperative, including using culturally relevant teaching resources and incorporating stories and important figures from diverse racial and disability backgrounds. They are also likely to have more direct communication and stronger relationships with the parents. Therefore, their commitment and buy-in remain key to building strong partnerships with parents.

Support staff create an inclusive environment, working with individual pupils, advocating for pupils, observing microaggressions and providing additional support in understanding cultural materials. Their role in building trusting relationships with pupils can shape a child's learning experience, as they are usually the staff who know the children best of all. Administrative and office staff also have extensive contributions to make – they support a welcoming school culture. They are usually the first point of contact for parents and help shape the school culture. Office staff can reinforce the school's anti-racist ethos through their interactions, ensuring communication is friendly, easy to understand and culturally sensitive for all families. They may support to ensure communication is available in different formats or languages.

The concept of intersectionality is crucial for understanding the specific and often unique challenges faced by ethnic minority children with SEND. Ensuring all staff are informed and receive relevant professional development leads to essential "buy-in" into anti-racist practices.

Overlapping identities: Intersectionality unpacked

Intersectionality examines how various forms of discrimination overlap and affect individuals' experiences. In the context of ethnic minority children with SEND, this means understanding how race, disability and socio-economic status intersect to create unique challenges. For example, ethnic minority children with SEND often face language barriers, cultural misunderstandings and socio-economic disadvantages, which can significantly impact their educational experiences.

Bias in plain sight: Recognising and addressing disparity

Leaders, teachers and support staff must know these intersecting factors to provide effective support. Teachers and support staff's access to comprehensive training on anti-racism, intersectionality and cultural competency can support the development of this knowledge. It is essential for staff to understand how their identities and unconscious biases could influence their teaching practices and possibly discriminatory practices and interactions with pupils. For example, we know that Black Caribbean boys and Mixed-race White and Black Caribbean boys are more likely to be labelled with behavioural issues, are overidentified as having social, emotional and mental health (SEMH) needs and are three times more likely to be excluded from school compared with their White peers (Gillborn, 2008). If staff are educated and aware of these trends, as well as their own potential unconscious biases that may contribute to these identified trends, they will be more informed and aware of how any potential bias can affect their judgements and actions. They will be more aware in recognising their privileges and understanding how systemic racism operates within educational settings.

Cultural competence for all: Training beyond the classroom

Ethnic minority children with SEND also face unique challenges that stem from a range of socio-economic and cultural barriers. These barriers can include language differences and cultural misunderstandings between educators and families, which can significantly impact the educational trajectory of pupils. Strand and Lindsay (2012) indicate that ethnic minority pupils with SEND are often under-identified for special needs services, frequently due to teachers misinterpreting cultural differences as learning disabilities or behavioural issues. This can lead to misidentification, which can delay crucial support and intervention, causing further marginalisation.

It is also equally important that admin and office teams receive training to better support communities with their communication strategies and interactions with parents. Informed admin teams may display more empathy, patience and support for parents who may require signposting, additional information, support and clarity regarding school and any processes related to Education Health Care Plans, setting dates for Annual Reviews.

Building bridges through engaging communities in the School Improvement Plan

Sharing the School Improvement Plan with the community can also be hugely beneficial. Communicating relevant goals, how achieving the goal will benefit the school and how the community can support the work provides an opportunity for collaborative work. It also extends the development of anti-racist practices beyond the school, developing alignment, a shared sense of ownership and commitment to anti-racist work.

To develop initial buy-in, school staff and community leaders must know the "why". Why is this work important and meaningful, as opposed to being perceived as a reactive response to the Black Lives Matter movement?

As previously discussed, training may include explanations of the meaning of key terminology, as this can often be misconstrued in the media. Professional development is essential for equipping staff with the skills and knowledge they need to begin to consider an anti-racist curriculum. In reviewing the four strands of an "anti-racist curriculum", it is straightforward and less contentious to start with reviewing "multicultural education", which schools can begin with by reviewing their festivals and celebrations calendar. In diverse communities, this can move to the next phase, to ensure the school offers a range of cultural celebrations, reflecting the pupil and staff population, thus increasing representation. In less diverse communities, this may consist of providing opportunities to widen "knowledge of, and respect for, different people's faiths, feelings and values" and developing a "sense of enjoyment and fascination in learning about themselves, others and the world around them" (Ofsted, 2024)

The limits of multiculturalism and surface solutions

Schools must move beyond the "multicultural stages" and, after accessing anti-racist CPD, consider what "anti-racist" practices may look like in their school. Embracing the "multicultural" aspects, without considering how to develop anti-racist practice, focuses on surface-level celebrations and occasional days to celebrate the community. While these are essential, developing knowledge and understanding of the deeper issues, through CPD, develops cultural competence, providing a lens into the systemic racism ingrained in society. Without this knowledge, ethnic minority families will continue to be celebrated through the "food and festivals" approach but continue to have their wider needs unmet.

Confronting silence through navigating difficult conversations

As discovered from the initial stages of this work, there were areas of challenge and difficulty that I had not anticipated, as each person contends with their own experiences, beliefs and views. Views that can sometimes be masked when working in an establishment bound by a code of conduct or similar policies. However, when topics such as race are presented to discuss, providing a safe space to ask questions, express opinions and create dialogue is imperative. Pupils and staff should be able to share their experiences and perspectives. These discussions can help to explore their thoughts and opinions, be challenged to identify issues, develop solutions and agree on ways forward collaboratively. Providing forums for open and honest conversations about race can foster a more inclusive and supportive school environment. Examples of initiatives to create these safe spaces may include:

- Diversity committees
  Pupils, teachers and parents meet regularly to discuss diversity and inclusion and review how the school is progressing with its SIP focus on these issues.
- Discussion circles
  Facilitated conversations where participants can talk about their experiences with race and racism in a safe and supportive setting.
- Peer support groups
  These are groups where pupils can support each other in dealing with issues related to race and identity, where applicable and relevant, with SEND pupils.

CASE STUDY: ESTABLISHING A DIVERSITY GROUP

In leading the anti-racist work within a school, establishing the "diversity group" was, by far, the most successful strategy to establish and implement the work. The group comprised of volunteer staff from the school, teacher, and support staff, who displayed brilliant enthusiasm and commitment to allyship. They attended the half-termly meetings after school and within their own time, again showing great support and dedication to the work. The project led to establishing and running the diversity group, with members taking on roles such as creating surveys and posters, consulting with the external diversity coach and attending training sessions.

Challenges in discussion circles

Although a discussion circle was also created, the conversations veered towards sharing personal opinions on the Black Lives Matter movement and contentious opinions on behaviours at the time, such as whether they believed in "taking the knee". There were also opinions expressed about staff not wishing to create an anti-racist curriculum, as well as feeling that there was too much national and school focus on Black and Asian cultures. Despite these ethnic groups being the most prevalent in the school, it was suggested that we focus on Romania or Poland, as we also had one or two children from these countries. The conversations did not always feel safe, and some staff did not feel safe. Conversations were rushed because they were before or after school, so staff could voluntarily leave when the conversations became too heated, as a "fight or flight" response, meaning those left behind were also left with a debate which provided no conclusion or closure. Some staff were left with feelings of frustration, anger and sadness, as they felt that their experiences, their identity and the work we are focused on were meaningless to other staff.

Upon reflection, I would now suggest that these groups are identified and initiated as "safe spaces" with group rules to protect and keep everyone safe emotionally and psychologically. Group rules may include:

1. Respect all voices
   Everyone's experiences and perspectives are valid. Listen actively and without interruption. Avoid making assumptions about others' thoughts or experiences and be mindful of your tone and body language. Respect for diversity of opinion is essential, and disagreements should be addressed respectfully.
2. Confidentiality
   What is shared, stays in the room to foster openness and trust. Ensure that personal stories, feelings and sensitive information shared during conversations are confidential.
3. Speak from personal experiences
   Use "I" statements when sharing to avoid generalisations and focus on your perspective.
4. No blame or judgement
   Be open to hearing different perspectives and avoid blaming or shaming other's opinions, even if you disagree. Focus on understanding.
5. Take responsibility for growth and impact
   Words and actions can have unintended effects. If something you say or do causes harm, take responsibility, even if unintentional. Be open to feedback and willing to apologise.

I would also suggest that, if possible, the groups be led by an external consultant detached from individuals, negating feelings of personalisation or targeted attacks. This person would be skilled and experienced in facilitating large group debates and discussions, creating openness and safety, managing contention, maintaining respect for all and navigating big feelings without them spilling into a messy debate. They would be skilled in ensuring everyone felt heard and safe and the debate was concluded in a manner that was respectful to all. If hiring a consultant is not within a school's budget, there could also have been some group rules or guidelines for all present to follow to ensure respect and professionalism in creating a safe and respectful space. A trained colleague could lead the sessions, however, it would be important for them to access supervision, to manage any contention or their own feelings, from facilitating the group. This action would ensure their wellbeing is supported.

I also feel that in leading this work, I was constantly "grabbing" for time. Although the work was part of the SIP, there was no scheduled CPD time to hold the discussion groups or the diversity groups as part of the directed time. Therefore, this sense of voluntary contribution, as opposed to non-negotiable attendance, lessened the feeling of importance and gravitas of the work. This was a missed opportunity, as the project felt optional. Discussion groups could have been identified as part of the School Improvement Plans and built into CPD time and directed hours – staff would not have easily been able to leave the situation. As it is directed time, they would have needed to remain on-site. If there were an issue, it would have been addressed with immediate input from the group leader or SLT.

Some recognition and rewards could have been provided to boost the morale and motivation of the staff who volunteered to form part of the diversity group. Thompson (2024) in "The ultimate guide to employee wellbeing in 2024" states that recognition and incentives effectively enhance staff engagement. Examples could have included awards, public acknowledgement, or professional growth opportunities or even a wellbeing day.

A coordinated effort: The power of collaborative planning

Support systems for staff, such as mentoring programmes and peer support networks, could be established to help teachers navigate the challenges of implementing an anti-racist curriculum. These support systems can provide a space for staff to share experiences, seek advice and receive encouragement. In addition, collaborative planning involving all staff in the planning and development of an anti-racist curriculum can foster a sense of ownership and commitment.

Cooper-Gibson (2019) in "School and college staff wellbeing evidence from England, the UK and comparable sectors" suggests that collaborative planning enhances staff engagement and curriculum effectiveness. Collaborative planning sessions and regular staff meetings can allow staff to share ideas, voice concerns and contribute to the curriculum development process. They can also plan, create and share resources, which may reduce their workload.

As most teachers are White, they must understand their diverse community and ensure that the opportunities they plan in their medium-term planning (MTP) are meaningful, impactful and relevant to the pupils in their care and their families. Beresford (2013) highlights that many teachers feel underprepared to address the complexities of meeting the needs of ethnically diverse pupils with disabilities. Therefore, teachers will need comprehensive training and someone to support and lead the direction in providing them with the confidence and skills to create practical strategies for inclusive classrooms.

Gillborn (2008) argues that the role of educators in anti-racist initiatives is critical, especially in diverse societies like the UK. The racial inequalities within the UK system are evident. Therefore, there is a vital need for educators to actively engage in anti-racism work to challenge and change entrenched biases and systemic structures. Professionals who are well-versed in intersectionality can advocate more effectively for inclusive policies and practices that acknowledge and cater to the complex identities of their pupils.

The journey towards an anti-racist curriculum in SEND settings is complex and demands a committed effort at every level of the educational system. These efforts must be underpinned by a robust understanding of the issues and a dedicated approach to addressing them. Through focused education, representation, community engagement and continuous evaluation, schools can begin to dismantle systemic barriers and create a more inclusive, equitable educational environment.

The intersection of race and disability presents unique challenges that require sophisticated understanding and committed intervention from teachers and leaders in schools, as there is little research available that illustrates these complexities with clarity. Through targeted professional development and proactive leadership in anti-racist work, staff can better support their pupils' diverse needs. A commitment to intersectionality and anti-racism should be essential and practical in preparing all pupils to thrive in a diverse and inclusive society. Schools must, therefore, prioritise comprehensive training, engage deeply with their communities and ensure that anti-racism is woven into the fabric of their school's educational practice.

Chapter summary

This chapter highlights the importance of staff engagement and leadership in successfully implementing an anti-racist curriculum in SEND schools. It discusses the intersectionality between race, disability and socio-economic status and how these overlapping challenges affect ethnic minority pupils with SEND. The chapter emphasises that comprehensive professional development, active leadership and fostering inclusive environments are essential for staff to understand and address systemic racism within educational settings. Strategies for involving the wider school community and creating safe spaces for dialogue are also explored, along with practical steps for integrating anti-racism into everyday school practices.

TIFFIN TAKE-AWAY

1. **Create safe spaces for open dialogue**
   Establishing safe spaces for honest discussions about race and inclusion can foster a more collaborative school culture and deeper engagement in anti-racist work.

   - You could consider what your school can do to create and sustain safe spaces where staff and pupils feel comfortable discussing race, bias, and inclusion.

2. **Align school improvement plans with anti-racist goals**
   Embedding anti-racist work into the school improvement plan ensures that it becomes a strategic priority with measurable goals and accountability.

   - How can your school improvement plan more effectively prioritise and track progress on anti-racist initiatives and inclusive practices?

3. **Incorporate anti-racism into staff appraisal targets**
   Embedding anti-racism into performance management helps ensure that all staff actively contribute to creating an inclusive environment. This can include setting specific cultural competency goals, engaging with ethnic minority families or integrating diverse perspectives in lesson planning.

   - You might consider adjusting staff appraisal targets to include measurable contributions to anti-racism and inclusion efforts.

References

Beresford, P. (2013) "Beyond the usual suspects". Research Report. Shaping our lives. https://shapingourlives.org.uk/report/beyond-the-usual-suspects-research-report/

Cooper-Gibson (2019) "School and college staff wellbeing evidence from England, the UK and comparable sectors". Department for Education. https://assets.publishing.service.gov.uk/media/5fbbe98d8fa8f559da0f168e/Wellbeing-literature-review_final18052020_ap.pdf

Gillborn, D., Rollock, N., Warmington, P. and Demack, S. (2013) *Race, Racism and Education*. The University of Birmingham

Ofsted Inspection Handbook (2024) www.gov.uk/government/publications/school-inspection-handbook-eif

Strand, S. and Lindsay, G. (2012) "Ethnic disproportionality in the identification of speech language and communication needs (SLCN) and autistic spectrum disorders (ASD). 2005-2011". London: Department for Education.

Thompson, S. (2024) "The ultimate guide to employee wellbeing in 2024". www.workhuman.com/blog/employee-wellbeing/

4
What does an anti-racist curriculum mean to parents of SEND children?

"We can barely get through the days …"

The paradox of parental engagement in anti-racism

Parents play a pivotal role in their children's education; their support and involvement are critical in shaping a school's culture and ensuring the successful implementation of an anti-racist curriculum. Parents' unique perspectives and insights can contribute to creating a curriculum that meets the diverse needs of all pupils.

Exploring whether parents "care" about an anti-racist curriculum is complex and multifaceted. Data is limited. From the initial parent surveys on the school project, it was felt that parents felt it was irrelevant to their child with severe learning disabilities. Labelling the work as "anti-racist" seemed to have more negative connotations with parents and staff than "increasing representation", as the term "racist" or "anti-racist" seemed inapplicable and irrelevant in a SEND school.

> "I can't even go to the temple… the priest tells me to take my son and go home… they say I must have done something in a past life to deserve this…"
>
> *Parent*

Creating an anti-racist curriculum for pupils with SEND goes beyond simply increasing representation of ethnic minority communities within the curriculum, celebrating a wider array of festivals and celebrations across the year or embedding a decolonised curriculum. While increasing representation through multicultural experiences can be a positive step, it often only addresses the surface level and could be viewed as in response to an "educational initiative". As we have discussed, we need to adopt "roots and branches" measures.

Moving beyond festivals: Roots, branches, and representation

The root of this work is to identify the ingrained racism within various strands of society and the complex array of challenges, both cultural and socio-economic, that affect ethnic minority families with disabled children and their ability to engage with schools.

> If we are to improve the lives of BAME families dealing with what can initially be a devastating diagnosis, it's vital that decision-makers, service providers and faith and

community groups listen to those families and work together to produce effective, culturally appropriate support.

(Cockburn, 2015)

Disability across cultures: varied lenses, varied stigmas

Understanding how disability is viewed across different cultures is also crucial in providing valuable insights for school staff, allowing them to understand how to create a more inclusive and effective educational environment for ethnic minority pupils with SEND. According to Ingstad and Whyte (1995), the perception of disability varies significantly across cultures, influencing how disabilities are addressed and managed within communities.

Western societies often approach disability through a medical lens, emphasising assessment and diagnosis. While this medical perspective can drive advancements in health, it also risks stigmatising those with disabilities. This view can lead to the assumption that people with disabilities need to be "assessed and labelled" through clinical and biological perspectives, with a focus on treatment through therapeutic intervention.

In education, applying a medical model to disability can support children with disabilities to fit into existing educational frameworks, embed therapeutic strategies into the classroom and ensure teaching and learning meet the needs of all pupils. Using this model, any deviation from the "norm" triggers a process of assessment, quest for a diagnosis and label and placement in "the correct educational setting" which is less accommodating to diverse needs.

The reality of this, is that we have an overwhelming number of children and young people in mainstream schools who cannot access the curriculum offer, or are in alternative provisions, or out of education completely, as there is no "correct educational setting" for these pupils who don't fit into recognised boxes. Special schools remain overwhelmingly over-subscribed.

Many non-Western cultures approach disability holistically, integrating social, spiritual and community elements in their understanding and approach to disability. This model is based on community values, traditional beliefs and superstitions. For example, some African cultures view disability within the broader family and community life context. These cultures often place a stronger emphasis on shared responsibility and community-based support. In these settings, families and local communities take on caring for and integrating individuals with disabilities.

Invisible chains: Stigma, superstition, and silence

In some Asian cultures, disability is sometimes perceived through a spiritual or religious framework, where disability can be seen as a reflection of past actions or failures. Although this may provide a sense of purpose and acceptance, it can also lead to stigma and the ostracisation of the family.

> A lot of people felt sorry for me because I had a disabled child… My mum turned around and said to me, "Don't mix Sayed's clothes with theirs (other children's) because he's different… Don't put the baby near him… Asian people don't understand… People kept on saying take him down to the healers, do this, do that… like in Pakistan or India a lot of people say 'Oh he's got the devil's in him'…"
>
> (Hatton, 2003)

Ethnic minority parents of children with SEND can often face deep-seated isolation and cultural conflict. This sense of disconnection stems from multiple factors, including:

1. Cultural taboos: In some communities, disabilities are subject to unspoken rules or restrictions based on long-standing social norms. For example, pretending the disability does not exist.
2. Stigmatisation: There is often a negative perception associated with disabilities in certain cultures, including feeling sorry for families if they have a disabled child, or believing the family are cursed, therefore reducing all contact with them.
3. Misconceptions: Many communities hold inaccurate beliefs about the causes of disabilities, including karma or the actions of the woman while pregnant and carrying the baby.

These factors can create a challenging environment for ethnic minority parents of children with special needs. In numerous communities, disabilities are frequently viewed through the lens of

- superstition – attributing disabilities to supernatural causes.
- stigma – associating disabilities with shame or disgrace.
- shame – feeling embarrassed or dishonoured due to a child's condition.

> As a result, some parents often find themselves isolated from their cultural communities, lacking the support and understanding they need to navigate their unique challenges.

In certain cultures, disabilities are believed to result from past wrongdoings or curses, either in this life or in their past (Hatton, 2004). Parents may be blamed for their child's condition, with accusations that they have done something wrong in a previous life or have failed in some way (Cerebra, 2021). These beliefs can lead to parents being blamed for their child's condition, increasing their sense of isolation and guilt.

Families frequently navigate a labyrinth of cultural expectations and misconceptions about disability, which hinders their engagement with available educational and community resources. The National Autistic Society (2014) confirms that misconceptions about autism and other developmental disorders are widespread, particularly in minority communities. Additionally, the relationship between cultural representation and these parents' experiences is complex, with some feeling that a sole focus on increasing cultural representation does not sufficiently address their unique challenges.

Following on from karma from previous lives, in some cultures disability is viewed through a spiritual lens, where individuals are made to feel they are being "tested" or "punished" by having a child with additional needs by a higher power. While these beliefs can offer some families a sense of purpose or explanation, they can also contribute to feelings of blame and isolation.

Ali, Fazil, Bywaters and Wallace (2001) found that stigma is a significant barrier to seeking help for many ethnic minority parents of children with disabilities. The stigma associated with disabilities can lead to social exclusion. Parents may be ostracised by their communities, leading to a lack of support and understanding. The social stigma can be particularly pronounced in tight-knit communities where the social norms are strongly maintained.

In some cultures, there is a tendency to maintain silence about disabilities to avoid shame, which can prevent open discussions and seeking necessary support and resources. The fear of judgement or ostracisation can also lead parents to withdraw from social interactions, causing further isolation from potential support networks. The isolation can be compounded when parents are already marginalised within their communities due to race or ethnicity.

Many ethnic minority parents avoid community gatherings to prevent exposure to judgement and criticism. The constant burden of stigma and isolation can take a toll on the mental and emotional health of parents. Feelings of shame, guilt, and helplessness are common, leading to higher levels of stress and anxiety. Hatton et al. (2004) highlight that ethnic minority parents of children with special needs are at a higher risk of experiencing mental health issues due to the compounded stressors of stigma and isolation.

Misconceptions and blame can also lead to isolation from extended families and community support networks, which can be particularly devastating for parents who rely on these networks for emotional and practical support. Many minority parents and carers are less likely to receive support from their communities compared with White families. There can be an observable difference in attitudes towards disability between the generations. Older generations may hold more traditional views, while younger parents might be more open to seeking support. The generational clash can create additional stress and isolation within families, and parents may experience conflict with extended family members who hold different beliefs about disability, leading to further isolation.

The UK government, in its report of "Review of Evidence of disability programmes in South Asia" (2019), estimate that 80% of the world's population with disabilities live in developing countries, where there can be high rates of discrimination and stigma, and any policies or laws which may have recently been passed, remain "on paper only". Thakkur found that in countries such as Afghanistan, disability can be viewed as two different names, "malul", those who suffered injuries in the war and "mayub" those with disabilities caused by birth accidents, malnutrition, and so on. The "malul" is "to be respected, admired, and celebrated, as they are considered heroes, whereas the 'mayub', are regarded to be cursed". "Intellectual and developmental disability that cannot be attributed to a specific cause is perceived as a curse, shameful, punishment or bad lack; children may be locked up or given food but no affection or care".

Ingstad and Whyte (1995) found that in Somalia, disability is regarded as a "disease", which is flexible and subject to improvement depending on the intervention. There is no specific term for "disability", but the term "naafo" is ascribed, meaning "rehabilitation", and people with disabilities are called "sick people". As there is no one term to describe disability, disabled people tend to be addressed according to the specific disability they have; for example, a person missing a limb may be called "gacanley", meaning "missing limb", deaf people are called "dhegoole" meaning "without ears" and blind people "indhoole" meaning "without eyes".

Like the Afghan culture, there is more tolerance for physical disability than learning disabilities or cognitive disabilities, where the culture is far less accepting; people with cognitive learning disabilities are told to "be normal" or "not be crazy". Research from other non-Western cultures has found similar approaches to labelling disabilities. In India, names such as "bawla" (simple), "bhola" (innocent) or "paagal" (mad) are given to cognitive challenges and disabilities.

Similar to South Asian culture, religious healers, herbal treatments, traditional healing techniques and surgical procedures can be sought.

> In English they say disability, but in our language, they say mental… The English say the child is special, but if we tell people outside that she is disabled, they say she is mental. No one believes that she is any different. Instead, they tell me I am mad, and she will be cured.
>
> (Quote from a South Asian parent, Hatton, 2004)

The response to disability in Somalia can be identified into three main categories:

1. "dawa Soomaali" – Somalian medicine
2. "dawa casriga" – modern medicine, and
3. "diin" – religion

Hatton (2004) states that when questioned on support from religious leaders, over 45.6% of parents stated that they did not feel that support from religious leaders, organisations or healers was helpful.

A review available on the DfE website, entitled "Review of evidence on disability programmes in South Asia" (Kalyanwala, Singh and Iqbal, 2019), explores the intersection of race and disability, and gender, specifically the vulnerability of females in some South Asian countries. Where some countries may have special schools, in countries such as Bangladesh, India and Nepal, it is reported that girls with disabilities tend not to be sent to school due to fears of "emotional, physical and sexual abuse". Girls with disability are at increased risk of this kind of abuse, and the review stated that there was "reported abuse by traditional healers during treatment or therapy... these instances go unreported because of social stigma or threats".

The review continues to highlight that many researchers have found that, horrifyingly, in India, 100% of women with a disability had experienced physical abuse, and 25% experienced sexual abuse and rape. Women are denied their right to sexuality and are forcibly sterilised; disabled women can experience neglect, abandonment and the administration of electric shocks and chemical, physical or mechanical restraint without consent.

Research on cultural interpretations and views of disability reveals significant disparities in understanding and responding to children with SEND across different cultures but also within cultures. These differences can contradict contemporary Western approaches to SEND support and inclusion.

Shifting perspectives: The generational divide on disability

Hatton (2004) found that South Asian families in the UK often interpreted their child's cognitive disability through a religious or supernatural lens, which influenced their actions in seeking help from schools and services. Attitudes towards SEND vary and are not synonymous with any specific culture – they can vary significantly. Raghavan, Pawson and Small (2013) observed that while traditional views on disability still exist amongst the South Asian community in the UK, there is a growing acceptance of medical models of disability among the more educated, middle-class families.

The intersection of class and education with cultural attitudes is further supported by Bywaters et al. (2003), who found that socio-economic status significantly influenced how British Pakistani families understood and responded to their children's disabilities. There is a gradual shift in beliefs and perspectives and a development of more progressive attitudes towards disability in many communities. Hussain, Atkin and Ahmad (2002) observed that there are changing and more inclusive attitudes amongst the younger generations in Pakistani communities within the UK.

CASE STUDY: JAY

I spoke to a mid-30s Indian male who acquired a spinal cord injury in his early 20s after being involved in an accident, which caused paralysis from his shoulders down. He is the only son with four sisters and has always been fiercely ambitious. He is physically disabled, but his cognitive capacity is unchanged, except for a recent diagnosis of injury-induced dyslexia. Despite this, and through his sustained injury, Jay qualified as a lawyer and works as a junior lawyer.

We spoke of the immediate response to his injury from his family and friends. Desperate remedies were sought from prayers, fasts and touching grains and fruits so these could be fed to the birds or cast into rivers, all with the promise that he would heal from his injuries and walk. He spoke of his own beliefs, that "maybe these would work", torn between his educated and logical brain, but also with the deep-seated wish and the want for there to be a positive result – maybe these remedies would work. It was a hybrid model of medical and therapeutic interventions, as well as a spiritual model of exhausting all options and never giving up hope.

Jay spoke of both the immediate but then prolonged support from his family and friends. He understood that his loved ones had an overwhelming desire to help, be helpful and somehow make it better. Before reaching for a cup, he had the cup brought to his face, a straw put in between his lips so he could drink. This went on for longer than it should have. There was a conflict between his therapists, who pushed for him to be more independent and to act himself to promote this independence, and his family, who over-supported through their care. In Indian culture, these acts of giving are acts of service – it is how you show you care.

"The Indian community wants to help," he says. "They are abundant, lots of them, and that's how they show their love and support. But it is disabling. I needed to learn to do things myself, and my independence was prolonged because too many people were doing too many things for me."

However, his shock came from the prejudiced attitudes and assumptions of social services, who informed him that he would not be entitled to independent living packages, "as surely, he is going home to live with his parents – that's what Indians do?" He felt denied his privilege and right to access an independent lifestyle, which was afforded to White patients, due to the stereotyping of the social worker. Furthermore, they then insisted that he remain living in the allocated nursing home, as "this was easiest".

There is an abundance of research that illustrates Jay's experience, as racial profiling by social services, particularly when assigning care packages, is of significant concern.

> Various studies and reports indicate the substantial disparities ethnic minorities face in how care services are allocated, leading to unequal access and support.
>
> He did not take the easy route. He fought to live independently, complete his studies and qualify as a lawyer. He fights every day to travel via the London Underground, as he is expected to commute to work several days of the week to be office-based. The London Underground has been long-criticised for its lack of accessibility, with one-third of stations still lacking any accessibility to disabled people. On most days, Jay is unsure whether the ramp will be out for him to use at one of the more disability-friendly stations.
>
> "Race is not the issue," he tells me. "I see lots of brown faces at work; there's lots of us there now.""It is the systemic biases towards disability, through social services preventing independence, transport limiting independence, lack of reasonable adjustments on job descriptions to create a more equitable practice. These barriers affect career progression, job satisfaction, and quality of life. It's having to travel to work, to work 7.30 am to 7 pm, three days a week, which leaves me exhausted because I am manually wheeling myself around all day, as I was refused an electric chair to navigate around, which would have helped me greatly."
>
> The frustration of the systemic bias within these several systems is letting him down because there is a lack of prioritisation, accountability and commitment to ensure they support equity for all. Some changes, quite minor, would have a colossal impact on not just his wellbeing but also his ability to fulfil his potential while maintaining his hard-earned independence.
>
> When an individual has demonstrated such a colossal amount of resilience, hard work and sheer determination to sustain a path of continued success, attainment and achievement despite some significant hurdles in life – as a society, don't we all owe it to each other, to help identify and remove barriers, offer support and become an ally in our fights for freedom and accessibility?
>
> A fight against injustice remains the same – whether it is a race riot on the street or ensuring a disabled person can get onto a tube in London without being told to "just squeeze on somehow ..."

Cultural understanding, response and acceptance of disability are complex landscapes that require culturally sensitive approaches from schools and SEND support services. Lindsay and Edwards (2013) argues that "tailored interventions that consider diverse cultural interpretations of disability" should be considered.

With many ethnic minority communities becoming isolated from their community groups, there is less support from extended families, and parents become increasingly isolated both within themselves as well as understanding how to support their child with additional needs fully. Ethnic minority parents, with additional barriers such as English as an additional language, are at risk of challenges around mental health. For example, South Asian families of children with SEND have higher rates of visits to the GP and hospitalisation for their own needs, including high levels of stress, distress, hypertension and diabetes.

Ethnic minority parents of children with SEND encounter distinct socio-economic and cultural barriers that intersect with their educational experiences. These include differences in language, cultural misunderstandings between educators and families and socio-economic disadvantages. Strand and Lindsay (2012) have shown that minority children with SEND are often under-identified for special education services, frequently due to educators mistaking cultural differences for learning disabilities or behavioural issues. These pupils usually lack access to culturally competent support, exacerbating their challenges. Economic hardships disproportionately affect families, limiting their access to necessary educational resources, healthcare and other critical support services outside school.

Coard (1971) identified that Black children have been disproportionately identified with various labels. In his seminal work, Coard identified that four out of every five immigrant children in "Educationally Subnormal schools" were Black. These schools were a part of the UK education system from the 1940s until the 1980s and introduced a "tiered system of education". Children who were identified as "educationally subnormal" were placed in these early "special schools", which were meant for pupils with intellectual disabilities or learning difficulties.

Coard (1971) argues that there are several biases in the assessment processes administered by the UK education system, which include personal biases, cultural bias, middle-class bias, emotional disturbance bias and IQ tests. It is argued that these biases form an assessment process which is structured in a way that allows White, middle-class children to "pass", and Black children do not have the same life experiences, culture or use of language and will be observed to have "failed" assessments.

Black children continue to experience similar prejudice. Almost 60 years on from Coard's research, we find that Black Caribbean and Mixed White and Black Caribbean pupils are twice as likely to be identified with Social, Emotional, and Mental Health (SEMH) needs than White British pupils. While there are socio-economic factors, such as poverty and deprivation, that account for some of the disproportionality observed, the data and research suggest biases in school policies and practices, as well as under-identification of other possible needs such as autism as teachers are more biased in their interpretation of behaviours for example citing SEMH needs as opposed to identifying any possible other needs.

Bridging the gap and cultural competence in practice

Many Black parents feel that the education system is ineffective in addressing and rectifying racial biases. Despite school, authority or national commitments to change, parents continue to feel that there is a lack of concrete action, accountability or substantial changes, leading parents to believe there is a lack of commitment. The mistrust of educators and authorities among parents of Black children is rooted in historical and ongoing experiences of discrimination, systemic biases, cultural misunderstanding and inadequate support.

Recent research and statistics also demonstrate that there is a significant under-identification of autism in the Asian community in the UK. Research shows that cultural perceptions within Asian communities can significantly impact the identification of special needs; there is often a lower level of awareness and understanding of conditions like autism among Asian parents. Cultural attitudes towards disability, which might include stigma or viewing it as a family shame, can lead to reluctance in seeking diagnosis and support services. This cultural backdrop influences parents' willingness to acknowledge and address special educational needs.

Additionally, language barriers play a crucial role in the underrepresentation of Asian children with special needs. Many Asian families might face difficulties communicating effectively with educators and healthcare providers due to limited English proficiency. This can result in a misunderstanding of the child's needs and a lack of proper advocacy for their children's needs. While socio-economic factors and status do influence educational outcomes, research indicates that it does not fully explain the underrepresentation of Asian children in special needs categories such as autism. Factors such as early educational attainment and the levels of deprivation in the area are considered, but they do not account for the entire display.

The education system may contribute to the under-identification of children with SEND in the Asian community due to biases and a lack of cultural competence among educators. Schools lack the knowledge and skills to recognise and address the needs of different ethnic groups of children, especially if those needs manifest differently due to cultural behaviours. There is a vast difference in cultural variations and social attitudes towards disability, and schools tend to ignore these.

However, ethnic minority families often face systemic failings, such as feeling as though any potential difficulties that the school has identified are not adequately explained to them. They continue to feel overwhelmed through the assessment and diagnosis processes, as they do not have information adequately explained. Essential information about diagnosis or how to best support and advocate for their child is not shared through any translation – no efforts are made to help parents understand their child's needs (Hatton, 2004). Additionally, they face lengthy waits for Education Health Care Plans or inadequate support from local authorities. Research indicates that ethnic minority children frequently receive a later diagnosis of SEND, resulting in delayed support and intervention (Strand and Lindoff, 2010). Due to experiences of discrimination within the health care systems, minority communities can show a general mistrust of medical professionals, which can prevent parents from seeking medical advice or early interventions for their children.

Perepa, Wallace and Guldberg (2023) found that ethnic minority parents, either due to fear of blame, stigma or judgement, are less likely to seek help or services for their children.

Misconceptions that minority families may hold regarding their child's disabilities can also significantly affect the educational experiences of the child. Systemic bias and confusion in navigating the SEND processes can make it difficult for parents to advocate effectively for their children due to their lack of knowledge and understanding.

Ethnic minority families can mistrust professionals due to the misalignment between a firm and final medical diagnosis by professionals and the more fluid, interchanging religious explanation of disability. Minority families often feel that professionals do not fully understand their unique cultural contexts and needs, which barriers in language can further exacerbate. Research does also show, however, that there is a lower level of understanding of autism in ethnic minority communities. It could also be explained that if English is a second language, there is a great deal of emphasis on diagnosis labels or medical jargon, which people will not understand, especially those with English as a second language. Families can feel that professionals are not providing appropriate or effective explanations or support, further eroding trust. With recent and historical experiences of discrimination and systematic racism within healthcare and education, there can be deep-seated mistrust among minority communities.

CASE STUDY: SEN SCHOOL, OXFORDSHIRE

There was a significant lack of parental engagement with the school from minority communities and parents. Communications were digital, with links to weekly newsletters and emails sent to parents.

Due to the schools' locations, parents do not tend to engage with in-person events and typically attend Annual Reviews via virtual meetings. Due to challenges with digital literacy, parents can often have difficulties logging on and remaining engaged in the meeting.

Parent surveys were not responded to; the average response was up to 10 parents.

Translating the survey into the home languages using Artificial Intelligence and printing the surveys to go home as paper copies increased engagement responses by four or five times. Additionally, recorded videos explaining the school's curriculum are emailed and sent to parents so they can click on a link to access key information about the school.

In addition, offering satellite coffee mornings in the community and more central locations to parents who cannot drive ensured they could attend by using more frequent public transport or through another parent attending the sessions. The coffee mornings were received very well, and parents were grateful for the attempts made to support their engagement.

> Ethnic minority parents can be labelled as "hard to reach", as these efforts are beyond what is expected. However, as the headteacher of this school and leading this work nationally through BAME ED SEND, I felt it my duty, and within my role of service to the wider community, to find ways to engage with the whole community—regardless of any perception of strategies being "too much".
>
> The efforts are driving and securing sustained engagement – therefore, I would say, have been initially successful.

Empowering parents: From isolation to advocacy

An anti-racist curriculum is crucial to confront and challenge racism within the education system actively; a curriculum which creates an inclusive environment that respects and acknowledges the diversity of all pupils, including those from all racial and ethnic groups. However, in leading this work in SEND schools, and working alongside parents of children with SEND, we examined what significance creating and implementing an anti-racist curriculum held for them.

An anti-racist curriculum should integrate anti-racist principles into all aspects of education, including the content taught through the curriculum, the pedagogical approaches used, the training of teachers and support staff and the school policies. The curriculum should identify, address and dismantle systemic racism, promote equity and ensure that all pupils, regardless of their racial background, have equal opportunities to succeed (Ladson-Billings, 1995).

Various research demonstrated that ethnic minority children with SEND are often double-marginalised. They face not only the challenges associated with their disabilities but also the added layer of racial discrimination, known as "dual marginalisation". This can lead to under-identification in some racial groups, over-identification in other racial groups, misdiagnosis of need, inappropriate placements and a lack of adequate support (Strand and Lindorff, 2018).

One of the primary reasons parents of children with special needs might value an anti-racist curriculum is its potential to address specific systemic biases that affect their children. As we know, research indicates that Black Caribbean and Mixed White and Black Caribbean pupils are over-represented in categories such as Social, Emotional and Mental Health (SEMH) needs due to biased perceptions, assessments and disciplinary procedures. An anti-racist curriculum can help staff recognise and potentially mitigate these biases by creating spaces for discussion, parental input, and engagement, leading to fairer assessments and, essentially, better support for all children.

A focus on developing cultural competence of staff should also be maintained. Creating an "anti-racist curriculum" should ensure professional development opportunities for teachers to develop their knowledge, understanding and cultural contexts of the pupils in their schools. This would lead to better understanding and relationships with pupils and their families, thus improving communication between teachers and parents through developed trust and ensuring that educational strategies are culturally relevant and practical (Gay, 2000).

Some parents report being more concerned about the practical support their children require than about curriculum intentions or changes. They communicated that ensuring their child accesses therapy, medical support, behavioural support and appropriate resources is more important. However, some ethnic minority parents of children with SEND face unique challenges that they may not be aware of but will influence their priorities and concerns. These parents will not always be aware of the systemic discrimination they and their child may experience or how these will affect their child's later life. Therefore, while cultural presentation in the curriculum design is an essential aspect of an inclusive education system, many parents primarily focus on their children's immediate, significant needs.

As we have seen, parents are navigating a complex education system. They face multifaceted challenges in securing appropriate support, assessments, and diagnoses to explain their child's specific needs or, in some cases, what levels of progress to expect.

Schools developing an anti-racist curriculum must begin by acknowledging the intersection of SEND and race and reviewing the needs of their community, including parents' knowledge, understanding, and engagement in the school.

The primary focus and concern for all parents is usually ensuring the child's immediate and most significant needs are met. Navigating the special education system, securing adequate support and dealing with ongoing discrimination and bias are urgent priorities that can overshadow broader issues like cultural representation in the curriculum. Research supports the notion that the immediate needs of children with special needs take precedence over other concerns for their parents.

A study by Satherley and Norwich (2021) found that parents of children with special needs prioritise securing adequate support and navigating the educational system above all else. Strand and Lindorff (2018) also highlight the significant challenges ethnic minority parents face in ensuring fair treatment and appropriate identification of their children's needs, which often require immediate attention. Therefore, we may conclude that while cultural representation is essential for an inclusive education, the pressing needs of their children in a complex system demand immediate attention and resources.

While cultural representation in the curriculum may be a lower priority for families struggling with daily survival, its significance cannot be understated. A curriculum that reflects various racial groups' diverse histories, cultures and contributions can significantly enhance the self-esteem and identity of ethnic minority pupils and their families. It also provides all pupils with a more comprehensive and inclusive worldview for the whole school community, fostering mutual understanding and respect across racial divides.

For White families, it provides opportunities to learn about the cultures that make up the school community, and for ethnic minority communities it provides a space and place to be seen, heard and celebrated. Thus, it creates a sense of belonging and community that may otherwise be lacking due to cultural stigmas and interpretations of special needs.

For ethnic minority parents of children with special needs, cultural representation can play a complex role in their experiences of isolation and support. While cultural representation in the school is viewed positively, it may not be viewed as sufficient in extending and supporting the reality of the challenges these families face, such as the stigma and misconceptions about disabilities from their respective communities. These cannot be addressed merely by increased cultural representation within the school (O'Hara, 2018).

Research by Pearson and Parentkind, "Diversity and inclusion in schools report" (2022) identified a similar trend in that many ethnic minority individuals view tokenistic representation of their culture as superficial and ineffective in addressing more profound issues of inequality and exclusion. Some parents perceive efforts at cultural representation as tokenistic, lacking genuine understanding or a commitment to addressing their needs, leading to cynicism and disengagement from available support services.

With a White majority in teaching and leadership positions, schools risk reinforcing stereotypes and superficial opportunities that do not genuinely reflect community experiences. Building trust with ethnic minority families is fundamental to the success of any anti-racist initiative in schools. Trust can be fostered through consistent and transparent communication, building relationships through coffee mornings and workshops, and showing genuine respect for the disadvantages experienced by minority communities. Each family's cultural and personal backgrounds, and involving them in decision-making processes related to their child's education is imperative. Cultural competence training for staff is essential to help them understand and respect these cultural differences.

In the UK, the relevance of intersectionality is particularly pronounced given the diverse nature of the pupil population. Crenshaw's framework illustrates how when race and disability intersect to create unique challenges, educational policies tend to overlook the additional barriers faced by ethnic minority families of children with SEND. These issues can range from discriminatory attitudes to inadequate support services, requiring a nuanced, informed approach considering these overlapping identities.

While the immediate daily realities of minority families with SEND children might not prioritise educational reforms such as an anti-racist curriculum, the long-term benefits of this work are crucial. Schools have a significant role in supporting these families by addressing not only the child's individual needs and supporting the parents in understanding how to help their child but also the cultural and emotional wellbeing of their pupils and their families. Schools can transform educational settings into sanctuaries of understanding, empowerment and holistic support by fostering an inclusive environment and directly engaging with these families' challenges.

Providing culturally competent services that respect and understand the unique cultural contexts of families can create more supportive environments and improve the health and wellbeing outcomes for minority families. In SEND schools, or pupils with EHCP, these services include the local authority, psychologists, CAMHS, nurses, speech and language therapists, possibly physiotherapists and occupational therapists, nurses, doctors and consultants, as well as the education teams of headteachers, leaders, teachers and support staff. Parents will encounter a wealth of professionals, each with their advice, strategies, and reports to make sense of and implement. These services need to access training to provide culturally competent and accessible services.

Parents should be supported and empowered through support groups, forums, coffee mornings and access to resources to help them navigate the challenges of raising a child with special needs. Empowerment can reduce isolation, build resilience, develop wellbeing and increase engagement. Strengthening community support networks can provide ethnic minority parents with the social and emotional support they need, including peer support groups, community centres and online forums where parents can connect and share experiences.

Schools could offer outreach coffee mornings, as per my previous case study. Offering outreach services to parents within their community can increase attendance significantly, providing valuable opportunities for discussion, checking in and identifying parents' priorities. Some schools create specific groups based on languages spoken so parents can network and communicate with one another more freely. Using these groups as platforms and forums to discuss and make decisions provides opportunities for ethnic minority parents to enable advocacy and representation, ensuring their voices are heard and their experiences are considered in policies, practice and the development of services.

Support groups allow parents to share their unique needs and challenges. Furthermore, support groups can provide access to information such as respite care, financial assistance and educational support, which may alleviate some of the pressures parents face. Ensuring these resources are culturally appropriate and accessible can enhance their effectiveness, as there is a demonstratable effort of equitable resource allocation.

Meaningful cultural representation involves the visibility and inclusion of culturally relevant services and supports, including bilingual staff, culturally sensitive support and community-specific programs. Engaging ethnic minority communities in the design and delivery of services can ensure that their specific needs and perspectives are addressed, develop trust and reduce feelings of isolation.

Creating an inclusive school environment for parents to come together could be created by implementing these strategies, as well as ensuring the diverse backgrounds of the community are reflected in the school materials and curriculum. The school could offer ongoing coffee morning and workshops, to provide safe spaces for conversations and support.

These shared spaces can provide support and develop understanding, reducing stigma, which is important in some cultural groups. Non-English-speaking families face further isolation due to significant barriers to engaging effectively with schools because of language differences and a lack of translated resources. Schools must address these barriers by providing translation services and bilingual staff to communicate effectively with all families.

Chapter summary

This chapter explores the crucial role of parental engagement in the development and implementation of an anti-racist curriculum for children with special educational needs and disabilities (SEND). It delves into the cultural, socio-economic and systemic challenges faced by ethnic minority families, who often experience additional barriers in accessing educational support for their children.

The chapter emphasises the need for schools to go beyond token representation and foster a deeper understanding of intersectionality, focusing on how race, disability and culture intersect. Schools must prioritise creating culturally competent environments and listen to parents' voices, ensuring that the curriculum and support services are relevant and responsive to their unique challenges.

 TIFFIN TAKE-AWAYS

1. **Tailor support for ethnic minority families in SEND settings**
   Schools need to recognise the unique barriers ethnic minority families face in navigating the education system for their SEND children, which is challenging for all parents. Offering tailored support through culturally sensitive communication, services and community outreach programmes should be considered.

   - You might think about how to improve your engagement with ethnic minority parents and ensure that support systems are culturally appropriate and accessible.

2. **Empowering parents with SEND knowledge**
   Ethnic minority parents often face cultural and language barriers that affect their understanding of SEND pedagogy. Schools could offer culturally tailored workshops, resources and training that address these challenges.

   - What culturally responsive resources and training can your school offer to help minority parents better understand SEND and support their child's learning? For example, the Early Bird programme with translators is offered. The Early Bird programme is a supportive and information providing series of workshops designed by the National Autistic Society. Parents and carers learn more about autism and how to support their child following a diagnosis.

3. **Empowering ethnic minority parents as advocates in the SEND system**
   Empowering ethnic minority parents with knowledge about SEND pedagogy, support services, school policies and practices and their rights in the education system can help them to become stronger advocates for their children. Schools should provide ongoing opportunities for parents to engage with SEND experts, peer support groups, and so on.

   - You might consider how your school can better empower ethnic minority parents to become confident advocates for their child's educational and SEND needs.

References

Ali, Z., Fazil, Q., Bywaters, P., Wallace, L. and Singh, G. (2001) "Disability, ethnicity and childhood: A critical review of research". *Disability and Society*, 16(7): 949-967.

Bywaters, P., Ali, Z., Fazil, Q. and Wallace, L. (2003) "Attitudes towards disability amongst Pakistani and Bangladeshi parents of disabled children in the UK: Considerations for service providers and the disability movement". *Health and Social Care in the Community*, 11(6).

Cerebra (2021) "Institutionalising parent-carer blame" - https://cerebra.org.uk/download/institutionalising-parent-carer-blame/

Coard, B. (1971) *How the West Indian child is made educationally sub-normal in the British school system*. McDermott Publishing.

Cockburn, Dr L. (2015) "BAME families are missing out on autism support". *SEN Magazine*.

Department for Education (2023) "Special educational needs and disability: An analysis and summary of data sources". GOV.UK

Gay, G. (2000) *Culturally responsive teaching: Theory, research and practice*. Teachers College Press.

Gay, G. (2002) "Preparing for culturally responsive teaching". *Journal of Teacher Education*, 53(2)

Hatton, C., Akram, Y., Shah, R., Robertson, J. and Emerson, E. (2004) *Supporting South Asian families with a child with severe learning disabilities*. Jessica Kingsley Publishers.

Hussain, Y., Atkin, K. and Ahmad, W. (2002) *South Asian disabled young people and their families*. The Joseph Rowntree Foundation. Policy Press.

Kalyanwala, S., Singh, S. and Iqbal, M. (2019) "Review of Evidence on Disability programmes in South Asia". GOV. UK. - www.gov.uk/research-for-development-outputs/review-of-evidence-on-disability-programmes-in-south-asia-amaltas-consulting-new-delhi

Ladson-Billings, G. (1995) "Toward a theory of culturally relevant pedagogy". *American Educational Research Journal*, 32(3): 465-491.

Lindsay, S. and Edwards, A. (2013) "A systematic review of disability awareness interventions for children and youth". *Disability and Rehabilitation*, 35(8).

O'Hara, J. (2018) "Learning disabilities and ethnicity: achieving cultural competence". *Advances in Psychiatric Treatment*, 9(3).

Perepa, P., Wallace, S. and Guldberg, K. (2023) *The experiences of marginalised families with autistic children*. University of Birmingham.

Raghavan, R., Pawson, N. and Small, N. (2013) "Family carers' perspectives on post-school transition of young people with intellectual disabilities with special rference to ethnicity". *Journal of Intellectual Disability Research*, 57(10).

Satherley, D. and Norwich, B. (2021) "Parents' experiences of choosing a special school for their children". *European Journal of Special Needs Education*, 37(6).

SEN Magazine (2014) "BAME families are missing out on autism support". https://senmagazine.co.uk/content/specific-needs/autism-asd/1779/Ethnic minority -families-are-missing-out-on-autism-support/

Strand, S. and Lindorff, A. (2018) "Ethnic disproportionality in the identification of Special Educational Needs (SEN) in England: Extend, causes and consequences". University of Oxford. Department of Education.

Strand, S. and Lindsay, G. (2012) *Ethnic disproportionality in the identification of speech language and communication needs (SLCN) and autism spectrum disorders (ASD)*. University of Warwick. Department for Education. www.researchgate.net/publication/265906644_Ethnic_disproportionality_in_the_identification_of_speech_language_and_communication_needs_SLCN_and_autism_spectrum_disorders_ASD_2005-2011

The National Autistic Society (2014) "Diverse perspectives: The challenges for families affected by autism from Black, Asian and Minority ethnic communities". www.autism.org.uk/advice-and-guidance/what-is-autism/autism-and-Ethnic minority -people

Part II

Collaborative action

Empowering communities and schools

5
Ensuring your community is informed to resist racism, empower change and shape an inclusive society

"Black Lives Matter is a political movement.

What's it got to do with schools?"

The fires of injustice: A legacy of resistance

I was six months old when the National Front clashed with the Asian and Black population of Southall, led by the Southall Youth Movement, which included my dad.

> all of a sudden, I heard shouts and glass smashing. A brick was thrown into the window and just missed you in your baby bouncer... your dad was out marching with the others... I looked out of the window and saw hundreds of people, running and shouting, and everything was on fire... everything looked red.

We lived above a shop, a few shops down from the Hamborough Tavern pub. This pub was famously set alight in full violent protest of the ongoing intimidation and brutal racist attacks against the minority population of Southall. Protests, the institutional racism of the police, and their lack of support for the ethnic minority community were not new. There have been the Notting Hill riots in the 1960s and ongoing riots across the country in the 1980s in Brixton, Toxteth, Handsworth, Chapeltown and Broad water Farm. Further race riots in Tottenham in 2011, caused by the police killing of Mark Duggan, who was shot dead by police, across Hackney, Brixton, Walthamstow, Ealing, and several other parts of London. These riots spread in several other large towns and cities across the UK.

BLM: A modern movement with deep roots

The Black Lives Matter movement was not new.

It gained monumental global attention following the death of George Floyd in May 2020 and profoundly influenced various sectors, including education. The movement, initially perceived by some as purely political, prompted all strands in society, including schools across the globe, to re-evaluate their stance on institutional practice, systemic racism and their commitment to breaking these persistent biases. Fights, riots and stands against racism, often violent and life-threatening, have been frequent in UK history.

DOI: 10.4324/9781003416081-8

In the UK, the movement prompted the education system to critically examine the systemic racism embedded in the content and curriculum offered to young people. Schools began exploring ways to create an "anti-racist curriculum" or "decolonise the curriculum", dissecting the importance of these changes and the challenges faced in the UK.

The BLM movement brought widespread attention to issues of racial inequality and injustice, which were pre-existing but brought to the forefront. In the UK, this led to increased social and political pressure on institutions to address systemic racism. The public demanded action from educational institutions, a commitment to make a change and to ensure they were not perpetuating racial biases and inequalities but fully fostering equality and inclusivity. There was widespread recognition that racism is ingrained within our society – and there was a clear call to make significant changes. In a 2020 article in *The Telegraph*, the president of the NEU claimed that the government was 'dragging its feet' in ensuring there was representation within the UK curriculum, including teaching of Black history. In response to many similar articles, studies and calls to action, many schools started to review ways to incorporate more comprehensive studies of Black History, colonialism and the contributions of various racial groups to society.

Invisible histories: The exclusion of ethnic minority narratives

The National Curriculum, established in 1995, has long been criticised for its lack of representation of ethnic minority communities, thus raising concerns about perpetuating systemic biases experienced by these communities. More of a "traditional curriculum", it overlooked the histories and contributions of ethnic minority communities. While the curriculum may not be considered overtly racist, its lack of inclusive content and focus on a Eurocentric position and perspective side-lines the histories, culture and contributions of diverse communities and contributes to a form of institutional racism (Tomlinson, 2008). Additionally, the curriculum focuses on the benefits and achievements of the British Empire for Britain. It fails to offer alternative perspectives of this period of history, including the economic exploitation of colonialism, the resistance and impact of colonial rule or the lingering feelings of those from these communities.

As this content is being taught to ethnic minority children, they still fail to see themselves reflected in the teaching materials, causing feelings of being invisible and feeling inferior. When pupils cannot see their histories and cultures reflected in their education, it can lead to feelings of exclusion and alienation. Lack of representation can also perpetuate stereotypes and reinforce racial biases amongst all pupils (Ladson-Billings, 1995). Ethnic minority children cannot see themselves reflected in the content they are learning each day, either through role models, notable figures in history, and so on. Therefore, the curriculum does not reflect the diverse society of modern Britain.

The summer of 2024 felt like a heart-breaking and terrifying déjà vu of stories from the past. I could not help but feel a surge of fear. The race riots, with their stark and violent display of racial hatred, echoed the dark chapters of history that we had hoped were long behind us. Yet here we were again. My greatest concern now was that my children, who had so far been shielded, would be exposed to the same hatred and prejudice that I had endured growing up.

In the aftermath, I turned to my professional communities, listening to a podcast for teachers and scrolling through social media groups for headteachers and educators. What I found was disheartening. The conversations missed the mark. Instead of addressing racism directly, many schools were promoting "values-based" responses and discussions on kindness, respect and tolerance without explicitly naming or confronting the racial violence that had unfolded.

I thought of the children from minority backgrounds sitting in assemblies, feeling invisible. What would it have meant to hear someone say, clearly and firmly, that what had happened in the summer riots was wrong, that it was a violation of human dignity and that racism would not be tolerated? To tell those children that they belong and that it's those others who were doing wrong. Schools have an opportunity to name the problem and align their values explicitly with anti-racism, which could make all the difference.

Reading and listening to the responses from fellow educators, it became clear to me that although there was empathy and a will to want to "do the right thing", many were disconnected from the lived realities of minority communities. For those of us who have lived through racism, the failure to directly confront it feels like a missed opportunity for healing and education. These conversations must be about more than just "values" – they must name the harm and commit to action.

The fact is that the majority of these leaders are White, and through their attempts to demonstrate some semblance of allyship, they are still missing the mark by not calling out the behaviour as being wrong. I would implore staff to think that despite not having lived experiences, you can demonstrate empathy and know what a hurting or scared child would need to hear.

Breaking the bias and embracing an anti-racist curriculum

An anti-racist curriculum is essential for promoting equity and inclusion in education. It ensures that all pupils, regardless of their racial or ethnic background, feel valued and respected. A curriculum can help dismantle prejudices and stereotypes, fostering a more inclusive school environment. By addressing and incorporating diverse perspectives, schools can create a learning environment where every pupil can succeed. Although previous efforts to diversify the curriculum have often faced political and institutional resistance, some policymakers and educators argue that an increased focus on minority histories and contributions could "dilute the traditional British narrative", hindering the implementation of a more inclusive curriculum (Lander, 2016).

Teachers may also lack the resources and training to effectively teach about diverse histories and cultures. Without adequate support or CPD, educators may struggle to incorporate diverse perspectives into their lessons for fear of "getting it wrong" and, thus, further perpetuating the underrepresentation of ethnic minority communities in the curriculum. The BLM movement allowed educators to open the dialogue and access CPD to ensure they were "saying and doing the right things". Teachers and leaders were being celebrated and hailed as "progressive" if they were tackling an anti-racist curriculum in 2020/2021.

Critical Race Theory (Delgado and Stefancic, 2017) suggests that racism is embedded in the fabric of society and that tackling this requires persistent and sustained efforts. Therefore, any work schools undertake must be embedded in the curriculum, not performative "tick-box" exercises. Providing anti-racist training to stakeholders is essential for several compelling reasons, all contributing to fostering a more inclusive, equitable and effective educational environment.

Building an anti-racist school: The four pillars of change

We reviewed the potential four strands of an anti-racist curriculum, including

1. multicultural education
2. increasing representation
3. decolonising the curriculum and
4. anti-racist practices.

Creating the optimised environment to build these blocks of the anti-racist curriculum, training and CPD to incorporate the following themes is vital.

1. Understanding unconscious bias
   Everyone holds unconscious beliefs about various social and identity groups, and these biases stem from one's tendency to organise social worlds by categorising. Anti-racist training helps staff identify and mitigate their unconscious biases, which can influence their behaviour and decisions regarding pupil discipline, academic expectations, classroom interactions and understanding parents' perspectives and pressures. Understanding these biases is crucial for staff to create equitable learning opportunities and to prevent discrimination through practice.
2. Cultural responsibility
   Anti-racist training equips teachers with the skills to develop culturally responsive teaching strategies that acknowledge and value the cultural backgrounds of all pupils. This is important because research shows that culturally responsive teaching improves pupil achievement, fosters a greater sense of belonging and inclusion and reduces cultural conflicts. When teachers understand and relate to their pupils' cultural backgrounds, they can tailor their teaching methods to more effectively meet the diverse needs of their classrooms.

3. Promoting equity
   Research has consistently highlighted disparities in the achievement and outcomes of pupils from different ethnicities. Anti-racist training identifies these differences, recognising the systemic factors that contribute to these disparities. By gaining a deeper understanding of the root causes, staff can review policies and practices to promote fairness and ensure equal access to aspirational and positive teaching and learning opportunities for all pupils, regardless of their racial background.
4. Supporting a positive school culture
   Antiracial training creates a positive school climate where all pupils feel safe, supported and included. Research indicates that a positive school climate can lead to decreased absenteeism, reduced incidences of bullying, and improved academic outcomes. Training staff to effectively address racial tensions and foster an inclusive environment is crucial for achieving these outcomes.
5. Preparing pupils for a diverse world
   Schools are crucial in preparing pupils to succeed in an increasingly diverse and connected world. Anti-racist training helps staff foster a curriculum and a school culture that respects and celebrates diversity, which is essential for helping pupils develop the interpersonal skills they need to navigate and thrive in diverse environments. Through multicultural events, multi-lingual opportunities are created in the school.
6. Community and parental engagement
   Anti-racist training also helps build trust and strengthen partnerships with diverse community groups and parents. Educators training in anti-racist practices are better prepared to engage with parents and community members in respectful and culturally sensitive ways, thereby enhancing involvement and support for the school.

Anti-racist training is not just about preventing overt acts of racism; it transforms educational environments in profound ways that uplift all pupils. It equips educators with the understanding and tools they need to dismantle the barriers to learning and success that racism creates for many pupils. As such, it is a critical professional development component supporting schools' ethical, legal and educational goals.

Creating and sustaining an anti-racist school curriculum requires the active involvement and support of all stakeholders, including governors, parents, the wider community, staff and pupils. Each group is crucial in fostering an inclusive and equitable educational environment.

Governors' role in steering anti-racist education

School governors have a significant influence over policy and decision-making within schools, and their support is crucial for the successful implementation and sustainability of an anti-racist curriculum. Governors can ensure that anti-racist policies are integrated into the schools' strategic plans. The process should involve not only initial adoption but also regular reviews and updates to maintain relevance and effectiveness over time.

Governors also play a pivotal role in resource allocation, ensuring sufficient funds and resources are available to support training and curriculum development to foster an anti-racist educational environment. Their strategic oversight can help prioritise initiatives that promote equity and inclusivity, thus reinforcing the school's commitment to anti-racist education.

To effectively champion an anti-racist curriculum, school governors must undergo comprehensive training that encompasses various aspects, including understanding the historical and systemic roots of racism, developing and implementing anti-racist policies and equipping them with practical tools and strategies for supporting anti-racist education.

Governors need a deep understanding of the historical and systemic aspects of racism to address it within the education system effectively. Workshops and seminars can provide this foundational knowledge by exploring the following topics:

1. Historical context of racism, including a detailed exploration of the history of racism, including slavery, colonialism and segregation. They should also participate in an analysis of how historical events have shaped contemporary societal structures and educational inequalities (Gillborn, 2005),
2. Systemic racism in education should include training that examines how systemic racism manifests in educational policies, practices and outcomes. They should also hear case studies highlighting the impact of systemic racism on ethnic minority pupils, particularly those with SEND (Ladson-Billings, 1995).

Governors should gain an understanding of anti-racist policy development and implementation. Effective anti-racist education requires robust policies that are well-developed and diligently implemented, and the training sessions for governors should include the following:

1. Guidelines for developing anti-racist policies should be included for creating comprehensive policies that address various aspects of school life, from curriculum content to disciplinary practices.
2. Developing strategies for effectively implementing anti-racist policies must be reviewed, including setting clear objectives, timelines and accountability measures. Techniques for monitoring and evaluating the effectiveness of these policies, ensuring they lead to meaningful change, are also imperative.

Governors could be equipped with practical tools and strategies to support anti-racist education. Through interactive workshops and seminars, governors could access practical insights into implementing anti-racist policies and practices and have opportunities to engage with experts in anti-racist education and learn from their experiences. Case studies are also helpful, especially from SEND schools, which have successfully integrated anti-racist curriculum meaningfully. Governors should support leaders through discussions on the challenges they face and the strategies employed to overcome them; mainly, as we have gathered, the work can be provocative, challenging and immensely emotional.

Governors need ongoing professional development that adapts to evolving educational contexts and challenges to ensure sustained commitment and effectiveness. Access to CPD and regular training updates through workshops that revisit key concepts, consider and debate new research and best practices and provide a platform for sharing experiences and strategies allow governors opportunities to exchange ideas and learn from the diverse experiences of other schools.

Governors could demonstrate responsibility for reviewing the effectiveness of anti-racist policies and measuring their impact. Initiatives must be regularly assessed to ensure they are achieving their intended outcomes. We have already explored that it would be beneficial to have a designated governor to link to the development of anti-racist practices and review ethnic minority achievement and feedback on the wellbeing of pupils, families and staff. They could also monitor racist incidents and review reactive strategies for managing them and proactive strategies on what the school has implemented to prevent future incidents.

Parent power and partnership for anti-racist education

Parents play a crucial role in shaping their children's attitudes, behaviours and perceptions. Understanding the critical role of anti-racist education in their child's development and in creating an inclusive society is essential. However, they should be provided the opportunity to explore why they must invest in this work through targeted training sessions and workshops. Engaging parents effectively in anti-racist initiatives creates reinforcement and alignment that bridges school and home life. This collaboration is crucial for reinforcing anti-racist values and practices across all aspects of a child's life.

Epstein's (2011) research highlights that aligning home values with a school's commitment and focus on inclusivity significantly impacts the child's beliefs, values, and outlook. Therefore, parental involvement in promoting and embedding anti-racist education is crucial. By creating consistent messages about being committed to anti-racist thoughts, beliefs, and actions, parents align themselves with the school ethos. This supports learning because parents and children can discuss key concepts and ideas within safe spaces, and children will feel empowered to apply this learning to real-life situations.

Workshops and interactive sessions are effective methods for engaging parents in anti-racist education. These sessions can allow parents to learn, share experiences and collaborate with other parents and educators. Workshops can focus on the principles and practices of anti-racist education, helping parents understand why and how these principles are applied in the school curriculum and how they might support these efforts at home. Sessions could include role-playing exercises, group discussions and case studies to help parents practice what they learn and apply it to real-life situations.

Creating a focus group of parents representing the community is essential, as this will provide deeper insights into their perspectives and experiences and what an "anti-racist" curriculum means for their children. Creating focus groups, or support groups, for parents of similar backgrounds can be useful, as parents can form support networks. For some parents who may be an ethnic minority, have English as a second language and have experienced some of the social isolation outlined in previous chapters, these groups can be a lifeline of support, developing understanding, knowledge, skills and acceptance. They can see that disability is present in their community, and this does not need to be associated with negative connotations, and they do not have to feel as though it is their fault or they have done anything wrong.

Schools could offer interactive sessions on cultural competence, including activities to promote cultural awareness and understanding, such as cultural fairs, cooking classes featuring diverse cuisines and storytelling sessions with community elders (Banks, 2015). These sessions can also provide a platform for parents to share their cultural experiences and learn from each other, fostering a sense of community and mutual respect (Ladson-Billings, 1995).

Family engagement programmes are critical for promoting collaboration between parents and schools. These programmes can include specific initiatives to involve parents in the educational process, curriculum design and activities to support anti-racist education. Organising family reading nights that feature books by diverse authors and about different cultures can help parents and children learn together. Reading lists and sensory stories with ideas for sensory props can be provided to parents to use at home. They can extend the impact of these events and encourage ongoing conversations about race and diversity.

Parent-teacher meetings could also be forums for deeper and more sustained conversations about the curriculum. Improving representation, reviewing culture and ensuring parents are heard in their views on the school's anti-racist policies can inform the curriculum and school processes and policies. For example, can parents access school correspondence, including the website, letters, newsletters, curriculum information, and so on?

Involving parents in assemblies, trips and projects can provide practical opportunities to apply, lead and observe the anti-racist principle in action. These can include celebrating cultural events in the autumn term, with Diwali, bonfire night, Eid, Hannukah and Christmas all within the same term, which could provide opportunities for termly "multicultural events". Projects that involve families can strengthen the connection between the school and the community, creating a united effort to promote inclusivity and equity. Several schools I have worked in are successful in creating this celebratory sense of belonging through "International evenings", where food and drinks are brought into school by families and enjoyed by children, staff and families. In the most successful examples, the invitations extended beyond to include the wider community, including the local mayor, governors and local shop owners and businesses.

Feedback from parents is also imperative. Regular surveys and feedback forms can help assess parents' attitudes toward the school, the curriculum and how inclusive they feel the school is. Parents can also get feedback on their views of the school and how successfully the school is promoting inclusivity to all cultures, including accessibility to resources, workshops, training and engagement with the school. Collecting this feedback allows schools to make necessary adjustments and improvements to their programmes (Epstein, 2011).

Schools can create a cohesive and supportive environment for all pupils through engaging parents through workshops and interactive sessions, family engagement programmes, and so on. Measuring the impact of these initiatives ensures their effectiveness and allows for depth of action, review and continuous improvement. Through these efforts, parents can help foster a broader community acceptance of anti-racist initiatives, contributing to a more inclusive and equitable educational environment.

Extending the reach of anti-racism through community partnerships

The wider community, including local organisations, businesses, and cultural institutions, play a vital role in supporting schools and providing real-world contexts for learning. Bronfenbrenner's (1979) ecological systems theory emphasises the importance of these external environments in the educational development of children. Engagement with the community can offer pupils diverse perspectives and learning opportunities beyond the classroom and provide real-life applicability and context. This is essential in supporting the understanding, experience and ability to transfer skills and knowledge beyond the school. Strong community ties can provide additional support and resources for successfully implementing an anti-racist curriculum.

Community connections and real-world learning for ethnic minority pupils with SEND

Working with the local community, businesses and organisations can provide ethnic minority pupils with SEND practical learning experiences. These experiences can involve changes in the culture of settings and learning to identify, understand and celebrate differences and similarities. These experiences can also provide insights into history, art, RE and social issues, which could support bringing the curriculum alive with meaning, experience and relevance. This community-based learning project can help pupils apply classroom knowledge to real-world problems, enhancing their learning experience and relevance (Epstein, 2011).

Exposure to different perspectives encourages critical thinking and empathy amongst pupils, an essential skill in navigating a multicultural society (Gay, 2002). Community involvement brings a wealth of diverse perspectives into the educational environment, which helps pupils understand, appreciate and develop an awareness of their own culture and viewpoints, as well as that of others. These processes foster a more inclusive mindset, as engaging with community members from different backgrounds allows pupils to challenge stereotypes and preconceived notions, promoting a more nuanced understanding of social dynamics and cultural diversity (Banks, 2015).

Local businesses can also play a crucial role in supporting anti-racist education by offering internships, sponsorships and mentorship programmes. For example, a technology company might partner with a SEND school to provide STEM educational resources and mentoring for pupils from underrepresented backgrounds.

These collaborations can help bridge the gap between education and the workforce, preparing pupils for future careers while promoting diversity and inclusion in various industries (Gay, 2002).

Community engagement could be promoted with strategies for building partnerships between schools and community organisations. These partnerships can take many forms, from collaborative projects to joint efforts and regular interactions that reinforce the importance of anti-racist education ✣ for example, offering work experience opportunities in different restaurants and experiencing different smells, foods and cooking styles.

Advanced technology now offers simulated work experience placements for pupils with SEND, who can apply their knowledge and skills to a new environment before a work experience placement. This provides a "warm-up" and insight into the expectations of any given role.

Social media provides fantastic opportunities to network with and link with organisations and businesses that may be able to support SEND settings. Community links can provide schools with resources that may not be available internally, such as guest speakers, mentorship programmes and extracurricular activities. Local businesses and organisations can offer funding, materials and expertise to support anti-racist initiatives and curriculum development. For example, having a LinkedIn page for your school and networking with the wider community, coaches and mentors may result in wonderful opportunities for the school that may not have come about without the means of outreach via social media.

Collaborative projects between schools and community groups can provide practical applications of anti-racist principles. For example, community clean-up events, cultural festivals, and celebrations such as colour fun runs are linked with the celebrated Holi and collaborative arts projects that celebrate diversity. These projects can help build stronger relationships between pupils, schools, and community members, creating a shared purpose and mutual respect (Banks, 2006).

It is important to consider that when planning for engagement, developing critical thinking and metacognition, and facilitating deeper levels of thought, pupils with SEND will be able to access content dependent on their individual needs, disability or condition and its severity. Their accessibility to content also depends on how we present material, adapting with the use of resources, props and visuals. While we should not limit opportunities depending on disability, we must adapt and ensure the content is meaningful, engaging and useful to young people. We will explore some strategies and approaches in working with more moderate to severe learning disabilities in the latter sections of the book. However, the case study below highlights how to celebrate a cultural event, meeting the diverse range of needs in a SEND school.

 CASE STUDY: WINDRUSH DAY ART PROJECT

As a collaborative community commitment to increasing representation and cultural awareness beyond Black History Month and Diwali, several schools joined together to plan, create and deliver a borough-wide art exhibition of several mainstream and SEND schools focused explicitly on Windrush Day. As the only SEND school participating in this work, we had to think creatively about accessibility to the topic and ensure it was relevant and meaningful work and not tokenistic. Maintaining integrity and remaining true to cause was imperative.

We decided to focus on ships, recreating ships in 2D multi-media art, and creating 3D sculptures. We facilitated in-house art projects, used multi-sensory stories to chart the journey from the Caribbean to the UK, used torches and heaters for the sun and heat, and used fans to indicate the change in weather. We retold the story of Windrush, using aided language boards to teach essential vocabulary at that time and a range of props.

We observed the "same" and "different" aspects of life in the UK compared with the Caribbean. We also used zones of regulation to observe how the Windrush generation might have felt about their journey. Members of the public who were part of the Windrush also talked about their experiences.

Adapted versions of Coming to England by Floella Benjamin were also shared with children across schools, as they each learned a chorus of "One Love" by Bob Marley. A collaborative video with the children singing was created and edited to showcase the entire project.

The final art project was displayed with collaborative pieces from across the Local Authority, and various stakeholders were invited to observe the showcase over different days.

Schools that become further along in their journey of embracing and embedding anti-racist practice can offer workshops and seminars for community members and help raise awareness about the importance of anti-racist education. These sessions can cover topics such as their starting points and the process of their journey towards becoming more inclusive. Engaging local experts and activists to lead these workshops can enhance their impact and further support the community in raising awareness about the importance of anti-racist education. There could be avenues for continued support through establishing networks for resource sharing to support schools with access to resources and materials and signposting to help schools implement their own anti-racist curriculum effectively.

Support networks could take the form of online problem-solving meetings, sharing information and collaborating on projects. Support networks can also provide emotional and social support to educators and pupils engaged in anti-racist work, helping them to sustain their progress over time.

Community engagement should be promoted with strategies for building partnerships between schools and community organisations. Educating the community and raising awareness about the importance of anti-racist education is also imperative. For example, partnering with local museums and culture centres can create rich, immersive learning experiences by providing hands-on learning about the contributors of various ethnic groups to society. These partnerships also help pupils understand the history of their community and the relevance of this to their lives today.

There is also scope to develop links between community service projects, as involving pupils in community service projects that address social justice issues can provide practical applications of their classroom learning. Projects such as organising food drives, advocating for local policy change or participating in environmental justice initiatives can empower pupils to become active, engaged citizens. These projects can also provide valuable opportunities for pupils to develop leadership skills and learn about the impact of collective action.

The wider community plays a crucial role in supporting schools and providing real-world contexts for learning. By building strong partnerships between schools and community organisations, raising awareness about the importance of anti-racist education, and engaging in collaborative projects, communities can significantly contribute to successfully implementing an anti-racist curriculum. These efforts enrich pupils' educational experiences and foster a more inclusive and equitable society. Through continuous engagement and collaboration, schools and communities can work together to ensure pupils receive a high-quality, anti-racist education that prepares them for a diverse and interconnected world.

From theory to practice: Staff training for cultural competence

Educators must model anti-racist behaviours and attitudes, influencing the lives of pupils, their families and their colleagues, supporting all to foster and celebrate an inclusive school environment. Staff training ensures that educators are well-prepared to understand the importance of anti-racist work and work together with the wider school to manage discussions about race and integrate anti-racist principles into their teaching (Howard, 2003).

To effectively support an anti-racist curriculum, staff must receive comprehensive "cultural competence" training, including anti-racist principles or "culturally responsive teaching".

This involves recognising, addressing biases and integrating diverse perspectives into their pedagogy. Culturally responsive teaching consists of identifying the cultural backgrounds of pupils and incorporating this understanding into teaching practices, helping to create a more inclusive classroom environment where all pupils feel valued and respected. Teachers and school staff are on the front lines of implementing the curriculum and directly interacting with pupils, and their commitment is critical to the success of anti-racist education (Gay, 2002).

Staff should focus on developing techniques for integrating diverse perspectives into lessons, including using multicultural literature, examples and case studies that reflect various experiences and viewpoints. Although this can be a difficult concept for children with additional needs, developing a theory of mind and providing alternative views is essential in developing one's thoughts, feelings and opinions. For pupils with severe learning disabilities, teaching these concepts can be more challenging due to relevance and applicability. However, staff can work on recognition of self, recognition of others, feelings of self and feelings of others, using various communication strategies and approaches such as comic strip conversations and aided language boards.

> Educators should adapt their teaching methods to meet the diverse learning needs of their pupils, ensuring that all pupils can access the curriculum effectively.
> (Banks, 2006)

Staff should access specific training on implicit and explicit biases, as recognising and addressing biases is crucial for creating an equitable classroom environment. Training sessions can help educators identify their biases and provide strategies for mitigating their impact on teaching and interactions with pupils. Practical exercises, such as role-playing, reflective journaling, as well as facilitated discussions in small group sessions, can help staff to become more aware of their biases, identify how these impact pupils or the ethnic groups they belong to, as well as develop strategies for fostering an inclusive classroom.

Ongoing training sessions and facilitated discussions on key topic areas are essential to keep educators informed and engaged with the principles of anti-racist education. Workshops and seminars can provide in-depth training on specific aspects of anti-racist education. These sessions should be interactive, allowing educators to practice new strategies and receive feedback from peers and trainers. Topics should include strategies for the four strands of creating an anti-racist curriculum, including:

1. multicultural experiences,
2. representing the school community,
3. decolonising the curriculum, and
4. anti-racist practice through policy and practice.

A collaborative approach through peer learning and support

Peer learning communities are one of the most essential forms of CPD for staff, as this type of learning is vital for sustaining anti-racist education efforts. Peer learning groups allow educators to share best practices, discuss challenges and develop new strategies collaboratively. These groups can meet regularly to discuss topics related to anti-racist education and support each other in implementing new practices. Facilitating structured discussions and collaborative projects can help maintain focus and ensure productive outcomes from these meetings.

Peer learning communities could also offer mentorship programmes, where less experienced educators could be paired with professional mentors who have expertise in anti-racist education and can provide valuable support and guidance. Mentors can offer insights, feedback and encouragement, helping mentees develop their skills and confidence/regular check-ins and goal-setting sessions can help maintain momentum and track progress in the mentorship relationship.

CASE STUDY - NETWORKS, EDUCATION FESTIVALS AND CONFERENCES

Networks such as BAME Education aim to ensure that diverse communities are represented in the curriculum and the education workforce for teachers and leaders. The network also seeks to address the inequity in the recruitment and career progression of those from ethnic minority backgrounds.

Through regional and national seminars, workshops and talks, school staff can access current research and progressive "how-to" pedagogies led by experts in the field, including voices from ethnic minority communities. The valuable network allows staff to access professional learning communities, attend events, share their CPD experiences, discuss challenges and maximise collaboration opportunities.

Education festivals and conferences also provide significant benefits to CPD, including giving inspiration and motivation through being surrounded by like-minded professionals. This can re-invigorate passions with new ideas for their school communities.

Empowering pupil voices as agents of change

Pupils are at the heart of any curriculum, and their active engagement is crucial in creating an inclusive school culture. An anti-racist curriculum not only benefits the pupils and the whole school community but also empowers their identity and, for some, promotes their voice to become agents of positive change within their school community. Ladson-Billings (1995) highlights that an anti-racist curriculum fosters critical thinking skills and empathy in pupils. Pupils are encouraged to understand themselves, others and different perspectives and experiences better.

When pupils embed and actively demonstrate anti-racist behaviour, we expect to see them contribute to a welcoming, respectful and inclusive school ethos and environment. We would also see them advocate for "right" and "wrong" discriminatory behaviours when they encounter them, and we would also observe them positively influence their peers through modelled attitudes of acceptance and allyship. This is why the 2024 summer race riots were an opportunity to promote discussion and commitment to anti-racism to groups of pupils in SEND schools.

Empathy and understanding are critical components of anti-racist education. Pupils can develop these skills through activities that promote the acceptance of diverse perspectives. Activities such as role-playing and perspective-taking exercises can help pupils understand the experiences and feelings of others from different backgrounds. These activities foster empathy by encouraging pupils to put themselves in others' shoes. Literature and storytelling are powerful tools for building empathy. Reading and discussing stories from diverse perspectives can help pupils understand and appreciate different cultures and experiences; guest speakers sharing their own experiences can bring lived experience and awareness that this is not just tokenistic and "happens from afar" but can have a profound impact on people's lives.

Pupils benefit from facilitated and interactive workshops that involve pupils in discussions and activities related to anti-racism can be highly effective. These sessions can involve projects, hands-on activities such as art, cooking and crafts, as well as guest speakers that engage pupils in learning about race and equity. Workshops can also focus on current events and historical contexts, helping pupils connect past and present issues of race and racism.

Encouraging pupil leadership and voice is crucial for actively empowering pupils to promote anti-racist values within their school community. Pupil voice initiatives such as student councils and diversity committees can allow pupils to express their views and contribute to school policies and practices. These groups can lead anti-racist campaigns, organise events and provide feedback on the curriculum.

Encouraging pupils to participate in decision-making helps them feel valued and respected, fostering a sense of ownership and responsibility for their school environment. Therefore, school councils or pupil forums are useful ways for pupils to make decisions and contribute to what is happening in their school and what makes them happy. These are also successfully embedded in some SEND school settings, using various communication systems to promote pupil voice.

Creative expression through drama, art and music can give pupils powerful ways to explore and communicate their experiences and ideas about equity and race. School performances, exhibitions and competitions focused on anti-racist themes can engage the wider school community and promote awareness. Integrating anti-racist themes into the arts curriculum can help pupils develop a deeper understanding of social justice issues and inspire them to advocate for change. For example, in one SEN school, I led anti-racist work, and a group of primary-aged pupils with moderate to severe learning disabilities led an assembly on Rosa Parks through a dramatic re-enactment. Although the historical significance of the event may not have been fully understood, the pupils were aware that the behaviour towards Rosa was "not right" and "unfair" and this was an appropriate level for this group of pupils and the rest of the school.

Educational institutions' response to the Black Lives Matter movement and the broader challenge of racial injustice is not merely a political consideration but a crucial element in the mission to educate and prepare all pupils in all settings to thrive in a diverse and equitable society. Through a commitment to anti-racist work, schools embrace a role beyond traditional education, acting as positive areas for social change. This work is necessary for fostering a future where all community members can succeed and be recognised as valuable contributors to society.

Through raised awareness using CPD, the collective effort of all stakeholders – pupils, staff, parents, governors and the wider community ‡ will help dismantle systemic racism within the education system and promote a culture of equity and inclusion for all pupils. By providing targeted training and fostering a collaborative approach, schools can ensure that all stakeholders are equipped to contribute to and support anti-racist education. A comprehensive and sustained commitment is essential for creating a genuinely inclusive educational environment that prepares pupils to navigate and contribute to a diverse and interconnected world.

Chapter summary

This chapter reflects on the deep-rooted history of racial tensions in the UK, starting from riots in Southall to the global Black Lives Matter movement. It explores how these events have influenced the education system's focus on implementing an anti-racist curriculum and the need to challenge Eurocentric content that marginalises ethnic minority communities.

The chapter underscores the importance of reshaping education to be inclusive, reflecting diverse histories and cultures, and breaking down systemic barriers. Additionally, it highlights the role of educators, pupils, and school leaders in fostering equity and inclusion while addressing potential resistance from stakeholders who view anti-racist efforts as unnecessary or politically motivated.

TIFFIN TAKE-AWAY

1. **Challenging Eurocentric narratives in the curriculum**
   Eurocentric perspectives often dominate the curriculum, side-lining the histories and contributions of ethnic minority communities. By incorporating diverse perspectives, schools can ensure a more inclusive education for all pupils.

   - You might consider the relevance of a "Eurocentric narrative" in SEND settings; however, you could consider whether your current curriculum truly represents the pupil and school community you serve.

2. **Opportunities for dialogue on racism**
   Following the 2024 UK race riots, many school leaders failed to engage directly with the racial context of the unrest. Debates, online forums and social media discussions centred around promoting general "values-based education" responses instead of using these events, where relevant and appropriate, to have vital discussions on race, inequality and systemic discrimination.

   - You could consider the impact of conversations about race during pivotal events, which could support empathy and understanding in a community and demonstrate support and allyship to ethnic minority pupils and their families to support their sense of inclusion and belonging.

3. **Navigating resistance and building consensus**
   Resistance to anti-racist initiatives may arise from stakeholders who perceive these efforts as "political" or "woke". Schools must find ways to engage these stakeholders in meaningful dialogue, helping them understand the educational necessity of anti-racism.

   - You could consider how your school could build understanding and consensus around the need for anti-racist initiatives, even when faced with resistance.

References

Banks, J. (2006) *Cultural diversity and education: Foundations, curriculum and teaching*. Pearson.
Banks, J. (2015) *Multicultural Education: Issues and Perspectives* (9th ed.). Wiley.
Bronfenbrenner, U. (1979) *The Ecology of Human Development: Experiments by Nature and Design*. Harvard University Press.
Delgado, R. and Stefancic, J. (2017) *Critical Race Theory: An Introduction*. NYU Press.
Epstein, J.L. (2011) *School, Family, and Community Partnerships: Preparing Educators and Improving Schools* (2nd ed.). Westview Press.

Gay, G. (2002) "Preparing for culturally responsive teaching". *Journal of Teacher Education*, 53(2).

Gillborn, D. (2005) "Education policy as an act of white supremacy: Whiteness, critical race theory and education reform". *Journal of Education Policy*, 20(4): 485-505. https://doi.org/10.1080/02680930500132346

Howard, T. (2003) "Culturally relevant pedagogy: Ingredients for critical teacher reflection". *Theory into Practice*, 42 (3): 195-202.

Ladson-Billings, G. (1995) "Toward a theory of culturally relevant pedagogy". *American Educational Research Journal*, 32(3): 465-491.

Lander, Vini. (2016) "Introduction to fundamental British values". *Journal of Education for Teaching*, 42(3): 274-279.

Tomlinson, S. (2008) *Race and education: Policy and politics in Britain*. Berkshire: Open University Press.

White, N. (2020) "Ministers 'dragging feet' on adding Black history to curriculum, teaching leader warns". *The Independent*.

6
How to create allyship with colleagues

"Can you do it? You're BAME! I might say the wrong things..."

"Dad, who is Blair Peach? Is he from a Roald Dahl book? Why does it say he died here? Did that really happen? What did he die from?"

I was about 8 or 9 years old, playing hopscotch on the pavement in front of my grandparents' house in Southall, a cul-de-sac. It was always the best fun as I had several cousins living on the road, and it was a chance for us to see each other. I enjoyed coming back and playing with them. Living over the bridge in Hayes seemed a million miles away, with faces that looked different to mine and were sometimes hostile. In Hayes, I would ride my bike around the block by myself, watching the other girls go off to Brownies after school; there was no "space" for me to join. We lacked the sense of community that was evident when we went to Southall. There was no community in Hayes – not for us, anyway.

I jumped on the pavement, one foot, two feet... I noticed a new memorial tile on the corner of the pavement next to a lamppost. I recall it as pink and white with a gold inscription. Blair Peach. The name "Blair Peach" stayed with me for a long time, as it was such an unusual name, I thought. I felt great sadness for someone I did not know anything about. I wonder why he died and what happened. Why did he get a special tile for dying? And why did he die outside my grandma's house? Why didn't she save him when she must have been just inside the house? Death felt a little too close to home and as a young child. It felt scary.

Blair Peach. His name is woven into the tapestry and timeline of my life. Every now and then, I would learn a little more about who he was and what happened to him. I would learn a little bit more about life, as it was, for my parents and relatives, for the community, during the times in which he died. It would fill me with nerves, despair and sadness because I realised that nothing, or little, had changed as I grew and attended secondary school.

The horrendous bullying was initiated and was sustained for years when I started in Year 7 at a girls' school in an outer London borough. The incessant, collaborative efforts by a group of girls, "tag-teaming" their relentless verbal, emotional and racist abuse, was overwhelming in the first few years of school life. I would hate the unstructured times of the day – breaks and lunches – as I knew that was when they would have free rein to unleash hell. Sometimes, to avoid them, I would hide in the toilet cubicles for the entire time.

DOI: 10.4324/9781003416081-9

it was worse in our day... we used to leave school early, to run home from Greenford to Southall, because if we waited until the end of the day, we would have got jumped and they would have beaten us with pipes and sticks, calling us wogs and p*kis, telling us to go home. The girls weren't any better – they would pull your mum's hair.

My parents tell me it is better now; at least things are not as bad as they were back then. Only sometimes it feels as if they are not. It feels more covert now. There were no allies in my time in school either – just facial expressions of friends frozen with fear, anxiety and relief that "at least it isn't me". In the absence of an ally, I learned to hold my own. I learned how to fight back.

The concept of an "ally" felt like a glorious, true friend. And this is what drew me to the story of Blair Peach.

The call for allyship

He was an ally of the minority community in Southall, demonstrating solidarity during an intense time of overt racism, crisis and indescribable violence, including from the institutionally racist police.

He did not need to be in Southall, protesting the National Front's presence and intimidation towards the community. He did not need to be supporting the South Asian community. But he did.

He died from a blow to the head with a weapon. Witnesses reported this was delivered by the Special Patrol Group (SPG), a controversial and violent unit of the Metropolitan Police. He fell outside my grandparents' house from the blow to the head and was picked up and whisked into the house opposite. He died later that night in the local hospital.

An "ally" can be someone who supports and advocates for the rights of those from underrepresented and marginalised groups, or an individual. An "ally" may not be from the same group experiencing discrimination but actively works and advocates for their right to equity.

The integration of an anti-racist curriculum in schools, particularly those serving pupils with SEND, necessitates robust support from a diverse spectrum of stakeholders – it absolutely needs allies from everywhere. I have touched upon the tendency for ethnic minority educators to spearhead these initiatives, which highlights a significant gap in the distribution of responsibilities. Robin DiAngelo, in *White fragility: Why it's so hard for white people to talk about racism* (2018), explains how racial dynamics in education settings discourage non-minority individuals from engaging in anti-racist efforts, often leaving this crucial work to their ethnic minority colleagues.

Cultivating a school culture where anti-racist work is understood as a shared responsibility requires a commitment from all stakeholders, not just those from ethnic minority backgrounds. Through strategically integrating anti-racist objectives into every facet of school operations, from policy and leadership to professional development and community engagement, schools can create a more equitable and inclusive environment. A collective approach not only alleviates the disproportionate load on ethnic minority educators but also enriches the educational experience for all, fostering a community that actively challenges racism, promotes inclusivity and demonstrates solidarity with the diverse community.

Establishing a robust anti-racist framework in schools where leadership is predominantly White poses unique challenges. For such initiatives to be effective, it is crucial for White leaders to understand, embrace and advocate for anti-racist policies and practices.

Allyship in anti-racist work involves more than just passive support; it requires proactive engagement and commitment to understanding and addressing systemic racism within educational settings. For White leaders, this begins with a deep personal and professional commitment to learning about racial issues and their impacts. According to DiAngelo (2018), White individuals often struggle to engage with racism due to having been protected from it, having a little concept of what racial stress is, feels like or how it impacts our lives. She describes this as "White fragility". Overcoming this requires a conscious effort to engage with and understand racism beyond individual prejudices.

White fragility and the challenge of change

Strategies for White leaders to foster buy-in include education and self-reflection. The first step in creating buy-in is for White leaders to become educated on issues of race and intersectionality. Leaders must engage with varied work on racism and intersectionality to understand how overlapping social identities relate to systems of oppression. Understanding these concepts is crucial for leaders to frame anti-racist work within their schools meaningfully. However, this investment in gaining knowledge and understanding is vital for ALL leaders, as it cannot be assumed that even if you are a leader from an ethnic minority background, you have a developed and extensive knowledge and understanding of the complexities of sub-cultures and groups.

Therefore, for all leaders to effectively foster support for anti-racist initiatives, a two-pronged approach focusing on education and self-reflection is essential. Generating this buy-in begins with their commitment to their education on racial issues and intersectionality, involving

1. Reading diverse literature and research on racism.
2. Understanding intersectionality, the variations, and its impact.

Training and development should include sessions on recognising and addressing unconscious biases and understanding microaggressions and their impact on pupils and staff of minority backgrounds. This can be instrumental in helping leaders and teachers understand the daily experiences of their ethnic minority colleagues and pupils. They should then learn how to support their diverse communities, including finding out how their communities would like to be supported with issues identified through data and research.

Leaders should lead by example and actively build relationships with stakeholders, including the local community, particularly those that are racially and ethnically diverse. The information gained through open forums, coffee morning discussions or even surveys can provide valuable insights into the cultural contexts of the pupils and families and help them understand how they might be served better.

Research indicates that ethnic minority staff usually lead this work. While their leadership is invaluable due to perspective, lived experience and potential personal insight, it also brings challenges. Ethnic minority staff leading this work in schools can become further isolated, as they tend to operate within White teams; they can be vulnerable and exposed as they lead a potentially contentious topic, of which the rest of the team may not have any lived experience.

We also know that research suggests that ethnic minority teachers and leaders are disproportionately tasked with spearheading diversity and inclusion efforts, and this is documented globally across various professional fields, not just in education. For example, research conducted by the Runnymede Trust in the UK highlights a trend where ethnic minority staff often feel pressured to take roles centred around diversity and inclusion, which, while important, may not necessarily align with or contribute to their professional advancement within educational intuitions (Bhopal and Pitkin, 2019). I have a brother who works in law, a sister who works in finance, I work in education, and my husband works in the arts. Within the past five years, all of us, as ethnic minority leaders in our respective fields, have spearheaded Equality and Diversity projects at work through having been asked.

Historically, educational institutions have been sites of both overt and covert racial discrimination. Ethnic minority staff and leaders often take on anti-racist work due to a personal and historical commitment to addressing these longstanding issues. We feel obliged to make a difference by making it a better place for future generations. The history of segregation and systemic racism in education systems around the world, including the UK, has laid down the groundwork for this dynamic. According to Ladson-Billings (1995), the deep-seated inequalities in education systems often require the lived experiences of those directly affected by racism to drive meaningful change.

The assignment of anti-racist initiatives to ethnic minority staff within employment settings often stems from a presumption that these individuals possess intrinsic insights into racial issues due to their backgrounds. While logical, this approach risks marginalising these professionals by confining their professional identities to their ethnic backgrounds rather than recognising their broader educational expertise. The specialisation of roles could not only reinforce racial divisions within educational leadership but also place a disproportionate burden on ethnic minority professionals, who are often expected to navigate complex issues of racial discrimination without adequate support or resources, or any assumed responsibility or personal commitment from those who did ask. This perpetuates a cycle where anti-racism work is viewed as the sole responsibility of those affected by racial discrimination.

It also assumes that all ethnic minority people are committed to the work of equity. We know from the recent ethnic minority Conservative leaders that this is not true. Many second- or third-generation ethnic minority people have not experienced any outward racism and have little experience. My husband grew up in Southall throughout the 1980s and 1990s. He tells tales of hard work, community, togetherness and support; everyone lived and functioned as extended families. Whole streets of people looking out for one another. He then went off to Drama school in Glasgow and Los Angeles. He claimed he had never experienced a racist incident… until I pointed out to him that many of the auditions he was put up for required him to use a thick, comedic Indian accent. He was not auditioning as, or for, a British-born Asian who authentically speaks with a London accent.

However, many ethnic minority people do lead anti-racist initiatives because they usually have personally experienced the effects of racism and are deeply committed to creating more equitable environments for future generations. Bradbury, Tereshchenko and Mills (2021) found that ethnic minority educators often feel a personal responsibility to address issues of racism due to their own experiences of marginalisation. My own story provides a personal connection stemming from the passion and resilience needed to tackle the deeply ingrained issues of racism in education.

Many White leaders in education are hesitant to take the lead on anti-racist work due to a lack of understanding, fear of making mistakes or discomfort in discussing race. The reluctance can stem from a lack of personal experience with racism and the fear of being accused of insensitivity or perpetuating racism unintentionally. According to DiAngelo (2018), White educators often exhibit this "White fragility", a defensive response to discussions about race and racism that can inhibit their ability to lead anti-racist work effectively.

White leaders can often lack the training, confidence and, sometimes, the will required to lead anti-racist work in their settings. Many educational leadership programs, such as the National Professional Qualification for Headship (NPQH), do not prepare leaders to address racial issues, leaving them ill-equipped to manage the complexities of "anti-racist initiatives". If Ofsted are not looking for it, and it is not statutory, is the work viewed as an additional workload or a "nice to have, if you have the time" but not a non-negotiable priority?

Due to their personal commitment and lived experiences, some ethnic minority staff become the leaders of anti-racist work as they may consider that undertaking this leadership work will provide them with opportunities for career advancement. However, it also places additional burdens on these staff, who may already face numerous challenges in their professional environments. Staff from minority groups often take on these roles as a pathway to leadership, although it can also lead to increased workload and stress, as well as navigating their personal journeys with the content, which they are left to manage without adequate support or supervision (Miller, 2016).

Ethnic minority employees who lead anti-racist work often face increased workload and stress, and the added roles of diversity and inclusion to their existing responsibilities can lead to higher levels of professional burnout. Leaders from minority backgrounds report feeling overwhelmed by the additional expectations placed upon them. Wallace (2019) supports the view that the emotional impact of confronting and addressing racism can be draining, and ethnic minority employees often must navigate their personal experiences with racism while advocating for systemic change without supervision or support, which can be emotionally taxing.

In many cases, ethnic minority staff step into leading anti-racist work because there is a noticeable vacuum in the leadership of this work from their White colleagues. We know this dynamic can lead to further isolation as these staff navigate these responsibilities within White teams. As ethnic minority employees are often expected to lead diversity initiatives due to their racial or ethnic background, this can lead to tokenism, which can cause further marginalisation. The professional identities and roles can be reduced to their ethnicity, and being constantly called upon to speak on racial issues can pigeonhole these staff into a narrow professional role, limiting their opportunities for career growth in other areas (Bhopal and Pitkin 2020).

Additionally, the sense of isolation felt by these leaders, especially when tasked with leading initiatives focused on anti-racism, is significant. Ethnic minority leaders may find themselves isolated in their efforts due to a lack of support and understanding from their colleagues. The feeling of isolation can be attributed to the perception that anti-racist work is an add-on or "side-line" activity rather than central to the leader's core responsibilities for the school.

Ethnic minority staff who find themselves advocating for fundamental values such as equity and inclusivity often do so without substantial backing from their institutions. The issue is compounded by the lack of comprehensive policy or practice to address racism, leaving these leaders to shoulder the responsibility in environments that may not fully acknowledge the systemic nature of racial issues.

A report by Education Support (2023) found ethnic minority educators frequently report feelings of isolation and marginalisation when working in predominantly White environments. The lack of diverse perspectives within these teams can make it difficult for these leaders to gain support and understanding for their initiatives. Ethnic minority staff may face a lack of support from their White colleagues, who may not fully understand the importance or complexity of anti-racist work, usually as they have not attended the training and lack knowledge on the key areas, data or research. This lack of support can hinder the effectiveness of anti-racist initiatives and place additional burdens on ethnic minority leaders. Many ethnic minority educators feel unsupported in their efforts to address racism, often due to a lack of understanding and commitment from their White colleagues.

Anti-racist work in schools must consider the socio-economic contexts of pupils and their families. Staff from minority backgrounds, due to their own lived experiences, are often more attuned to these issues. Still, they may struggle to address them comprehensively without support from the wider community. Furthermore, effective anti-racist work requires a deep understanding of cultural issues and the ability to navigate them sensitively. Ethnic minority staff often bring this cultural competence to their roles but may not always have the institutional support needed to implement culturally responsive practices.

Institutions may resist the changes required to implement effective anti-racist work, leading to frustration and burnout among ethnic minority leaders. This can manifest in various forms, including pushback from staff, lack of funding and a lack of buy-in. In some cases, schools may engage in tokenistic or symbolic actions that do not lead to meaningful change, which can undermine the efforts of ethnic minority leaders and contribute to feelings of frustration and disillusionment.

Distributing the load through shared leadership

Shared leadership models that involve all staff can enhance the effectiveness and sustainability of anti-racist work. These models promote collaboration, mutual learning, and shared responsibility, reducing the burden on minority leaders. Shared leadership can also signal a stronger intuitional commitment to anti-racism work, as it demonstrates that the entire school community is invested in this work.

Shared leadership allows for a more comprehensive approach to anti-racist work, incorporating diverse perspectives and addressing the multi-layered complexities of socio-economic and cultural issues, which can lead to more comprehensive and effective interventions. By involving both ethnic minority and White staff in leadership roles, schools can leverage diverse expertise and experiences to develop and implement anti-racist initiatives.

Shared leadership can also help reduce the isolation experienced by minority staff by creating more supportive and inclusive environments. This helps foster a culture of mutual respect, understanding and support among all staff members. Establishing mentorship and peer support networks can provide ethnic minority leaders with the support and guidance they need to navigate their roles effectively. These networks can also help build solidarity and collective action amongst staff.

Creating effective allyship from colleagues in anti-racist work is crucial for distributing the responsibility more equitably and fostering a supportive environment for ethnic minority staff.

Here are seven steps to create allies and share leadership among colleagues in anti-racist work in schools

1. Educate yourself and others

Colleagues should take the initiative to educate themselves about the history and impact of racism, current issues affecting ethnic minority communities and White privilege and its effects on and in education. This can involve reading books, attending workshops and discussing race and equity. Schools can provide resources and training sessions to help staff better understand these issues.

Schools can establish reading groups focused on key texts about racism and ethnic minority experiences, such as *Why I'm no longer talking to white people about race* by Reni Eddo-Lodge or *Brit(ish): On race, identity and belonging* by Afua Hirsch. Schools could also offer ongoing workshops and seminars facilitated by diversity and inclusion experts who can equip the staff team with practical tools and strategies for understanding and addressing racism.

According to Bhopal and Pitkin (2020), such professional development initiatives can significantly enhance staff understanding and empathy, fostering a more supportive and inclusive school environment. This research has indicated that professional development in diversity and inclusion can help build a more informed and empathetic workforce.

2. Self-audit your biases

Recognising personal biases and working to address them is a critical step in becoming an ally. Staff must be comfortable with feeling uncomfortable as they reflect on and challenge their attitudes and behaviours and consciously try to change them. Research by DiAngelo (2018) emphasises that understanding and addressing White fragility is essential for White educators to become effective allies.

Schools should offer regular implicit bias training sessions, including opportunities to work with external providers who can provide various resources and tests to help individuals identify their biases. Engaging in these tests can be very surprising for individuals and deliver content for further thought and exploration. Staff could be encouraged to keep reflective journals to help them track their progress in recognising and addressing their biases, as well as which specific strategies they felt most useful to help them address and overcome their biases. Establishing peer discussion groups where staff can share their experiences and strategies for overcoming biases can foster a culture of openness and continuous improvement.

3. Supporting ethnic minority colleagues

Ethnic minority colleagues' anti-racist efforts require support, which can include emotional support, initiative assistance and advocacy for their needs within the setting. To reduce feelings of isolation and increase valuable professional development opportunities, ethnic minority staff should be provided with supportive supervision, mentorship and coaching.

Schools should establish a range of support systems to ensure a feeling of support and safety. Mentorship, supervision and coaching programs for ethnic minority staff can be supportive in providing platforms and spaces for staff to share their experiences, receive peer support and benefit from experienced mentors who can offer further guidance and support. However, it is imperative to review "how" individuals may wish to receive this support to ensure they do not feel disempowered and "rescued"'

4. Promoted shared leadership of anti-racist work

Encouraging shared leadership models that involve both ethnic minority and White staff can enhance the effectiveness and sustainability of anti-racist work; these opportunities provide collaboration, mutual learning and shared responsibility. Shared responsibility prevents the burden of anti-racist work from falling solely on minority staff while allowing for diverse perspectives and addressing the multi-layered complexities of socio-economic and cultural issues.

5. Foster an inclusive environment

Creating an inclusive environment where all staff feel valued and respected is crucial, as this actively promotes diversity and inclusion in all aspects of school life, from recruitment processes to classroom interactions. Through group discussions, schools should review policies collectively to determine what works well and what needs to change. Implementing policies and practices that support diversity and inclusion, such as examining career progression opportunities and helping with steps into leadership as a part of the appraisal processes, should also be prioritised.

Implementing recruitment practices that seek to increase staff diversity can help create a more inclusive environment. Developing policies that promote inclusion, such as flexible working arrangements and support for career progression, can help retain diverse talent. Providing cultural competency training can also help staff understand and respect the diverse backgrounds of their colleagues and pupils.

6. Challenge discrimination

Ladson-Billings (1998) emphasises the importance of challenging discrimination to create equitable educational environments. Being an ally involves standing up against racism and discrimination whenever it occurs, challenging discriminatory behaviour and policies, and advocating for systemic change, no matter how uncomfortable. Schools should establish clear protocols for reporting and addressing discrimination, ensuring that all staff feel safe and supported in speaking out against racism.

A range of anti-discrimination strategies, such as clear reporting protocols, should be implemented. Establishing transparent and accessible reporting mechanisms for discrimination can ensure that issues are addressed promptly and effectively. Developing comprehensive anti-discrimination policies that outline the consequences of discriminatory behaviour can deter such actions. Supporting those who report discrimination and advocating for systemic changes can help create a more inclusive environment.

7. Commitment to ongoing learning and action

Allyship is not a one-time effort or project but an ongoing commitment to learning and action. Seeking out new knowledge, reflecting on one's practice and striving to make a positive impact is essential. Schools should provide regular opportunities for staff to engage in professional development related to anti-racism and encourage a culture of continuous improvement.

Implementing continuous learning, including professional development opportunities focused on anti-racism, can help staff stay informed and committed to equitable practices. Reflective practices and encouraging staff to engage in reflective practices, such as peer discussions, can help them continuously improve their understanding and actions. Implementing feedback mechanisms to evaluate the effectiveness of anti-racist initiatives and make necessary adjustments can promote continuous improvement.

While leading anti-racist work, it offers significant opportunities for ethnic minority employees to influence positive change, it also places substantial demands on them, both professionally and personally. Addressing these challenges requires a collective effort from all setting members to support and share the responsibility of diversity and inclusion initiatives.

Anti-racist work in schools is essential for creating inclusive and equitable educational environments. While ethnic minority staff can often lead these efforts, it is crucial to distribute the responsibility more equitably and foster a supportive environment for all staff. By educating themselves, addressing biases, supporting ethnic minority colleagues, promoting shared leadership, fostering an inclusive environment, challenging discrimination and committing to ongoing learning and action, all staff can become influential allies in anti-racist work.

A collective effort will help dismantle systemic racism within the education system and promote a culture of equity and inclusion for all pupils. By fostering allyship and distributing the workload more equitably, institutions can create more supportive environments that empower ethnic minority employees and advance the goals of anti-racial work.

Chapter summary

This chapter explores the significance of allyship in anti-racist efforts within schools, drawing on the story of Blair Peach, a White teacher from New Zealand killed during his standing in solidarity with the Southall community during times of intense racism and violence. The narrative discusses the ongoing challenge of building anti-racist school cultures, especially when leadership fails to address systemic racism head-on. The reluctance of White leaders and headteachers to engage fully in anti-racist work, often side-lining the lived experiences of ethnic minority pupils and staff, reinforces the importance of shared responsibility in these efforts. It underscores how missed opportunities to create inclusive spaces can perpetuate racial inequities and highlights the need for proactive allyship from all school community members.

TIFFIN TAKE-AWAY

1. **Allyship: The importance of active engagement**
   Blair Peach's legacy is a powerful reminder of the need for active and vocal allyship in school. While many leaders understand the importance of inclusivity, some remain hesitant to address racial issues directly, often avoiding uncomfortable conversations around racism, particularly during times of social unrest. Silence or avoidance can be interpreted as complicity, and failure to act on racial matters reinforces systemic inequities. Active engagement from all school staff is crucial to dismantling racism in educational settings.

   - You might consider how schools can encourage proactive allyship amongst staff members, ensuring that racial issues are addressed openly and inclusively.

2. **Shared responsibility**
   Anti-racist work is disproportionately led by ethnic minority staff, placing an undue burden on individuals who may already face challenges in White environments. While educators from minority groups often feel personally committed to this work due to their lived experiences, shared leadership across settings is essential for long-term sustainability. True allyship from all staff, particularly White educators, and leaders, is needed to ensure this work is equitably distributed and supported.

   - How can your school develop systems that ensure anti-racist work is a shared responsibility?

   How can educational institutions ensure that anti-racist work is a shared responsibility among all staff members, rather than disproportionately relying on ethnic minority individuals, and what impact might this have on the overall effectiveness of anti-racist initiatives?

3. **Supporting the emotional wellbeing of ethnic minority staff**
   Ethnic minority staff often take on the emotional and professional burden of spearheading anti-racist efforts, which can lead to burnout and isolation. Schools must provide mental health support, peer mentorship and shared leadership to ensure these staff members are not left vulnerable or overburdened in this critical work.

   - You should consider what strategies you can implement to better support the emotional and professional wellbeing of ethnic minority staff leading anti-racist initiatives.

References

Bhopal, K. and Pitkin, C. (2019) "Same story, just a different policy: Race and policy making in higher education in the UK". *Race, Ethnicity, and Education*, 23 (4).

Bradbury, A., Tereshchenko, A. and Mills, M. (2021) "Minoritised teachers' experiences of multiple intersectional racisms in the school system in England: 'Carrying the weight of racism'". *Race, Ethnicity and Education*, 26(3): 335-351.

DiAngelo, R. (2018) *White fragility: Why it's so hard for white people to talk about racism*. Beacon Press.

Eddo-Lodge, R. (2017) *Why I'm no longer talking to white people about race*. Bloomsbury Publishing.

Education Support (2023) "Mental health and wellbeing of ethnic minority teachers". www.educationsupport.org.uk/media/painjg2z/mental-health-and-wellbeing-of-ethnic-minority-teachers.pdf

Hirsch, A. (2018) *Brit(ish): On race, identity and belonging*. Vintage.

Ladson-Billings, G. (1995) "Toward a theory of culturally relevant pedagogy". *American Educational Research Journal*, 32(3): 465-491.

Miller, P. (2016) "White sanction, institutional, group and individual interaction in the promotion and progression of Black and minority ethnic academics and teachers in England". *Power and Education*, 8 (3): 205-221.

Part III
Shaping futures
Transforming the curriculum and preparing students for lifelong success

7

A window and mirror
How to create a curriculum offer of multicultural representation

"Anti-racist curriculum doesn't mean anything to our children…"

The problem of cultural generalisation

"Mummy, we were learning about Diwali in school today, but they showed us things that we HAVE TO do for Diwali, and we don't do those things! We're not doing Diwali properly."

I spoke with the school about the lesson on Diwali. They shared that Diwali is celebrated in a Mandir with traditional prayers led by the priest, lots of Diva lights, huge family gatherings, getting dressed up in traditional clothes, mountains of food everywhere, and an abundance of fireworks. They also invited an Indian mother to talk about the snacks made at Diwali, including "pani puri" and "rangoli".

This is not Diwali in our household, and I had a conversation with my daughter about how festivals and celebrations are interpreted differently and not everyone does the same thing.

"But my teacher said, 'This is what Indians do at Diwali.' We aren't doing it right!"

Maybe. But we are doing it our way, and that is OK.

A curriculum that reflects the diverse cultural backgrounds of the community and provides meaningful connections between home and school environments is crucial for pupil's cognitive, social and emotional development. Educational and neuroscience research demonstrates that by providing a curriculum with opportunities to reflect diverse cultural backgrounds, pupils can build neural pathways, foster a sense of identity and belonging and enhance the transfer of skills and knowledge across different settings.

The neuroscience behind culturally responsive teaching

It is difficult to understand the relevance and applicability of this work to SEND settings and whether leading this work in these provisions provides substance and

DOI: 10.4324/9781003416081-11

meaning. We have already identified that an "anti-racist curriculum" should incorporate four strands

1. multicultural education
2. increased representation
3. decolonising the curriculum and
4. anti-racist practice

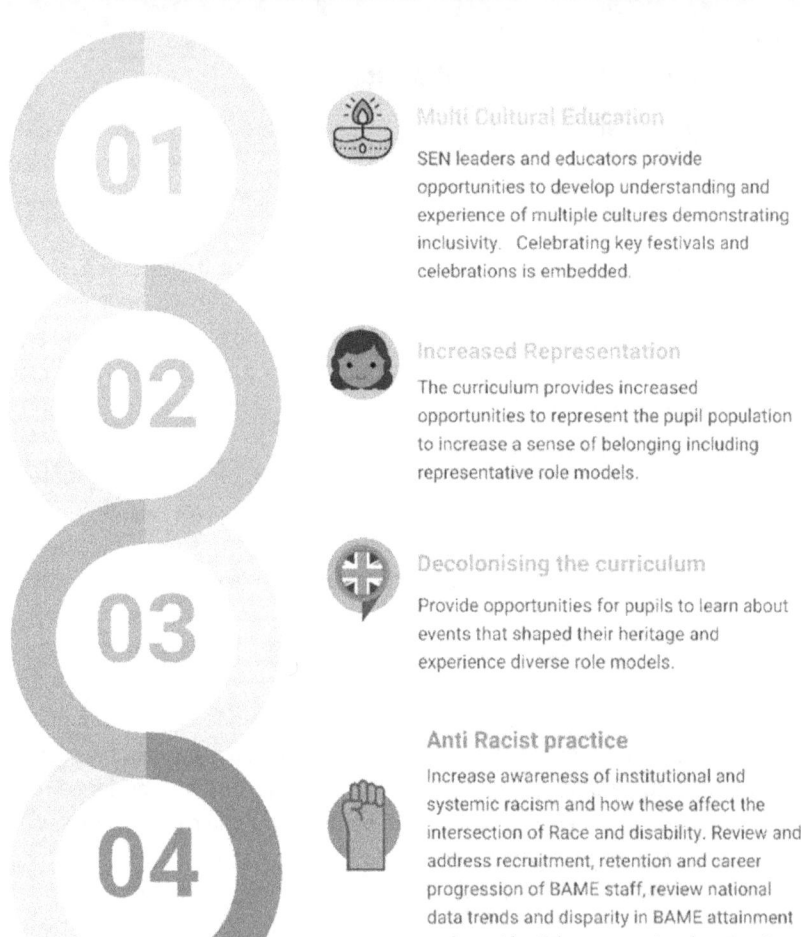

Figure 7.1 Creating an anti-racist curriculum for SEND

In most SEND settings, a three-pathway curriculum is presented to ensure it meets the broad range of needs and abilities. The pathways are usually pre-formal, semi-formal and formal. Children tend to access the pathway depending on the severity of their learning disability, their cognitive levels of understanding and the relevance of the content.

Pathways of learning: A tailored approach for SEND

The "formal curriculum" is designed for pupils who can access and engage in subject-specific learning, and this is often for pupils with more mild-moderate learning disabilities. The pathway tends to follow the National Curriculum. It focuses on core subject learning, including phonics, reading, writing and maths, with a wider focus on applying their knowledge to the wider community. They also develop their skills to access internships, work experience, further education, employment or independent living.

Pupils accessing the formal curriculum could benefit from all four strands of the "Anti-racist curriculum" offer, including decolonising the curriculum, which could, for example, include learning about the British Empire but also the perspectives and opinions of those who were colonised, how they might have felt about what was happening. "Anti-racist" practice may include promoting equal opportunities in education and career opportunities and accessing increased opportunities for job coaching, interviewing, presenting and interaction skills. Teaching and learning could also include applications to their feelings, such as if they have ever felt "out of control" or had to do what others tell them. They may learn to identify with marginalised groups as they learn about their own needs and diagnosis. They may learn how to advocate for themselves and identify situations where they feel included and supported and what discrimination against their disability and/or would look and feel like.

The "semi-formal curriculum" is a blended approach with a subject-specific focus, with the development of holistic and functional skills, including following everyday routines and drawing on strategies to promote self-regulation. The semi-formal curriculum tends to be aimed at pupils with more moderate to severe learning disabilities, and the focus tends to be more on "functional skills", including practical activities such as personal care, cooking, shopping and so on.

Learning in this pathway tends to be more structured, with increased use of visuals, visual timetables, now-and-next boards and task schedules. Pupils in this pathway would benefit from multicultural experiences that increase and promote representation, bridging links between home and school through these experiences. Decolonising the curriculum or understanding the principles behind anti-racist practice would not be suitable for this pathway's pupils.

The "pre-formal curriculum" focuses on the early stages of learning and development, focusing on sensory experiences and engagement. This pathway is focused on pupils with profound and multiple learning disabilities (PMLD) or severe learning disabilities (SLD).

The curriculum focuses on this pathway and the development of basic skills, including communication, fine and gross motor skills and social interactions. Developing an anti-racist curriculum in this pathway should focus on sensory stories, sensory-based learning, music and movement, interactive storytelling and experiences from different cultures. The focus would be to represent the pupil's cultural background and support the development of a sense of "self" reflected and celebrated in school.

The power of repetition: Strengthening neural pathways through cultural learning

Repetition and reinforcement are key approaches in all SEND teaching, as increased repetition of experiences strengthens neural pathways in the brain, aiding knowledge retention and skill transfer (Caine and Caine, 1991). Learning is a process that involves the creation and strengthening of neural pathways in the brain; it is enhanced and strengthened when new information can be connected and added to existing knowledge and experiences (Bransford, 2000). Therefore, when children are exposed to new information, their brains form new connections to build on their previous learning experiences.

Connecting home and school: The neuroscience of skills transfer

Repeated exposure to similar stimuli strengthens these connections, making information retrieval more efficient and effective. For example, when a child with learning disabilities learns a new concept in school, such as using an aided language board, the repeated use of that concept strengthens the neural pathways associated with it, and this process is known as "synaptic plasticity", where the brain's connections become stronger and more efficient with use. Therefore, studies confirm that repeated use of augmentative and alternative communication (AAC) devices, including aided language boards, improves the communication abilities of children with disabilities (Light and McNaughton, 2015).

Dehaene (2010) found that the brain can reorganise itself by forming new neural connections, which are essential for learning and memory; this plasticity is important for children with additional needs, as they may require more repetition and reinforcement to solidify their understanding. Neuroscience also emphasises the importance of transferring skills and knowledge between different settings. When children can relate learning to their lived experiences and aid in transferring skills across settings like home and school, the repetition strengthens neural pathways, supporting overall learning and development. For example, when working in specialist settings, liaising with parents and carers is good practice to find out what areas their child finds tricky at home. As a result, their family's quality of life may be compromised. An example of this may be children being unable to sit at a table during dinner. Therefore, they are unable to go out for family meals or even around the homes of family and friends, as their child may not be able to settle. The school would frequently support by working on specific skills, usually focusing on communication and independence, helping the pupils develop their skills, which would then be shared with parents and carers to continue the strategies at home. Very frequently, we would see transference of skills from school to home and the pupils demonstrating learned behaviours and skills that have transferred between different settings.

Zins, Weissberg, Wang and Walberg (2004) also suggest that the ability to transfer skills across different contexts is a critical component of social and emotional learning. For children with additional needs, this transferability can significantly enhance their ability to function effectively in various environments. Therefore, providing opportunities for children to see their culture represented in school experiences and identified in the curriculum promotes opportunities to create connections and reinforce learning across different settings, from home to school.

Neuroscience research also supports the three-strand curriculum focus on SEND schools. It confirms that children with disabilities often benefit from learning experiences that are multisensory, repetitive and consistent across different contexts. These principles are critical for helping them consolidate and apply their learning in various situations. Therefore, these form the basis of teaching and learning experiences in SEND settings. Delivering multicultural learning opportunities, the first rung of the "Anti-racist curriculum" approach, therefore, should incorporate the following elements;

1. Multisensory learning
   Engaging multiple senses can enhance learning for children with disabilities. This approach can help reinforce concepts and aid in memory retention. Shams and Seitz (2008) found that multisensory learning and training lead to more effective learning than traditional approaches. This type of learning activates different neural pathways, making it easier for children to grasp and retain information. Children also retained learning better over time. For example, Greenside School in Stevenage offer a range of sensory stories travelling the world, with audio, on their school website. These stories, together with the use of props, can make wonderful sensory experiences for children as you take them on a journey around the world.

2. Repetition and consistency
   Repetition and consistent practice across different settings help reinforce learning. Studies have shown that repeated exposure to the same concepts in various contexts can strengthen neural connections for long-term memory, thus improving recall. For example, parents could also lead the stories with the children at home, building familiarity with the sensory experiences between home and school. Parents could record videos of reading the story of the week, which is shared daily with the class, hearing the story and their parents' voice in school.

3. Contextual learning
   Learning across different times and places helps children generalise skills and knowledge. This means that teaching should not be confined to the classroom but integrated into daily activities and routines. Wilson (2002), in "Six views of embodied cognition", presented that our cognition is related to our physical environment

and experiences and that learning is not confined to abstract mental processes but through real-life contexts. This research, therefore, suggests that for children with additional needs, learning should occur across settings, integrated into daily lives and experiences mirrored across places and times. For example, multisensory learning through hearing music or sounds in the environment at school and then while out on educational visits.

Ensuring access to a curriculum and learning opportunities, which "mirror" experiences at home, promotes representation by reflecting diverse cultural backgrounds and encouraging experiences that can help establish a sense of identity and belonging. Recognising and celebrating cultural diversity in the classroom and wider school allows children to have their experiences presented, become validated and experience an inclusive environment. It also acts as a bridge between home and school, giving children experiences that mirror their experiences and culture at home. Gay (2010) also emphasises that culturally responsive teaching improves academic achievement and social competence. This approach can provide the necessary scaffolding for children with additional needs to support their unique learning needs and foster a more inclusive educational experience.

When children see and experience their culture and experiences reflected in their education, they are more likely to feel valued and included. Including stories, songs, rhymes, and music from various cultures in the curriculum allows children to see themselves represented in their learning materials. This representation can boost self-esteem and help children feel more connected to their community and peers. Banks (2006) argues that a multicultural curriculum is essential for fostering pupils' sense of belonging and identity.

Creating an anti-racist curriculum and an inclusive environment for ethnic minority pupils with SEND is a complex and ongoing process. We know that there is also conflicting research that suggests a focus on "multicultural experiences" and "representing the culture" is superficial and surface level. Troyna (1987) argues that this "foods and festivals" approach trivialises cultural differences and fails to promote a deeper understanding of the complexities that ethnic minority communities face.

However, it is the easiest "win" in schools. If you have a diverse school community, there are opportunities to embrace, extend and reflect the community in various ways, and the community can be mirrored into curriculum enrichment opportunities quite easily. If the community is less diverse, schools can act as "windows" to the wider world, showcasing cultures and traditions the children have not experienced. However, we should also consider that when there is a reduced representation of the ethnic minority communities in pupils, teachers, leaders and headteacher roles, schools are reliant on White teachers promoting these experiences. Without role models who can provide support and insight into lived experiences and authenticity, there could be a heavy reliance on stereotypes or outdated views. As for how Diwali was presented at my daughter's school, there is added complexity with this, as we also know there is the effect of teachers' implicit biases on their interactions with diverse content and pupils. Therefore, we can assume that the quality, depth and richness of the multicultural school experiences will depend on the staff's knowledge and biases.

Neuroscience research suggests that for children with additional needs or learning disabilities, mirrored experiences from home to school can increase opportunities for neural pathways to form and strengthen and transfer knowledge between settings. Therefore, when considering how to start creating an anti-racist curriculum for children with SEND, start with increasing multicultural events, mirror and represent the school community, or provide a window into the world through the increasing representation of a diverse and mixed global population. To do this, we must consider:

1. Incorporating diverse perspectives throughout the curriculum is essential, as is creating dedicated opportunities to celebrate and explore different cultures, traditions and identities. We can do this through dedicated units, projects or events that promote cultural awareness and appreciation.
2. Hearing the native language spoken in school can create a sense of belonging and validation for children. It also supports cognitive development and language skills.
3. Incorporating music and food from children's home cultures can make the learning environment more inclusive and engaging. These elements evoke positive emotions and memories, aiding emotional and social development.
4. While it is essential to include cultural elements, it is crucial to avoid stereotypes. Each child's experience of their culture is unique, and education should reflect this diversity.
5. The use of technology, including virtual reality, music, videos, iPads, sound systems and global links with international schools can help provide multisensory learning experiences.

Promoting multiculturalism in schools, as part of a broader commitment to anti-racism, involves embedding diversity into the SEND curriculum and the school culture. Below are a range of ideas to support your school's development in this area:

- Integrate anti-racist lessons into daily routines and activities. Consistent exposure helps reinforce learning and promote the generalisation of skills. For example, good morning sessions, saying hello in different languages or having a transition song to indicate different parts of the day.
- Celebrating international days with sensory experiences can help SEND pupils appreciate cultural diversity through tactile and engaging activities. Coard (1971) emphasised how the education system failed to represent Black children's cultural heritage, suggesting that "a lack of cultural representation can lead to a diminished self-concept in minority students". Incorporating sensory elements from various cultures directly addresses this educational gap.
- Organising stay-and-play sessions focusing on cultural inclusivity allows for family involvement, which is crucial in enhancing the educational experience of children with disabilities. Hatton et al. (2004) suggests "Family involvement in education can

significantly enhance the educational outcomes for children with disabilities". Sessions encouraging families to share culturally significant items and fostering a deeper community connection and understanding can support the pupils and their families in fostering a sense of belonging by bridging the gap between community and culture with education, leading to deeper community connection and understanding.
- Guest speakers could be invited into the school, including community members or elders, experts and artists from diverse backgrounds, to share their experiences and insights. By exposing pupils to a range of perspectives, the curriculum can challenge dominant narratives, foster critical thinking and promote a more profound sense of belonging, understanding and appreciation of diversity.
- Participating in community festivals with accessible crafts and performances makes cultural celebrations part of the learning experience. The DfE's guidance on inclusive education stresses "the importance of community integration in enhancing educational outcomes for SEND students" by providing real-world learning opportunities.
- Implementing dance and music workshops adapted for all abilities, including wheelchair dancing, aligns with the DfE's recommendations to include expressive arts in the curriculum, which are essential for "fostering social inclusion and developing motor skills and self-expression".
- Storytelling in the native language using visual aids supports language development and cultural awareness. Props, puppets and music can provide wonderful experiences for children to hear different languages and benefit from visual resources. Grove (2021) emphasises "the benefits of storytelling in enhancing language skills for SEN students, particularly when visual aids are used".
- Conducting cultural assemblies with visual aids and sign language interpretation, use of props and resources can ensure various relevant festivals and celebrations are accessible, breaking down barriers of communication and fostering an inclusive school culture, aligning with the "DfE recommendations for accessible communication formats". Open invitations to the parents and carers could be provided so that parents can celebrate notable events with their child and their school community, thus further enhancing a sense of belonging.
- Trips to culturally significant local sites provide experiential learning opportunities, crucial for real-world understanding and engagement, known as "culturally relevant pedagogy" (Ladson-Billings, 1995). Trips to temples, such as the Mandir, Mosque, Church, Gurdwara, and so on, can further function as a bridge between parents/child and the local community group, where exposure, understanding and visible strategies can be implemented.
- Creating a diverse library with books that include various forms of delivery, books, audiobooks, videos, stories and props ensures that all pupils, regardless of their abilities, can see themselves and others in the stories they read, as part of inclusive education.
- Cultural heritage units, including focused units examining the histories, traditions, values and contributions of a specific racial, ethnic or cultural group, for example, Black women of influence, celebrating the contribution of Black women through various fields of maths, science, stories and poetry, social activism or the arts.

How to create a curriculum offer of multicultural representation 121

- Inviting diverse role models, alumni pupils, and their families who can communicate effectively with SEND pupils, sharing their stories in engaging and inspiring ways for all abilities.
- Establishing global school links offers a safe, accessible way for SEND pupils to explore different cultures directly from their classroom, promoting global citizenship, for example, through the British Council.
- Collaborative Art projects based on themes, festivals and celebrations allow tactile and visual exploration that caters to various learning needs. These also provide avenues for creative expression that are essential for cognitive and emotional development.
- Cultural cooking classes for parents and carers could be offered. Chefs of various restaurants can be invited into school to work with pupils to create easy-to-make dishes from different cultures, providing pupils with opportunities to experience different ingredients through their senses. They would also have opportunities to work alongside parents, showcasing expectations around developing life skills and promoting independence, allowing parents a window into how to best support their child at home and transferring the skills from school to the home environment.
- Exploring cultural clothing through touch and visual descriptions helps pupils understand cultural diversity, supporting sensory learning strategies. Schools can also invite the school community to dress in traditional clothing for key festivals and celebrations or host "International days", whereby the school community is invited to wear dress as is culturally relevant to them. Again, this supports bridging the gap between home and school, supporting a sense of belonging.
- Pupil enquiry projects that allow pupils to investigate and share aspects of their cultural backgrounds and identities.
- A music curriculum with various cultural music embedded in the curriculum delivery can enhance pupils' appreciation for different music and instruments through cultural and artistic appreciation. This aims to expand beyond initiatives such as hiring a steel drum band for Black History Month and branch further out to fully embed cultural diversity within the curriculum offered throughout the year instead of condensing within one month, once a year, as a tick box exercise.
- Diverse language experiences linked to music appreciation, songs and rhymes from different cultures, together with stories and rhymes, are relevant and applicable to pupils with SEND.
- Culturally diverse sports days could be offered consisting of feature games from various cultures adapted for all abilities to encourage physical development and teamwork.
- Cultural celebrations, including school-wide events, festivals or programmes that honour and experience diverse cultures through performances, foods, arts and customs.
- Many significant religions have key festivals and celebrations at the same time of year. Several international days planned throughout the year can promote inclusivity and celebrate the events collectively, for example, Winter International Day (Festival of

Lights) and Spring International Day (New Cycles), celebrating with food, music and dance.
- Develop outreach programmes that address specific needs identified within ethnic minority communities, such as parenting workshops, language classes, education and tutoring. Bhopal and Myers (2015) found that targeted outreach programmes increased engagement and positively impacted multicultural schools.
- Facilitating parental involvement in school activities enhances the community's feelings and investment in the school's successes.
- School open days foster transparency and trust between families and the educational setting. These events can demystify the education process, making it more accessible and inviting to families.
- Community partnerships and collaborations with local cultural institutions, museums, businesses or organisations to provide experiential learning.
- Create robust feedback mechanisms that allow ethnic minority parents and pupils to provide input and feedback about their school experiences. These may be through surveys, suggestion boxes, translators or parent forums. Ensuring this feedback is acted upon is crucial to establishing trust and two-way relationships.
- As per the festivals and celebrations calendar, the focus could be on the histories, contributions and experiences of specific cultural or ethnic groups.
- Interdisciplinary projects or assignments that allow pupils to explore and share their cultural backgrounds and traditions are essential, as are cultural events, festivals or celebrations that bring the school community together to learn about and appreciate different cultures.
- Schools can also build partnerships with local cultural organisations, museums and community centres to provide authentic learning experiences and resources.

It requires commitment from all stakeholders, including educators, parents and the wider community, to ensure their own biases, knowledge and curriculum are audited. Hence, they are fully aware of the gaps. By adopting an integrated approach that considers the cultural, social and economic contexts of disability, schools can better support their pupils and create a more equitable educational system.

Decolonising the curriculum: Tailoring content for SEND learners

"Decolonising the curriculum" is a term used frequently and has become popular, especially since 2020, in response to the Black Lives Matter movement. CPD on the topic tends to include the history of colonialism, the legacy of colonial thought, critical thinking around decolonial approaches and a review of the curriculum, usually with subject leads.

Coaching in how to "decolonise the curriculum" may include reviewing whether the curriculum discusses colonialism and focuses on not just the economic benefits of the colonisers but also the counter-perspectives of those colonised communities and the drawbacks and impact on their communities, both positive and negative. As previously mentioned, pupils accessing a more "core" strand of the curriculum could be exposed to this debate and this difference of perspectives and be supported to develop their understanding and processing of this information, developing their critical thinking skills. SEND-specific strategies could be used for pupils to dissect and make sense of understanding events from different perspectives, which some children struggle with. Through using approaches such as comic strip conversations, role play, or drawings, some pupils may be able to access viewpoints, such as those presented in books such as *Stolen history* by Sathnam Sanghera through these SEND-specific strategies.

Decolonising the curriculum also goes hand in hand with the "increasing representation" strand, as developing an anti-racist curriculum should represent and include contributions to science, maths, the arts, and so on, of notable figures from ethnic minority communities. For the relevance, applicability and critical skills required to understand some of the content around "decolonising the curriculum", this strand would be recommended for pupils in SEND settings working at formal levels and those with SEND who are working at similar levels and beyond.

Decolonising the curriculum work with the pre-formal and semi-formal pathways may include simplified versions of stories, for example, "Coming to England" by Floella Benjamin, using multisensory props:

"Coming to England" by Floella Benjamin

What you need:

Touch and feel	Hear	See	Smell
Sand, fabric, swatches (cotton/wool), small suitcase, toy plane and boa, torch and hairdryer, fan and ice.	Recorded sound buttons of the ocean, aeroplane noises, Caribbean music, English nursery rhymes.	Photos of Trinidad, sea, London landmarks.	Smells of coconut, spices (cinnamon/cloves), lavender.

Part 1: Leaving Trinidad

Narration: "Floella is a young girl who lives on the beautiful island of Trinidad. The sun is always shining and the air smells sweet like coconuts."

Touch and feel	Hear	See	Smell
Let the children feel the sand and coconut scented items. Hairdryer to feel heat and torch for sun.	Play sounds of the ocean and soft Caribbean music.	Show pictures of Trinidad, showing beaches and landscapes.	Pass around a small jar of coconut scented oil to smell.

Part 2: Packing for the journey

Narration: "Floella's parents tell her that they are moving to England. She feels excited but also nervous. She packs her suitcase with her toys and clothes."

Touch and feel	Hear	See	Smell
Children help to pack a suitcase.		Show pictures or physical examples of suitcases and packed bags.	

Part 3: The boat/plane journey

Narration: "Floella and her family board a large boat (or plane) that took them over the sea to England. The journey is long and filled with new sights and sounds."

Touch and feel	Hear	See	Smell
Let children hold/see a toy boat or plane moving. Spray water bottle to indicate ocean journey.	Play sound buttons or aeroplanes taking off.	Pictures of Windrush boat on the water.	

Part 4: Arriving in England

Narration: "After many days, they finally arrive in England. It's much colder than Trinidad and Floella can see her breath in the air."

Touch and feel	Hear	See	Smell
Fan and ice to experience cold. Wool jumper or blanket to keep warm.	Play English nursery rhymes.	London landmarks – Big Ben, red buses, etc.	Lavender smell.

Part 5: Settling into a new home

Narration: "Floella and her family move into their new home. Everything is different, but they slowly start to adjust. Floella makes new friends and learns new things every day."

Touch and feel	Hear	See	Smell
Let children feel different textures of fabrics representing new clothes or furniture. Fan for cold air, or include ice.	Play soft background music of English nursery rhymes.	Show images of typical English homes.	

Part 6: New experiences

Narration: "Floella experiences new foods, new holidays and new traditions. She starts to feel more comfortable and proud of her new home while remembering her beautiful island."

Touch and feel	Hear	See	Smell
Share spices like cinnamon or cloves to touch and smell.	Mix Caribbean music with traditional English nursery rhymes.	Show multicultural pictures, e.g., of carnival.	Smell all of the smells, mixing them up representing blending of cultures.

Curriculum audits: Ensuring representation and inclusivity

An essential aspect of creating an anti-racist curriculum is the curriculum audit. An audit ensures that the curriculum reflects diverse perspectives. You must know who makes up your community so that you can cater to their needs and reflect them in your curriculum.

Most audits question all four elements that make up the "anti-racist curriculum". They will ask about whether the curriculum includes a diverse range of reading materials, books, authors, characters and illustrations of characters who are from diverse backgrounds, a diverse array of ethnic minority voices and representation across subject areas, lesson plans and classroom activities to ensure they promote inclusivity and representation. However, a comprehensive audit will also question the school's "anti-racist practices" regarding advertising positions, shortlisting candidates, recruitment, retention and career progression.

A comprehensive audit is essential for creating an inclusive curriculum which serves the entire school community. Arday, Branchu. and Boliver (2021) found that despite a focus on promoting inclusivity in schools, there were still significant gaps in the representation of ethnic minority communities across the curriculum coverage, perpetuating a "White curriculum".

A thorough curriculum review is foundational for identifying gaps, biases and opportunities for greater representation. This review should involve a diverse team, including educators, SEND experts, pupils, parents and community members from diverse racial, ethnic, socio-economic, gender and ability backgrounds.

A comprehensive audit is crucial for creating an inclusive, anti-racist and culturally responsive school that benefits all pupils and staff. An effective audit would benefit key areas, including governance, curriculum content, community engagement, and so on, ensuring an integrated approach to promoting diversity and inclusion. The following questions in this audit are grounded in research to promote credibility and effectiveness in this framework.

Example of a curriculum audit for creating an anti-racist curriculum:

1. GOVERNANCE, LEADERSHIP AND STRATEGY

Area	1. Explore 2. Embed 3. Excel	Next steps	Evidence
A dedicated governor oversees the achievement and wellbeing of ethnic minority pupils, families, and staff.			
Governors and senior leaders are committed to embedding anti-racist approaches in all school policies and processes.			
The school has a clear strategy for managing and recording racist incidents, including monitoring and addressing negative trends.			
Achievement data is analysed by ethnicities to identify any disparities.			
Behaviour, suspensions and exclusions are reviewed for any potential implicit biases.			
Disciplinary data is reviewed for any potential racial biases.			

SCHOOL ENVIRONMENT AND HIDDEN CURRICULUM

Ethnic minority staff and pupils feel confident that racist incidents are investigated and addressed.			
A sense of belonging is actively promoted for ethnic minority pupils, staff and parents/carers.			
Images and texts on the school's website and promotional materials represent multicultural Britain.			
The physical environment respects the cultural and religious identities of pupils.			
Communal areas are managed and promote the safety and wellbeing of all pupils, including ethnic minority groups.			
Values are promoted across the school, including respect and tolerance.			

PROFESSIONAL LEARNING AND DEVELOPMENT

There is an open environment where staff can engage in meaningful conversations about race anti-racism and anti-racist practices.			
The school provides professional learning opportunities on race equality for all staff, governors, pupils and the wider community.			
There is ongoing professional development on cultural competence for staff.			

Copyright material from Priya Bhagrath (2025), *Creating an Anti-Racist Curriculum for Children with Special Educational Needs*, Routledge

Criterion			
Staff are trained to recognise and address their own implicit biases.			
The school identifies and supports the career progression of ethnic minority staff into leadership roles.			
CURRICULUM CONTENT AND PEDAGOGY			
The curriculum includes diverse authors, characters and perspectives across subjects.			
Contributions from non-western cultures are included in science, maths and other subjects.			
The curriculum challenges Eurocentric perspectives and addresses colonialism.			
Curriculum leaders and teachers incorporate the contributions of people of colour in their subject areas.			
Lesson plans and classroom activities promote inclusivity and representation.			
Diverse cultural perspectives are incorporated into daily teaching.			
Trips, visits, guest speakers and CPD are carefully selected to align with the school's commitment to anti-racism.			
CULTURAL CALENDAR AND EVENTS			
The school's cultural calendar reflects the diversity of the community.			
Cultural celebrations are authentic and go beyond the "food and festivals" approach.			
Families and community members participate in cultural events.			
Visiting speakers are selected from diverse ethnic backgrounds and communities.			
COMMUNITY ENGAGEMENT AND PARTNERSHIPS			
Families from diverse backgrounds participate in the educational process and curriculum.			
The school has partnerships with diverse communities and organisations.			
Community members are welcomed in various ways, times and methods to engage with the school.			
The school proactively engages parents and carers of colour to participate in strategic parent groups.			
Parents and carers from all backgrounds feel assured that the school will address racist incidents, complaints and concerns with fairness and equity.			
The school actively seeks and responds to the wider community's views, needs and concerns.			

Copyright material from Priya Bhagrath (2025), *Creating an Anti-Racist Curriculum for Children with Special Educational Needs*, Routledge

REPRESENTATION AND INCLUSIVITY			
Ethnic minority pupils are represented in councils and forums.			
Pupils can share their perspectives on diversity and inclusion.			
Recruitment practices promote diversity and inclusion.			
There are clear career progression opportunities for ethnic minority staff.			
SEND identification and support processes are culturally sensitive.			
SEND resources reflect diverse cultural perspectives.			
Ethnic minority parents receive additional support and signposting on the diagnosis and EHCP processes.			
TECHNOLOGY AND RESOURCES			
Digital learning platforms, resources and support meet the needs of ethnic minority families.			
Provisions are in place for multilingual learners and families.			

Copyright material from Priya Bhagrath (2025), *Creating an Anti-Racist Curriculum for Children with Special Educational Needs*, Routledge

Inclusive curriculum design – "a mirror and a window"

Inclusive curriculum design is a critical approach to education that serves as both a mirror and a window for the pupils of a school and perhaps the community of staff and parents, depending upon their own experiences. As a "mirror" it aims to reflect the diverse experiences, cultures and identities of the school community, allowing pupils to see themselves represented in the learning materials and experiences. As a "window" it aims to provide insights into the broader world, exposing pupils to perspectives, histories and cultures different to their own.

The curriculum audit should be reviewed to create an action plan based on the results, ensuring adequate targets can be set and resources allocated, including any funding for CPD, resources or recruitment drives. The above intentions of "mirror and window" should be at the heart of its development. Communication with all stakeholders on the next steps following the audit is vital, as this will also ensure continued focus, alignment and sustained momentum.

Subject leads could review their curriculum areas using the audit to ensure that it incorporates role models, notable people, diverse perspectives and experts from the ethnic minority community. These voices and experiences across subject areas should reflect the diverse cultures and experiences of the individual and the wider school community, including reviewing whether selected texts reflect the community. Diverse authors, characters and narratives are essential in creating an anti-racist curriculum. Moncrieffe (2022) describes how the University of Portsmouth embedded Black British histories and narratives throughout its curriculum, leading to greater relevance and a sense of belonging for its Black students.

The key elements of an inclusive curriculum design include:

1. Ensure authors, characters and narratives are from various backgrounds. This extends to illustrations. Children, especially those who rely upon visuals for a better understanding of the world around them, should have representation and insight into cultures through the images in books and stories. These stories should mirror and reflect the immediate community.
2. Ensure the curriculum and enrichment reflect the achievements of those from underrepresented community groups in science, maths, history and the arts. Ensuring this level of representation is embedded within the curriculum provides the lens shifts from Eurocentric to more global.
3. For some pupils, whose learning disabilities are "milder" or those with additional needs but no learning disabilities, providing access to a curriculum that presents complex historical and cultural themes of colonisation may be more relevant and meaningful.
4. Links and resources, such as the British Council, can be used to forge partnerships with schools in other countries, offering opportunities and insights into different cultures through partnership schools.

We know that to make learning more relevant and meaningful, the curriculum should connect learning to children's lived realities by incorporating culturally relevant examples and scenarios that mirror the pupils' home environment, experiences, culture and backgrounds.

Culturally relevant scenarios, case studies and real-world applications that resonate with pupils' experiences should be used as assets in the learning process. This should also include drawing upon pupils' existing cultural knowledge, practices and ways of problem-solving.

For pupils that can, they can be encouraged to draw upon their personal experiences, knowledge and cultural frameworks to make sense of new information. For those pupils without the cognitive ability to share this information, parents and carers can be involved in this planning and discovery stage, ensuring that experiences delivered in school are suitably mirrored for the pupils. This process is essential in exploring how different cultural perspectives and values shape how concepts are interpreted and addressed.

Providing opportunities for pupils to apply their learning to real-world problems or challenges within their communities makes the curriculum more engaging, accessible and empowering, as they can see the relevance and applicability of what they are learning to their lives. Gay (2018) highlights how contextualising academic knowledge within pupils' cultural experiences improves learning, engagement and skills transfer.

Curriculum resources: Tools for inclusive and representative learning

To support a representative curriculum, it is crucial to ensure that all learning materials, including textbooks, multimedia resources and classroom displays, are inclusive and representative of diverse backgrounds, abilities and experiences. Representation must not be tokenistic but embedded, creating equitable environments for pupils.

Teachers and leaders should evaluate and select materials accurately portraying diverse groups, challenging stereotypes and avoiding biased or insensitive language or imagery. Developing or curating supplementary resources that provide diverse perspectives and representation, such as videos, websites or digital tools.

It is also essential to ensure that resources are accessible to pupils with different abilities and learning needs, such as providing alternative formats or assistive technologies. For example, using switch-activated technology such as "big macs" to make choices and add comments.

All curriculum materials and resources should be carefully selected or created to be inclusive and accessible, as well as reflective of pupil diversity. There should be:

- Diverse representations
  Ensure books, videos, websites and other resources accurately depict diverse groups and avoid stereotypical portrayals.
- Accessible formats
  Provide materials in multiple formats, such as audio, large print, captioned and symbols, to accommodate different abilities and learning needs.
- Inclusive language and imagery
  Use inclusive, asset-based language and visuals that avoid marginalising or tokenising underrepresented groups.
- Pupil-centred resources
  Involve pupils in developing learning resources that authentically capture their voices, experiences, and perspectives.

Creating inclusive classroom displays and visuals that reflect the diversity of the pupil and wider school population promotes a sense of belonging.

Engaging families and communities in curriculum development

Parents are not just passive recipients of their children's education but active contributors who play a pivotal role in shaping the school's culture and ensuring the successful implementation of an anti-racist curriculum. Their support and involvement are critical. However, it is crucial to recognise the spectrum of nuances, beliefs, and cultural influences that many ethnic minority communities face regarding the interpretation, understanding and acceptance of special educational needs.

As educators, we must familiarise ourselves with how cultural factors could affect parental engagement with the school and cultivate an open-minded approach to how they differ according to individual cultures within families. It is important to avoid making assumptions about specific ethnic groups' practices, beliefs and traditions. Cultural experiences can vary significantly, even within intra-groups, depending on factors such as class, wealth and education. For example, my mother is from Singapore, but my dad is from India. I grew up putting soy sauce over my Indian food, which many people told me was disgusting and bizarre. However, culturally, this was just my experience of a fusion of two cultures, and thus, cuisine, which was unique to my family. Just as my daughter questioned why we do not celebrate Diwali in the way she had been taught, this demonstrated that culture can be quite different.

Therefore, it is not only meaningful but respectful to invite families to share their experiences. It is essential not to stereotype families based on what we think their cultural experiences are but to create an inclusive environment where they feel comfortable sharing their unique experiences.

Effective communication is not just a tool but a responsibility in building trust and collaboration with parents of children with additional needs. Establishing clear and open lines of communication between school and parents is essential and a commitment. Regular newsletters, emails and parent-teacher meetings can inform parents about curriculum changes and invite their input. However, research also shows that ethnic minority parents are frequently disengaged from the school as they have limited means to access, interpret or respond to the information on offer.

In an ever-increasing digital world, there are also school apps such as "Arbor" or "Tapestry", "Evidence for Learning", and so on, to navigate, as well as online forms, parents evening booking, virtual meetings, virtual training, and schools are increasingly requiring high levels of digital literacy as a sole means of interacting with schools. Schools must remember the communities they serve, though, and consider socio-economic factors around accessibility; for example, in modern society, with the range of technology on offer, it can be unfathomable that not everyone possesses a smartphone to be able to navigate the expectations of digital response to schools' communication easily. However, some parents may not have access to the internet or smartphones or may lack the digital literacy required to navigate these developments in school communication systems. You may need to consider how you will support these parents' access to your IT systems.

Organising workshops and training sessions on anti-racism for parents can increase their understanding and commitment to the curriculum. These sessions can cover topics such as reviewing their cultural experiences at home, the language spoken, heritage, levels of engagement, involvement and support from their wider networks, and understanding their child's specific needs, behaviour, communication and expectations for the future. The workshops could also facilitate involvement in curriculum design and development through curriculum development committees, which can ensure that information about what is being taught is shared, their voices are heard and any concerns are addressed. A collaborative approach can foster a sense of ownership and accountability among parents.

The necessity for accessible communication is undeniable. Turnbull, Turnbull, and Erwin (2010) highlight that "Effective family partnerships are built on clear and accessible communication". Employing AI tools like Google Translate ensures that newsletters, surveys, and other communications are understandable to all families, thus enhancing engagement and participation. Visual aids are also a powerful aid in education. Hornby and Lafaele (2011) argue that multimedia resources can help clarify educational practices for parents from different cultural backgrounds, making the educational process more inclusive and accessible.

Engaging families and community members in the curriculum development process is essential for ensuring that the curriculum accurately reflects and resonates with the diverse experiences and perspectives of the school community. This can take many forms, such as:

- Establishing curriculum advisory committees or focus groups with parents and carers, staff and community members from diverse backgrounds to provide ongoing input and feedback on the curriculum.
- Create opportunities for families to share cultural knowledge, practices and perspectives to bridge home-school learning.
- Conduct surveys, interviews or community forums to gather insights, suggestions and feedback on the curriculum's representation and relevance.
- Inviting family and community members to share their stories, traditions or expertise as guest speakers or contributors to the curriculum.
- Identify and leverage the expertise, resources and funds of knowledge within the local communities for curriculum enrichment. Partner with local cultural organisations, community centres and businesses to provide authentic learning experiences, resources or mentorship opportunities.
- By involving families and communities in the curriculum development process, educators can tap into valuable knowledge, perspectives and resources while fostering a shared ownership and investment in the curriculum.

Creating a curriculum that bridges the gap between home and school environments is vital for special needs children. Demie and McLean (2017) found that actively engaging parents and communities in developing culturally relevant curriculum improved educational outcomes for ethnic minority groups. Pupils can also feel more connected to their schools, as the experiences on offer enable them to feel more acknowledged (Suarez-Orozco et al., 2018).

Consistency and continuity in their learning experiences help reinforce skills and concepts, making them more applicable and easier to retain. Teachers can collaborate with parents to incorporate cultural traditions and practices from home into classroom activities, ensuring children encounter family elements, such as language, music, greetings, smells and foods, reinforcing their learning and making it more meaningful. Epstein (2001, in Campbell, 2001) highlights the importance of family-school partnerships in enhancing educational outcomes.

Implementing inclusive teaching practices focused on cultural diversity and representation can significantly benefit children with additional needs. Using culturally relevant examples and materials in lessons can help make abstract concepts more concrete and relatable for children with additional needs. Visual aids, storytelling, hands-on activities and off-site trips that reflect the pupil's cultural experiences can enhance comprehension and engagement.

Schools can focus on increasing pupil engagement and participation and enhancing identity and belonging among pupils, their families and staff. This leads to positive feedback from parents and the wider community. The curriculum could include opportunities to experience cultural storytelling sessions, music, dance and art from various communities in the planning and lesson delivery. Parents could plan collaboratively to strengthen relationships between families and the school and increase parental involvement in the educational process. This would lead to better academic and social outcomes for pupils.

Engage families and community members in the curriculum development process. Their insights, experiences and perspectives can enrich the curriculum and foster a sense of shared ownership and investment.

Chapter summary

This chapter explores the importance of creating a culturally responsive and inclusive curriculum in SEND settings. It highlights how diverse celebrations, like Diwali, can be misunderstood or misrepresented in schools by teachers who lack the knowledge and skills, potentially alienating pupils from their own cultural practices. Neuroscience and educational research demonstrate the benefits of providing a curriculum that reflects pupils' diverse backgrounds, enhancing cognitive, social and emotional development.

The chapter also emphasises the challenges of applying anti-racist practices within SEND settings, offering strategies to incorporate multicultural representation in ways that support the learning needs of all pupils. Ultimately, creating a bridge between home and school environments fosters a sense of identity, belonging and inclusivity for all pupils.

TIFFIN TAKE-AWAY

1. **Reflecting individual cultural practices in the curriculum**
   Recognising that cultural practices differ within communities, even for widely celebrated festivals, is essential. Schools must avoid generalising or stereotyping these practices and instead create opportunities for pupils to share and celebrate their unique cultural traditions. This fosters a sense of belonging and validates their personal experiences.

   - How does your school create space for individual cultural differences within broader celebrations, avoiding stereotypes and ensuring all pupils feel seen?

2. **Repetition and multisensory learning**
   Neuroscience research supports using repetition and multisensory experiences to enhance learning for pupils with disabilities. A multicultural curriculum incorporating sensory activities, such as cooking, music and storytelling, can help pupils engage with diverse cultures in meaningful ways that reinforce learning.

   - You could consider how multisensory learning strategies could reflect cultural diversity and strengthen learning for pupils in SEND settings.

3. **Parental involvement**
   Engaging families in the curriculum development process strengthens the connection between home and school, allowing children to experience consistency in their learning environment. Parents can offer valuable insight into cultural practices and their children's specific challenges, leading to more tailored and inclusive learning experiences.

   - You could think about how schools could involve parents more deeply in shaping a curriculum that reflects SEND pupils' cultural and learning needs.

References

Arday, J., Branchu, C. and Boliver, V. (2021) *What do we know about Black and Minority ethnic (BAME) participation in UK higher education.* Cambridge University Press.

Banks, J. (2006) *Cultural diversity and education: Foundations, curriculum and teaching.* Pearson.

Bhopal, K. and Myers, M. (2015) "Racism and bullying in rural primary schools: protecting White identities post Macpherson". *British Journal of Sociology of Education*, 38(2).

Bransford, J. (2000) *How people learn: Brain, mind, experience and school.* National Academy Press.

Caine, R. and Caine, G. (1991) *Making connections: Teaching and the human brain. Association for supervision and curriculum development.* Pearson Learning.

Campbell, C. (2011) *How to involve hard-to-reach parents: Encouraging meaningful parental involvement with schools.* National College for School Leadership.

Coard, B. (1971) *How the west Indian child is made educationally sub-normal in the British school system*. McDermott Publishing.

Dehaene, S. (2010) *Reading in the brain: The new science of how we read*. Penguin.

Demie, F. and McLean, C. (2017) *Black Caribbean underachievement in schools in England*. Lambeth Education and Learning.

Gay, G. (2018) *Culturally responsive teaching: Theory, research and practice*. Teachers College Press.

Grove, N. (2021) *Storytelling, special needs and disabilities*. Routledge.

Hatton, C., Akram, Y., Shah, R., Robertson, J. and Emerson, E. (2004) *Supporting South Asian families with a child with severe learning disabilities*. Jessica Kingsley.

Hornby, G. and Lafaele, R. (2011) "Barriers to parental involvement in education: An explanatory model". *Educational Review*, 63(91): 37-52.

Ingstad, B. and Whyte, S. (1995) *Disability and culture*. University of California Press.

Ladson-Billings, G. (1995) "Toward a theory of culturally relevant pedagogy". *American Educational Research Journal*, 32(3): 465-491.

Light, J. and Mcnaughton, D. (2015) "Designing AAC research and intervention to improve outcomes for individuals with complex communication needs". *Augmentative Alternative Communication*, 31(2): 85-96.

Moncrieffe, M. (2022) *Challenging, decolonising and transforming primary school history curriculum knowledge*. The Chartered College of Teaching.

Shams, L. and Seitz, A. (2008) "Benefits of multisensory learning". *Trends Cognitive Science*, 12(11): 411-417.

Suarez-Orozco, C., Motti, F., Marks, A. and Katsiaficas, D. (2018) "An integrative risk and resilience model for understanding the adaptation of immigrant-origin children and youth". *American Psychologist*, 73(6).

Troyna, B. (1987) *Beyond multiculturalism: Towards the enactment of anti-racist education in policy, provision and pedagogy*. Oxford review of Education. Routledge.

Turnbull, A., Turnbull, H. and Erwin, E. (2010) *Families, professionals and exceptionality: Positive outcomes through partnership and trust*. Merrill Prentice Hall.

Wilson, M. (2002) "Six views of embodied cognition". *Psychonomic Bulletin and Review*, 9(4): 625-636.

Zins, J., Weissberg, R., Wang, M. and Walberg, H. (2004) *Building academic success on social and emotional learning*. Teachers College Press.

8
How to create a cultural calendar to reflect your school community

"We can't celebrate everything..."

Cultural connections: The role of a diverse calendar

A cultural calendar that represents the diverse pupil population of a school aims to foster inclusivity, promote understanding and celebrate the rich tapestry of cultures within the school community. Implementing such a calendar requires thoughtful planning, collaboration and a commitment to recognising and valuing all cultures the pupils represent.

In the realm of special education, the development of a cultural calendar is paramount, not merely for celebrating diversity but for forging meaningful connections between the educational environment and the home.

> Involvement of families in the educational journey is not just beneficial; it is essential for creating tailored and responsive educational strategies that accommodate the diverse needs of SEN students.
>
> (Hatton, 2004)

Implementing a cultural calendar that reflects the rich tapestry of cultures within some school communities strengthens the educational pathways by fostering a profound connection between home and school environments.

The school's cultural calendar should identify various festivals and celebrations to promote cultural awareness and understanding. This would allow pupils to experience diverse cultural celebrations in diverse communities, experience their own culture within their school environment and increase their cultural competence from a young age by broadening their worldview.

Cultural competence in action: Fostering inclusivity

Exposing pupils to diverse cultural celebrations helps to broaden their worldview and develop cultural competence from a young age. Banks (2014) found that multicultural education, including learning about different cultural traditions, helps pupils develop more positive attitudes towards diverse groups, which prepares pupils to thrive in an increasingly diverse society and globalised world.

DOI: 10.4324/9781003416081-12

Experiencing a diverse cultural calendar fosters inclusivity and belonging. Pupils from minority backgrounds see their cultural traditions recognised and celebrated at school, which can support inclusion and a sense of belonging. Suarez-Orozco (2018) found that ethnic minority pupils felt more connected to their schools when their cultural backgrounds were acknowledged and valued, and this sense of belonging is linked to better outcomes and overall wellbeing.

Learning about diverse cultural celebrations authentically can help challenge stereotypes and reduce prejudice. Research has shown that increased intergroup contact and learning about other cultures reduce prejudice. Schools provide an ideal environment for positive intergroup interaction and learning. Exploring different cultural perspectives and traditions encourages pupils to think critically about their assumptions and worldviews. In multicultural areas, celebrating diverse festivals and cultural events in schools is particularly important for establishing a sense of belonging amongst pupils from various backgrounds. When schools recognise and celebrate the cultural traditions of their diverse pupil population, it sends a powerful message that all cultural identities are valued. There is little research on how the identities of pupils with learning disabilities are affected; however, Tatum (1992) identifies how affirming pupils' racial and cultural identities impacts their academic engagement and success. We also know from neuroscience research that it supports children in transferring their learning across settings and building faster and more embedded neural pathways, allowing them to build upon previous knowledge.

Celebrating diverse festivals together as a school community creates shared positive experiences that can bridge cultural divides. In multicultural areas, celebrating various cultural traditions helps normalise diversity as an everyday part of school life, and joint celebrations provide opportunities for pupils from different backgrounds to interact and form friendships.

Beyond stereotypes: Ensuring authentic cultural representation

However, ensuring that school cultural celebrations are not stereotypical is important. Schools must ensure that staff have adequate training, including thorough explanations of various events' history, significance and practices. This fosters more profound understanding and respect amongst the school community and prioritises authenticity in the delivery of teaching and learning opportunities.

Planning for diversity: Creating the cultural calendar

The steps to create an effective cultural calendar include:

- Leaders should understand the school demographics and gather data on the pupils' cultural backgrounds. Using the curriculum audit, they should identify the key focus areas by reviewing any disparities.
- Staff should engage with parents and carers to understand the cultural and religious festivals they celebrate.

Forming a cultural calendar committee:

- Establish a working party, including teachers, parents, and pupils, to ensure representatives offer diverse perspectives.
- Designate a lead coordinator to oversee the development and implementation of the calendar.

Identifying key festivals and celebrations:

- Research major cultural and religious festivals celebrated by the school's community.
- Consult with cultural and religious leaders to ensure accurate representation and understanding.
- Ask parents to provide information regarding their celebration of these events

Creating the calendar

- Develop a visual calendar that is bespoke for the school community. Include descriptions of each festival, its significance and how it is celebrated.
- Ensure the calendar is accessible to all school community members in print and online. Various educational resource sites offer easily downloadable calendars; however, they contain overwhelming information that may not be relevant to your school community.
- Planning school events and activities around these festivals to provide pupils with experiential learning opportunities
- Incorporate lessons about these festivals into the curriculum to enhance understanding.

Promoting the cultural calendar

- Share the calendar with the school community through newsletters, emails and websites.
- Use social media platforms to highlight upcoming festivals and celebrations.
- Encourage pupils and parents to participate in the planning and execution of cultural events.
- Host assemblies and special events to introduce and explain the significance of the festivals, either half-termly or termly.

Evaluating and updating the calendar

- Gather feedback from pupils, parents and staff about the cultural calendar and its impact.
- Regularly review and update the calendar to reflect changes in the school's cultural demographics or community preferences.
- Ensure that new and emerging cultural groups within the school community are represented.

Cultural celebrations can involve families and community members, strengthening home-school ties, as Epstein (2010) supports. Epstein highlighted the importance of school-family-community partnerships for pupil success, particularly in diverse contexts.

Implementing cultural calendars to celebrate diversity and promote inclusivity may include:

1. Dedicating specific months to celebrating different cultures, for example, "Asian Heritage Month" or "Black History Month", where the focus is on traditions, historical figures, music, art, dance and food from these cultures.
2. Schools often create calendars highlighting global festivals such as Diwali, Eid, Chinese New Year and Hanukkah, alongside more commonly celebrated holidays such as Christmas and Easter. This type of calendar ensures representations of various religious and cultural traditions. As previously stated, it is important not to provide stereotypical teaching and learning opportunities and move beyond the sarees and samosas.
3. Schools in areas with specific ethnic or cultural communities often create calendars that reflect the local population. For instance, a school in an area with a large Indian community might include more South Asian festivals and events.
4. Schools could also implement a system where each month or week focuses on a different culture or country, allowing in-depth exploration of various traditions throughout the year.
5. In schools with pupils from diverse backgrounds, pupils could contribute to the creation of a cultural calendar, ensuring authentic representation and fostering a sense of ownership and pride.
6. With the increasing use of technology in education, some schools have created interactive digital calendars that provide information about various cultural events and allow for easy updates and additions. Opportunities like the British Council offer abundant opportunities to engage with diverse communities abroad to observe and share cultural celebrations.

While celebrating diverse cultural traditions is crucial in multicultural areas, it is equally important, if not more important, in predominantly White areas as it prepares pupils for a diverse world. Exposure to different cultures through school celebrations helps prepare pupils for future interactions, as they will encounter diversity in higher education, work, and travel experiences as they grow older.

Some examples of how we can involve families in celebrating cultural experiences include

- Family culture-sharing sessions can be organised virtually or in person, and families can share cultural traditions, festivals and important dates through presentations, storytelling, or interactive workshops.
- Families could be invited into school to create and share their traditional or favourite recipes associated with their cultural celebrations. These could be compiled into a school cookbook and incorporated into the calendar, highlighting specific dishes during relevant cultural events.
- Families could be encouraged to bring in or share photos of cultural artefacts, traditional clothing or significant objects. These could be displayed in the school and featured in the calendar alongside explanations of their cultural significance.

- Parents or family members could become "cultural ambassadors" for their heritage. They could work with subject leads and teachers to plan and lead activities related to their culture's celebrations throughout the year.
- Events could be organised where grandparents or older family members can share stories about their cultural traditions and how celebrations have evolved; these stories could be recorded and incorporated into annual festivals and celebrations.
- The school could host art workshops where families create visual representations of their cultural celebrations.
- Schools can partner with schools in other countries through the British Council or regions to set up a penpal programme where families can exchange information about their cultural celebrations with families from different backgrounds.
- Schools could invite families to lead school assemblies or classroom sessions about their cultural celebrations, allowing for more direct interaction between families and pupils.
- The school could organise a fashion show where families can display traditional clothing from their cultures and explain the significance of different garments and when they are worn.

Use of technology in cultural calendars:

- Schools can create an online platform where families can contribute dates, descriptions and images of cultural celebrations. This platform can be a shared document, allowing easy updates and additions throughout the year.
- Families can create short videos, which the school can use to create digital content to share via their website, newsletters or social media, giving insight into their versions or adaptations of cultural celebrations throughout the year.
- Families can contribute to interactive digital maps (using Google Maps) to display the geographical origins of various communities and various cultural celebrations represented in the school community.
- The school can generate QR codes for digital creations, videos, songs and school content about cultural celebrations. These can be issued physically via home-school communication books and newsletters or digitally via emails and the school website.
- The family recipe book can be made into a collaborative digital cookbook of traditional recipes using platforms like Google Docs.
- VR headsets allow experiences to "visit" other countries and experience festivals and celebrations, such as Chinese New Year or Diwali, could be offered. Schools could also use tools like Google Tour Creator to provide immersive learning opportunities for the school community on cultural celebrations through lessons, music lessons or sharing assemblies.

Cultural celebrations in White areas: Expanding worldviews

Creating a cultural calendar celebrating diverse festivals and traditions in White areas can significantly enhance cultural awareness, foster inclusivity and promote a broader understanding of the world. Without this approach to appreciating cultural diversity, which is crucial in today's interconnected world, pupils may develop an ethnocentric worldview if not exposed to other cultures.

Celebrating diverse traditions can help counter this tendency. Learning about different cultures and celebrations can foster empathy and a sense of global citizenship among pupils. Without direct contact with diverse groups, learning about other cultures can help address implicit biases. Lai et al. (2014) found that exposure to counter-stereotypical examples can reduce implicit bias.

Incorporating diverse cultural celebrations enriches the curriculum, making learning more engaging and relevant to the wider world and ensuring that culturally responsive teaching continues to benefit all pupils (Gay 2018). The National Curriculum in England aims to prepare pupils for the diversity they will encounter in society. However, due to the lack of embedded diversity within the curriculum, the effectiveness of doing so requires continued review to ensure opportunities are apparent and not implied and to support and effect equity, inclusivity and change.

There are many challenges in teaching diversity in White community areas, in that there is an apparent lack of first-hand experience and exposure to diverse communities, as well as a lack of understanding of the relevance. Picower (2009) highlights how White teachers' limited multicultural knowledge can perpetuate stereotypes; therefore, teachers with limited first-hand experience may rely on simplified or outdated representations of cultural traditions and pass these on to their pupils.

A lack of diversity among staff means fewer opportunities for authentic cultural insights. Villegas and Irvine (2010) emphasise the importance of teacher diversity in providing culturally responsible education. Teachers must try to assess and understand the demographics of the school. Even in White communities, there are often minorities and some level of diverse backgrounds. Leaders should conduct surveys or use existing data to understand the cultural and ethnic makeup of the pupil population and their families. Leaders must engage with parents and guardians to gather insights into the cultural practices and the traditions they celebrate.

Without diverse community members, schools may rely heavily on textbooks or media representations, which can present stereotypical and outdated views. Sleeter and Grant (2012) critique the often superficial treatment of diversity in educational materials.

Critical evaluation: Avoiding the "Food and Festivals" trap

Schools may adopt well-intentioned but limited approaches, such as adopting a "food and festivals" approach to cultural diversity, which can reinforce stereotypes and fail to address deeper cultural understanding. Troyna (1987) critiqued this approach as trivialising cultural differences. Without guidance on critical cultural reflections, pupils and staff may accept stereotypical representations at face value. Additionally, White areas may lack the community resources and cultural organisations that could provide more authentic cultural experiences. This aligns with research by Nieto (2017) on the importance of community involvement in multicultural education.

Teachers' unconscious biases can also influence how they present information about other cultures. Leaders and teachers in these areas should identify major cultural and religious key festivals celebrated globally and conduct research and consultation work. Universally significant events such as Black History Month, International Women's Day, and so on, should be identified and included in the calendar. However, staff must consult with cultural organisations or representatives from community groups to ensure accurate representation and understanding of various cultural practices.

Additionally, to address these challenges further, schools in predominantly White areas can follow the following suggestions to create deeper educational experiences.

1. Establish connections with schools or organisations in more diverse areas for cultural exchanges and collaborative projects, as this can provide pupils with authentic interactions and experiences with diverse communities. If these are not local, create link opportunities with schools in diverse areas or use British Council partnership opportunities to forge links and collaborations with schools overseas.
2. Implement virtual cultural exchanges and experiences to bridge the gap in first-hand exposure to diversity, including video conferencing with pupils from different backgrounds or virtual tours of cultural sites.
3. Create strategic recruitment and retention practices to recruit and keep staff from diverse backgrounds. Villegas and Irvine (2010) emphasise the importance of teacher diversity in providing culturally responsive education.
4. Offer comprehensive training for staff on cultural competence, addressing unconscious biases and effective multicultural education strategies. This is crucial in White areas where educators may have limited multicultural knowledge.
5. Carefully assess textbooks and media representations for stereotypical or outdated references, language, or views, as these may need to be supplemented or replaced with more authentic and in-depth resources.
6. Engage pupils in research and projects that promote deeper cultural understanding.
7. Bring individuals from diverse backgrounds to share authentic experiences and insights, exposing pupils to different perspectives.
8. Encourage critical thinking and discussions about cultural representations and stereotypes.
9. Move beyond the "food and festivals" approach, which tends to be deeply embedded in SEND settings. Ensure the school moves beyond multicultural events and representation and incorporates anti-racist practices focusing on deeper aspects of culture, such as values, beliefs, and social structures.
10. Teachers should be aware of and actively work to counteract their own unconscious biases, which can influence how they present information about other cultures.

Celebrating diverse festivals and cultural traditions in schools is crucial for fostering inclusivity, challenging stereotypes, and preparing all pupils for a diverse world. While the approach and challenges may differ between multicultural and White areas, the importance of this educational aspect remains constant. Addressing current practices and curriculum limitations allows schools to provide more authentic and meaningful multicultural education that truly prepares pupils to thrive in a diverse society despite their limited local exposure.

Building a richer educational experience through diversity

A representative cultural calendar is more than just an annual schedule of events; it is a comprehensive approach that embraces diversity and promotes inclusivity. By following these steps and leveraging strong partnerships with parents and the community, schools can provide pupils with a richer, more engaging educational experience that respects and celebrates the diverse world in which they live.

Chapter summary

This chapter explores the importance of integrating a cultural calendar in special education settings to reflect the diverse backgrounds of pupils and their families. By incorporating festivals and cultural celebrations, schools can create a more inclusive environment that fosters belonging and respect for cultural diversity.

The chapter discusses how a well-designed cultural calendar connects the school and home, supports the development of cultural competence and promotes shared experiences among pupils from different backgrounds. It outlines practical steps for creating, promoting and evaluating a cultural calendar and strategies for ensuring authenticity and avoiding superficial cultural representations.

 TIFFIN TAKE-AWAY

1. **Connecting home and school through celebrations**
   Implementing a cultural calendar that reflects pupils' diverse backgrounds strengthens the connection between home and school, ensuring pupils see their cultures and traditions respected and reflected. It is important to consider how your school could foster deeper connections between cultural traditions pupils experience at home and those celebrated at school to strengthen their sense of belonging.

2. **Promoting authentic and inclusive cultural experiences**
   Schools must go beyond superficial "foods and festivals" approaches, ensuring that cultural events and celebrations reflect genuine traditions and values. Staff training on cultural competence and a commitment to authenticity can prevent

the reinforcement of stereotypes and provide meaningful learning experiences for all pupils.

- How can your school deliver cultural celebrations with depth and authenticity, avoiding tokenism or superficial representations?

3. **Encouraging pupil and family involvement**
Engaging pupils and their families in developing the cultural calendar can lead to more relevant, meaningful celebrations. By inviting families to share their cultural traditions, schools foster a more profound sense of inclusion and create opportunities for shared experiences that celebrate diversity.

- You could think about how you can involve pupils and their families in shaping your school's cultural calendar to ensure it reflects and celebrates their diverse backgrounds.

References

Banks, J. (2014) *An introduction to multicultural education* (5th ed.). Pearson.
Epstein, J. (2010) *School, family and community partnerships: preparing educators and improving schools.* Westview Press.
Gay, G. (2018) *Culturally responsive teaching: Theory, research and practice.* Teachers College Press.
Grant, C. and Sleeter, C. (2012) "Doing multicultural education for achievement and equity". www.researchgate.net/publication/286730251_Doing_multicultural_education_for_achievement_and_equity_second_edition
Lai, C., Marini, M., Lehr, S., Cerruti, C., Shin, J., Gaba, J., Ho, A., Teachman, B., Wojcik, S., Koleva, S., Frazier, R., Heiphetz, L., Chen, E., Turner, R., Haidt, J., Kesebir, S., Hawkins, C., Schaefer, H., Rubuchi, S., Sartori, G., Dian, C., Sriram, N., Banaji, M. and Nosek, B. (2014) "Reducing implicit racial preferences: A comprative investigation of 17 interventions". *Journal of Experimental Psychology*, 143(4).
Nieto, S. (2017) "Re-imagining multicultural education: new visions, new possibilities". *Multicultural Education Review*, 9(1).
Picower, B. (2009) "The unexamined Whiteness of teaching: How White teachers maintain and enact dominant racial ideologies". *Race, Ethnicity and Education*, 12(2).
Suarez-Orozco, C., Motti, F., Marks, A. and Katsiaficas, D. (2018) "An integrative risk and resiliance model for understanding the adapatation of immigrant-orgin children and youth". *American Psychologist*, 73(6).
Tatumn, B. (1992) "Talking about race, learning about racism: The application of racial identity development theory in the classroom". *Harvard Educational Review*, 62(1).
Troyna, B. (1987) *Beyond multiculturalism: Towards the enactment of anti-racist education in policy, provision and pedagogy.* Oxford Review of Education. Routledge.
Villegas, A. and Irvine, J. (2010) "Diversifying the teaching force: An examination of major arguments". *The Urban Review*, 42(3).

9
Knowing the difference between multicultural experiences and anti-racist practices

"... but this feels tokenistic and box-ticking ..."

Defining the difference: Multicultural v anti-racist education

We have explored a range of themes, from barriers faced by ethnic minority parents and families in understanding and accepting their child's additional needs to reviewing how schools can be more inclusive and how they can do this. However, it is crucial to distinguish between what constitutes "multicultural experiences" and what supports "anti-racist practices and curriculum". This distinction is vital in understanding how educational approaches can either perpetuate or challenge systemic inequalities.

The distinction between the two is not new or instigated by the Black Lives Matter movement. Both frameworks' debates and calls to action are longstanding and almost 40 years old. Troyna (1987) highlights the ongoing difficulties in determining the distinction between the two.

> the assumption that the priority was the management of problems thrown up by the presence of Black students rather than the mitigation of problems which they encountered precisely because they were Black citizens living in a racist society. Thus, the package of reforms introduced in the 1970s concentrated on trying to ensure that the schooling experiences of Black students were made more palatable. They were geared towards representing their (presumed) lifestyles in curriculum design and teaching aids. What they ignored were the formal and informal racist processes which constrained the educational opportunities available to these students.

The legacy of multicultural education

A focus on increasing multicultural experiences and opportunities to celebrate "culture" and "heritage" involves exposing pupils to various cultural traditions, practices and perspectives. Multicultural education involves recognising, valuing and incorporating different cultural perspectives within the educational setting. It aims to respect and celebrate the diversity of pupils' backgrounds by integrating various cultural experiences, histories and contributions into the curriculum.

These approaches broaden pupils' worldviews and promote cultural awareness, competence and inclusion. Cultural celebrations foster a sense of inclusivity and belonging amongst pupils from diverse backgrounds. We have explored the key components of multicultural experiences in SEND schools and why SEND settings focus more on cultural celebrations and festivals. We considered how to increase curriculum integration, family and community involvement and, where appropriate, developing critical thinking and reflection. Troyna (1987) identifies this as "microscopic", as the focus is on developing an understanding of the culture and developing increased understanding and "tolerance of members of minority ethnic and cultural groups". The focus is on the school and "the nature of change concerns removing ethnocentric material from the curriculum and teaching materials and their replacement by more culturally sensitive and appropriate educational aids and stimuli".

As we have explored, the benefits of these multicultural experiences include broadening worldviews, fostering inclusivity, establishing a sense of belonging, challenging stereotypes and strengthening home-school connections, which are crucial for pupil success. We have also explored the challenges of multicultural experiences, especially in areas that are White communities, and ways around these barriers.

Beyond celebrations: Why an anti-racist curriculum is essential

An anti-racist curriculum with anti-racist practice firmly embedded goes beyond celebrating cultural diversity to actively address and challenge racism and systemic inequalities within the education system and society at large. It seeks to dismantle the structures and practices that perpetuate racial discrimination and inequality. The approach aims to create a more equitable and just educational environment by confronting the root causes of racial disparities.

The framework of anti-racist practices

The key components of anti-racist practices involve:

- Critical examination of the history and impact of racism, both historically and in contemporary society. This includes studying the systemic nature of racism and its effects on various communities.
- Pupils are encouraged to become advocates for social justice and equity, including teaching them about their rights and responsibilities and empowering them to act against injustice.

- The curriculum is designed to include diverse voices and perspectives, particularly those of marginalised communities, helping pupils understand the contributions and experiences of these communities.
- Teachers receive ongoing training on anti-racist practices and how to effectively implement an anti-racist curriculum, including addressing their biases and learning how to create an inclusive classroom environment.
- Ensuring anti-bias approaches in the recruitment and retention process, including advertising positions, shortlisting, interviewing, induction, support, and so on, in school positions. Also, succession planning and promotion opportunities for ethnic minority staff should be reviewed.

Troyna (1987) argues that anti-racist education developments "deliberately seek to make a connection between institutional discriminations and inequalities of race, class, and gender" and that "aims of Anti Racist education to realise the issues of race and racism cannot be abstracted from the broader political, historical, and social processes of society which have institutional unequal power". Anti-racist education priorities "collective action and conceives strategies for change". Thus, Troyna argues that an anti-racist approach must involve a critical examination of power relations and systemic discrimination within educational settings.

In mainstream settings, anti-racist work may include incorporating critical discussions about race, racism and social justice into the curriculum, teaching materials highlighting marginalised groups' contributions and struggles, or encouraging pupils to engage in activism and advocacy for racial equity.

The benefits of establishing an anti-racist curriculum include:

- An anti-racist curriculum helps pupils understand and challenge systemic inequalities, promoting a more just and equitable society.
- An anti-racist curriculum teaches pupils about their rights and responsibilities and empowers them to become advocates for social justice.
- An anti-racist curriculum encourages pupils to think critically about the world around them and question the status quo.
- An anti-racist curriculum with diverse voices and perspectives helps create a more inclusive educational setting.

Although pupils working around the "formal pathway" cognitive levels of functioning, either in SEND settings or mainstream, may be able to access this content, these higher-level concepts, requiring critical thinking and debate, may not be appropriate for most pupils in SEND settings. SEND schools and settings tend to focus on "Multicultural experiences" as these are easier to implement, and staff assume these experiences are more relevant.

Multicultural v anti-racist: A side-by-side comparison

	Multicultural experiences	Anti-racist curriculum
Goals and objectives	- Aims to celebrate and respect cultural diversity - Focus on cultural awareness and inclusion - Enhance pupils' understanding and appreciation of their own and different cultures	- Aim to dismantle systemic racism and promote social justice - Focus on critical awareness and active resistance to racism - Empower pupils to challenge and change discriminatory practices and ideologies
Teaching practices	- Promote cultural awareness and sensitivity - Enhance social harmony and mutual respect - Foster a sense of belonging among pupils from diverse backgrounds	- Develop critical thinking and awareness of systemic issues - Empower pupils to advocate for equity and justice - Create a proactive stance against racism and discrimination
Challenges and criticisms	- Critics argue that multicultural education can sometimes be superficial, focusing more on cultural festivals and foods rather than addressing deeper issues of inequality and discrimination - Troyna (1993) warns that without a critical component, multicultural education risks becoming a tokenistic gesture that fails to challenge systemic racism - Integrating multicultural content into the curriculum can be challenging due to existing curricular constraints and a lack of teacher training - Teachers may feel unprepared to manage the complexities of cultural diversity in their classrooms	- An anti-racist curriculum can face resistance from various stakeholders, who may be uncomfortable with its critical approach - Teachers may also struggle with the demands of implementing an anti-racist curriculum, particularly in environments resistant to change - Addressing systemic racism requires a deep understanding of social, historical and political contexts, which can be challenging for teachers to convey effectively - Developing and maintaining an anti-racist curriculum demands ongoing commitment and professional development

A new approach for SEND school: Combining multicultural and anti-racist practices

When leading anti-racist work in SEND settings, it is imperative to consider both frameworks to meet the needs of all pupils, their families and staff. Specialist provisions tend to effectively cover a broad range of festivals and celebrations, using multi-sensory teaching and learning opportunities. We have explored that these are usually rehashed, passing around the "Diwali" box, consisting of clay divas and old sarees, a type of approach that has not changed much in the past 10-20 years.

Reviewing the multicultural teaching and learning opportunities to aim to celebrate the cultural diversity of the pupil community is essential, and doing so through immersive, multi-sensory, collaborative and progressive strategies is essential. There is still a place for using music, textures, scents and tastes from different cultures to provide immersive learning experiences. A proportion of pupils may also be able to comprehend anti-racist concepts if broken down and simplified into more accessible ideas that pupils with more complex disabilities can understand. These might include social stories, role plays and stories with repetitive rhymes and props, focusing on kindness, respect, fairness and acceptance.

In considering the "anti-racist" framework for SEND schools, pupils accessing the formal learning pathway could access the content. It is not unrealistic to work with the pupils in this pathway to "develop critical thinking and awareness of systemic racism and promote social justice" or learn to "take a proactive stance against racism and discrimination". We would, however, use the multicultural experiences for pupils who cannot access this content.

The role of professional development in empowering staff to demonstrate anti-racist practices

Leaders should focus on staff development of anti-racist practices, including prioritising their understanding of systemic racism and how this affects their ethnic minority community of pupils and their families. As part of establishing an anti-racist curriculum, staff should be aware of the cultural barriers some communities can face, which can lead to not only prolonged denial of their child's diagnosis and long-term need but also increased isolation from communities. As discussed in earlier chapters, schools can form a lifeline for families by providing sources of support, knowledge, information sharing and troubleshooting through collaborative discussions. By understanding these dynamics, leaders can better respond to and support the ethnic minority community, thus identifying systemic biases and implementing strategies to eliminate barriers. This creates meaningful anti-racist work in SEND schools, which is not tokenistic but essential and progressive, leading to sustained changes over time.

Additionally, staff who access ongoing professional development and training on anti-racial practices can further enhance their understanding of their biases and how they may appear in the classroom or wider school. Multicultural experiences and anti-racial curriculum are important in promoting diversity and inclusivity in education. However, they serve different purposes and address various aspects of systemic inequality.

Chapter summary

This chapter examines the distinction between multicultural experiences and anti-racist practices within SEND settings. While multicultural education promotes awareness and celebration of cultural diversity, anti-racist education actively addresses systemic racism and inequality. In special education, where pupils' needs vary widely, leaders must find ways to integrate elements from both frameworks, ensuring that inclusive and immersive experiences celebrate diversity while also challenging systemic biases.

The chapter emphasises the importance of staff training in anti-racist practices, acknowledging barriers faced by ethnic minority families, and the need for SEND settings to provide tailored approaches that reflect both cultural celebration and meaningful anti-racism efforts.

TIFFIN TAKE-AWAY

1. **Recognise the limits of multiculturalism in addressing inequality**
   Multicultural celebrations provide important cultural awareness, but they often fall short of addressing the deeper issues of systemic racism that impact ethnic minority families and pupils in SEND settings. Anti-racist practices go beyond recognising diversity by critically examining and dismantling discriminatory structures.

   - How can your school ensure its multicultural activities extend beyond celebrations and begin to address the systemic barriers faced by ethnic minority families?

2. **Adapt anti-racist concept to SEND teaching**
   While traditional anti-racist concepts, teaching and reflections may not fully apply to pupils with more severe learning disabilities, aspects of anti-racist education, such as promoting fairness, respect and inclusion, can be simple and integrated into lessons through storytelling, sensory activities, and social stories.

   - An important aspect of your curriculum planning will be considering how anti-racist principles can be made more accessible to pupils with complex needs, fostering a sense of belonging and communicating a culture of kindness, tolerance and equity.

3. **Embed anti-racist practices through reflective teaching**
   Anti-racist work in SEND schools requires staff to reflect on their teaching practices, recognising how biases may unintentionally influence their interactions with pupils and families. Building an ongoing culture of reflection and dialogue around anti-racism is essential to change.

   - You might consider how reflective teaching practices help you and your staff teams identify unconscious biases and how you might address these to ensure more equitable outcomes for all pupils.

References

Troyna, B. (1987) *Beyond multiculturalism: Towards the enactment of anti-racist education in policy, provision and pedagogy.* Oxford review of Education. Routledge.

Troyna, B. (1993) *The educational needs of a multicultural society.* Centre for Research in Ethnic Relations. University of Warwick. https://warwick.ac.uk/fac/soc/crer/research/publications/occasional/occasionalp_no.9.pdf

10
How to review recruitment and retention and ensure representation within the staff community

> *"... so, what, we should only recruit ethnic minority people?"*

The weight of bias: Leadership and perception in education

> sorry you have not been successful on this occasion. You were most definitely the most qualified and experienced candidate. Exceptional... it is just that you did not smile enough, so we could not figure you out... you might be risky... smile more next time

This was interview feedback from a leadership position I had applied for.

Bemusement. Apathy. Disbelief.

I felt these all for a few days while I retreated to lick my wounds. Growing up in West London and spending most of my 20s in Central London, I had perfected my "street-smart" face, which is known more commonly as a "resting b**ch face". It keeps you safe in London.

Ethnic minority women are often judged more harshly on their appearance, and this can include a range of biases which negatively impact their chances of being considered for leadership roles. Mirza (2008) found that the leadership capability of ethnic minority women is frequently called into question over subtleties in her professional demeanour. Perhaps racial bias, or maybe gender bias; either way, ethnic minority women are often judged as not fitting the "traditional" image of a headteacher.

Representation matters: The power of ethnic minority leaders

Representing ethnic minority individuals in leadership roles within the educational sector is crucial for fostering an inclusive and equitable learning environment. However, as we have explored, teachers and leaders from minority backgrounds often face significant career challenges, from securing teaching positions to advancing into leadership roles.

We have already explored the statistics illustrating the underrepresentation of ethnic minority headteachers and teachers in the UK. This disparity highlights a cultural and

DOI: 10.4324/9781003416081-14

experiential disconnect that can hinder the effectiveness of educational delivery and the ability to address the nuanced needs of a diverse pupil body.

Challenges on the path to leadership: Ethnic minority educators in crisis

The ascent of ethnic minority leaders within the UK educational system is marred by significant, multifaceted challenges that stem from systemic inequities and deeply ingrained biases that hinder their progression into leadership roles. Miller (2019) observes that ethnic minority teachers are disproportionately selected for leadership positions in schools facing academic, behavioural and overall community instability. There are usually vast challenges, where they encounter high stress with limited resources. This placement trend suggests a systematic issue where minority leaders are often set up for challenges and failure rather than success.

Furthermore, Henshaw (2022) reports that these roles come with significantly less support than their counterparts, exacerbating feelings of isolation and limiting professional development opportunities. These conditions deter career progression and increase staff turnover among ethnic minority staff.

According to Demie (2022), pupils perform better and are more engaged when they see themselves reflected in their teachers and leaders. Therefore, having ethnic minority educators in teaching and leadership positions ensures that the school environment reflects the diversity of the pupil population. This representation is vital for fostering a sense of belonging and validation among pupils from minority backgrounds. This can inspire pupils to pursue their ambitions and believe in their potential.

Ethnic minority teachers and leaders serve as role models for all pupils, demonstrating that success is achievable regardless of racial or ethnic background. Demie (2022) also highlight the positive impact of diverse role models on pupil aspirations and self-esteem. Therefore, this can inspire pupils to pursue their ambitions and believe in their potential. Additionally, as we have seen, ethnic minority educators bring valuable cultural competence by providing representation that reflects the community's diversity, helping pupils feel understood and valued. This representation is significant in diverse communities where pupils come from various cultural backgrounds.

Studies have shown that the presence of ethnic minority teachers can help reduce achievement gaps between minority and non-minority pupils. They are often more attuned to the challenges faced by minority pupils and can provide the support needed to overcome these barriers. A diverse teaching staff can create a more positive and inclusive school climate. When pupils feel understood and supported by their teachers, they are likelier to engage in their learning and school activities. Ethnic minority educators bring valuable cultural insights that can inform school policies and practices, and they understand the community's cultural norms, values and challenges that can help create a more inclusive and supportive school environment.

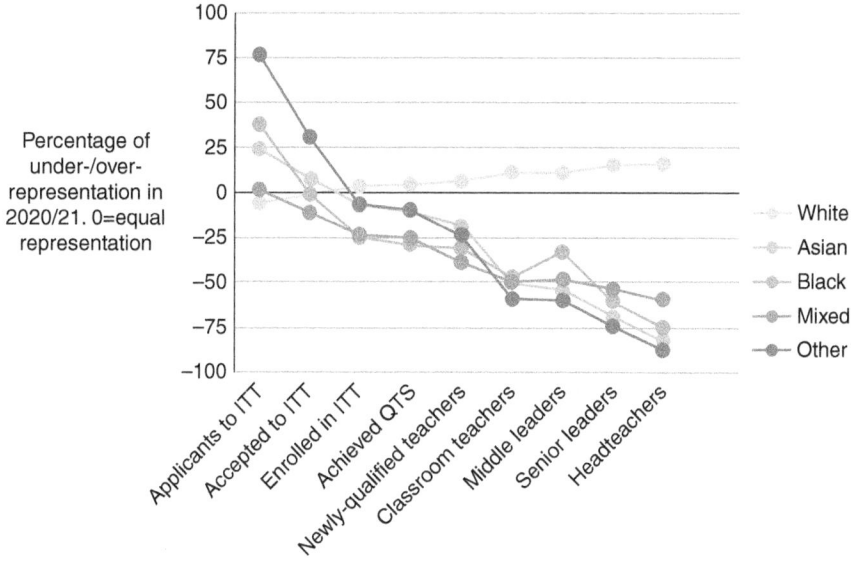

Figure 10.1 Career progression of teachers, per ethnicity
Source: Adapted from Worth, McLean and Sharp (2022).

Systemic barriers and Institutional racism: Ethnic minority leaders face a steeper climb

The Worth, McLean and Sharp (2022) research reveals that questions arise from the data around acceptance and entry-level to Initial Teacher Training (ITT) within the Black, Asian, Mixed and other backgrounds compared with the White groups. Therefore, we continue to see implicit biases within shortlisting, recruitment and interview processes. There are also barriers present in achieving QTS, therefore through the ITT training, which needs to be addressed. Even those who do go on to achieve their QTS, their downward and negative trajectory of career progression in all ethnic groups, except for White, which is a positive, upward trajectory, is of significant concern.

> Talent is everywhere. Opportunity is not.
> *(10,000 interns' foundation, 2024)*

Cultural disconnect: Navigating a White-dominated profession

Research suggests a series of explanations as to why the data is demonstrating these current patterns:

1. Institutional racism and structural barriers
   Ethnic minority educators frequently face overt discrimination and subtle biases that impede their professional advancement. Many face microaggressions, stereotyping

and discrimination that hinder their professional growth. These barriers are not merely anecdotal but are supported by extensive research, including how racial prejudices permeate hiring practices and promotional opportunities. The Runnymede Trust reports corroborate these findings, emphasising that racial discrimination within the school system profoundly affects career trajectories for ethnic minority individuals.

2. Isolation and lack of representation

    Ethnic minority teachers often feel isolated in predominantly White schools, where they may be the only person of colour on the staff team, which can lead to a lack of peer support and understanding of the unique challenges they face. These feelings can be further exacerbated if they are asked to lead on diversity work, as it can continue to highlight differences and the ethnic minority person being "the other".

3. Cultural disconnect

    There is often a cultural disconnect between teachers from ethnic minority backgrounds and their White colleagues who may not fully understand the multilayered challenges faced by diverse communities, including differences in lived experiences, cultural backgrounds or failure to see systemic racial issues in the environment. There could be misunderstandings of cultural norms and communication styles and undervaluing of diverse experiences, and ethnic minority teachers may also advocate for more culturally responsive teaching methods than their White colleagues. As it is not their lived experience, it may not be a priority for them. Anti-racist training embedded into teacher training course content is essential to develop understanding and allyship and create and sustain lifelong anti-racist pedagogy. Leeds Beckett University established an anti-racist framework for Initial Teacher Trainers.

4. Limited career advancement opportunities

    Ethnic minority teachers face significant challenges in advancing their careers within the education sector, particularly when applying to leadership roles. The barriers are multifaceted and rooted in systemic inequality. Ethnic minority teachers have limited access to professional networks and mentorship opportunities that can support their career advancement. These networks are crucial for gaining visibility, accessing resources and receiving career guidance. These teachers often find it challenging to advance to leadership roles due to limited opportunities and systemic barriers within the education sector. These barriers include a lack of professional development opportunities and networks that support career progression. They also tend to lack role models and mentors who understand their unique challenges and experiences. The scarcity of ethnic minority staff in leadership positions exacerbates this issue, limiting the pool of potential mentors who can relate to their specific circumstances.

Ethnic minority teachers may also find it challenging to gain visibility for their achievements and contributions. Franklin (1999) coined this as "invisibility syndrome", in that minority staff experience a lack of recognition. They tend to be overlooked and undervalued in White settings. Thus, they are not considered for promotion or further development or identified as "emerging talent" or "high performers" to nurture and further invest in.

Barriers to advancement: Limited career growth for ethnic minority educators

Miller (2019) identifies five factors that influence the career progression of ethnic minority leaders, including (a) unfair policy treatment, (b) racism, (c) institutional practices, (d) group membership or affiliation and (e) religion.

Miller also found that when ethnic minority teachers and leaders are promoted, they tend to have to "prove themselves", usually by taking on positions in challenging, high-risk environments where the chances of failure are significantly higher. Progression can also rely on "White sanction", in that a White person will need to endorse, act on behalf of or in the interest of, and act as a gatekeeper for the ethnic minority, almost as "vouching" for their abilities. Ryan and Haslam (2007) explore this phenomenon extensively, suggesting that such placements may be subtly influenced by racial biases that associate ethnic minority leaders with "crisis management capabilities" rather than leadership in more stable conditions.

Ethnic minority leaders are disproportionately more likely to receive leadership opportunities in schools that face significant challenges or are in crisis rather than higher-performing schools in more affluent areas. This is known as "the glass cliff phenomenon", which suggests that it is typically ethnic minority females who are promoted into leadership roles during times of crisis or unstable situations where the likelihood of failure is higher. They are expected to turn around failing settings, with often limited support or resources. This is typical across all industries, including education.

The dual burden: Leading and advocating for change

1. Expectations for racial advocacy
   Ethnic minority leaders in education also often find themselves in the challenging position of maintaining their professional responsibilities while leading anti-racist initiatives. This expectation to champion diversity efforts can compound the stress associated with their roles, as noted by researchers such as DiAngelo (2018), who discusses the additional "emotional labour" required from individuals who navigate these dual responsibilities. This dual role can detract from their primary responsibility and impact their wellbeing and professional efficacy.
2. Lack of support structures
   The support systems available to leaders from minority backgrounds are frequently inadequate, which can exacerbate feelings of isolation and burnout. The Institute of Race Relations highlights the need for robust support mechanisms, pointing out that supportive peer networks and mentorship programs tailored explicitly for ethnic minority staff are scarce yet critical for sustaining leadership.

Ethnic minority leaders can feel isolated, lack mentorship and understanding from colleagues or experience a failure to have their own needs met.

Solutions for equity: Overcoming the barriers for ethnic minority educators

1. Equitable practices and policies
   Settings must adopt and enforce equitable practices which progress beyond tokenistic and paying lip service. This also forms "anti-racist" practice, including reviewing and addressing biases in advertising positions, shortlisting, interviewing, induction, probation and appraisal processes.
2. Mentorship, support networks and career pathways
   Many ethnic minority teachers report a lack of mentorship and support during the early stages of their careers. This absence of guidance can make it difficult to navigate the complexities of the education system and advance professionally. Establishing dedicated mentorship programs and support networks for educators from minority backgrounds can mitigate the challenges they face. The benefits of such programs, which foster community support and provide role models, are well documented in educational research.
3. Distributed leadership models
   Encouraging a distributed leadership model that allocates responsibilities equitably among all staff can help alleviate the undue pressure on ethnic minority leaders. Such models promote shared leadership and ensure the drive for diversity and inclusivity is a collective effort.

The underrepresentation of ethnic minority educators can lead to a lack of role models and mentors for both staff and pupils from minority backgrounds, which is crucial for fostering a supportive and inclusive educational environment.

The predominance of White educators can lead to a cultural misalignment where ethnic minority educators may feel that their cultural perspectives and teaching styles are undervalued or misunderstood.

Strategies for enhancing ethnic minority recruitment, retention and representation

1. Mandatory bias training
   Implementing essential bias training for all recruitment panel members is crucial to ensuring fair and equitable hiring practices in education. The training should cover conscious and unconscious biases and provide practical strategies for mitigating their impact throughout recruitment and retention.
2. Diverse hiring panels
   Hiring panels should be diverse and include ethnic minority representation. These panels can provide different perspectives and help identify the best candidates based on merit rather than bias. Ethnic minority staff should be included in the panels, ensuring representation wherever possible.

3. Blind applications

   > Do you know that in our country today, even if they have exactly the same qualifications, people with white-sounding names are nearly twice as likely to get call-backs for jobs than people with ethnic-sounding names?
   >
   > *(David Cameron, 2015)*

   An insightful statement from David Cameron.
   Blind applications are designed to reduce bias and discrimination in hiring processes. By anonymising specific details, such as names and ethnicity, applicants are judged on their skills and experiences rather than demographic characteristics. This mitigates unconscious biases and increases equity for ethnic minority candidates.

4. Targeted recruitment initiatives
   Schools must actively seek to attract ethnic minority candidates through specialised recruitment drives that highlight growth opportunities and leadership pathways. Implementing targeted advertising campaigns and recruitment drives that specifically reach out to diverse communities should be adopted, offering clear, enticing career progression plans so schools can attract more ethnic minority candidates. These can be through job fairs, or partnering with networks, such as BAME education, the Network for Black and Asian Professionals, Women's Ed BAME leaders, Diverse Educators and Equaliteach. Further strategies could include attending cultural events, community gatherings and creating targeted marketing materials that showcase minority staff in leadership roles. Additionally, highlighting case studies of successful minorities in these roles, where there is clear support and mentorship to succeed and advance in their careers, is crucial.

5. Mentorship and support programs
   Establishing robust mentorship networks is essential for nurturing the careers of ethnic minority educators. Mentorship provides a supportive framework that helps new teachers navigate the educational landscape, offering advice and encouragement from experienced colleagues who understand the unique challenges educators face from minority backgrounds and providing guidance and support. These could include regular check-ins, goal setting and professional development opportunities.

6. Professional development opportunities
   Tailored professional development programs are crucial for preparing ethnic minority teachers for leadership roles. These programs should focus on leadership training, cultural competency and strategies to address race and equity issues within schools, equipping them with the skills needed for advancement.

7. Career progression pathways
   Develop and communicate clear career pathways for ethnic minority teachers to progress into leadership roles; these should include specific milestones, required qualifications, experiences and opportunities for professional development. Schools should ensure these pathways are equally accessible to staff from minority backgrounds and

include specific support mechanisms to help overcome any systemic barriers they may face. There could also be forms of sponsorship in which senior leaders advocate for the career progression of ethnic minority teachers, provide opportunities for visibility, recommend ethnic minority teachers for promotion and support their professional growth.

8. Inclusive school culture

    Cultivating an inclusive school culture involves more than celebrating diversity; it requires embedding inclusivity into every facet of school operations, from policymaking and curriculum design to staff meetings and pupil assessment, creating an environment where all staff members feel valued and supported. Developing and embedding policies that promote inclusivity and address discrimination within schools also promotes an inclusive school culture. These policies should include clear procedures for reporting and addressing incidents of racism and discrimination.

9. Monitoring and evaluation

    Regular monitoring and evaluation of recruitment, retention and promotion strategies are vital to identifying effective practices and areas for improvement. By continually addressing these strategies, schools can adapt their approaches to better support ethnic minority staff and promote a more equitable workplace.

10. Funding for further education

    Providing funding and scholarships for teachers from ethnic minority backgrounds to pursue further education and leadership training. The financial support can help remove barriers, increase opportunities, remove career advancement and ensure that ethnic minority educators have the qualifications needed for leadership roles.

Creating a diverse educational future

The importance of hiring teachers, leaders and headteachers from diverse backgrounds in schools cannot be overstated. Their presence ensures representation, cultural competence and advocacy for minority pupils, crucial for fostering an inclusive and equitable learning environment. However, ethnic minority educators face significant challenges in securing teaching positions and advancing to leadership roles, including bias in hiring practices, limited career advancement opportunities and discrimination.

To support ethnic minority teachers and leaders, the Department for Education (DfE) should implement mandatory bias training for hiring committees, develop mentorship and sponsorship programs, provide targeted professional development opportunities, establish clear career progression pathways to leadership, foster inclusive school cultures and collect and analyse diversity data. These measures can help create a more supportive and equitable environment for educators and ensure that schools benefit from the diverse perspectives and experiences they bring.

Addressing the underrepresentation of ethnic minority educators requires a comprehensive and strategic approach. Through focusing on their teachers' applications, support to sustain and complete their training, support with applications and recruitment and retention and professional development training for headteachers and governors, there can be growth and retention.

Implementing a strategic recruitment plan that targets initiatives, mentorship, professional development and an inclusive culture will support schools in significantly improving the diversity of their staff. Such efforts enrich the learning environment and empower pupils by providing them with role models with similar backgrounds and experiences. This enhances the educational environment and provides all pupils with role models who reflect the diversity of the society in which they live. Through a committed, strategic approach to enhancing diversity within their staff, schools can create an educational system that is truly inclusive, equitable and representative of the society it serves.

Chapter summary

This chapter delves into the systemic challenges faced by ethnic minority educators in their journey towards leadership within the UK education sector. It explores the intersection of race, leadership and institutional biases, highlighting the barriers that ethnic minority teachers face in securing leadership roles and the additional burdens placed upon them.

The chapter emphasises the need for anti-racist practices to counteract these systemic challenges. It offers strategies for schools to promote equitable leadership pathways, ensuring a more inclusive and diverse educational environment.

TIFFIN TAKE-AWAY

1. **Bias in recruitment and career progression**
    The underrepresentation of ethnic minority teachers in leadership roles is often the result of implicit biases in recruitment, promotion and hiring processes. Biases, both conscious and unconscious, can lead to capable ethnic minority candidates being overlooked for positions or being placed in high-risk roles where they are set up to fail. Addressing these biases is key to creating fairer and more equitable progression routes for ethnic minority educators.

    - You could think about what steps your school could take to address unconscious biases in recruitment and promotion, ensuring a more equitable process for all candidates.

2. **The dual burden of leadership and advocacy**
    Ethnic minority leaders often face the dual burden of fulfilling their leadership roles while being expected to spearhead diversity and inclusion initiatives. This additional responsibility can lead to emotional exhaustion and a sense of isolation, especially in White school settings.

    - How could you better support staff/leaders from minority backgrounds in their dual roles, ensuring that diversity work is shared across all staff rather than placed on a few individuals?

3. **Mentorship and professional development for ethnic minority educators**
    The lack of mentorship and professional development opportunities tailored for ethnic minority educators limits their career growth. Establishing strong mentorship programs and clear leadership pathways is essential for nurturing talent and supporting ethnic minority staff to excel in their leadership roles.

    - You might consider how your school can implement mentorship programs that actively support the career development of ethnic minority educators, ensuring they have access to the resources and guidance needed to advance.

References

DiAngelo, R. (2018) *White fragility: Why it's so hard for White people to talk about racism*. Beacon Press.

Demie, F. (2022) "Ethnic disproportionality in the school teaching workforce in England". *Institute for Educational and Social Equality*, 2(1).

Franklin, A. (1999) "Invisibility syndrome and racial identity development in psychotherapy and counselling African American men". *The Counselling Psychologist*, 27(6).

Henshaw, P. (2022) "Uncomfortable and disturbing: Report reveals substantial disparities in career progression for Ethnic minority teachers". Headteacher Update.www.sec-ed.co.uk/content/news/uncomfortable-and-disturbing-report-reveals-substantial-disparities-in-career-progression-for-ethnic-minority-teachers/

Miller, P. (2019). "Tackling race inequality in school leadership: Positive actions in BAME teacher progression – Evidence from three English schools", *Educational Management Administration and Leadership*, 48(5).

Mirza, H. (2008) *Race, gender and educational desire: why Black women succeed and fail*. Routledge.

Ryan, M. and Haslam, S. (2007) "The glass cliff: Exploring the dynamics surrounding the appointment of women to precarious leadership positions". *Academy of Management Review*, 32(2): 549–572.

11
How to review and improve the representation of all nine protected characteristics within policies and practice in SEND settings

> *"... what about the other protected characteristics?*
>
> *Aren't they all as important?"*

The Equality Act's nine protected characteristics

It is crucial to incorporate the nine protected characteristics defined under the Equality Act 2010, age, disability, gender reassignment, marriage and civil partnership, pregnancy and maternity, race, religion or belief, sex and sexual orientation, into the educational frameworks of special schools.

Embedding these characteristics into the curriculum and school policies is particularly important in special schools, where students with disabilities often face additional challenges and discrimination. These characteristics intersect uniquely for pupils with SEND from ethnic minority backgrounds, compounding their challenges.

Teaching about protected characteristics equips pupils with SEND with crucial life skills, enhancing their ability to navigate a diverse society. Roger Slee (2008) notes, "Inclusion isn't about making special arrangements; it's about the art of living together". Understanding these characteristics helps build empathy, respect and a deepened sense of community, preparing pupils for the broader societal interactions they encounter.

Embedding the nine protected characteristics into the curriculum

1. Disability awareness and inclusion

> *Focusing on disability is fundamental.*
>
> Tom Shakespeare (2013)

Disability awareness in schools is essential to fostering inclusivity and challenging stereotypes from an early age. Price (2018) found that early exposure to disability awareness can significantly reduce negative attitudes and misconceptions about disabilities. By integrating disability studies into the curriculum, schools can help pupils understand the diversity within disabilities and promote a more inclusive society.

Inclusive teaching materials play a vital role in this process. Materials representing people with disabilities in positive and diverse roles are crucial for challenging stereotypes and promoting a positive self-image among pupils with disabilities. Young (2020) found that children's literature featuring characters with disabilities in empowering roles can positively influence disabled and non-disabled children's perceptions of disability.

Awareness programs that teach pupils about different types of disability are also effective, as guest speakers, workshops and interactive activities can be delivered. Lindsay and Edwards (2013) found that when interactive interventions are used with groups of children, the attitudes towards disabilities among school-age children significantly improve. Therefore, disability awareness interventions can successfully improve children's knowledge about and attitudes towards peers with a disability.

Adaptive activities for school activities, including physical education, can also improve social interactions and physical skills for all children when playing together, both those with and without disabilities. Additionally, those teachers who accessed some teacher training on SEND also tended to be better equipped to meet various needs and demonstrated a more positive attitude towards supporting pupils with disabilities in their classrooms.

2. Sex, gender identity and sexual orientation

Addressing gender identity and sexual orientation in special schools requires a sensitive and inclusive approach that respects the diverse needs and abilities of all pupils.

> Involvement of families in the educational journey is not just beneficial: it is essential for creating tailored and responsive educational strategies that accommodate the diverse needs of SEN students.
>
> Hatton (2004)

Collaboration with families on this topic is crucial to ensure that the education, content, and approach are appropriate and respectful of individual family values and appropriate to the needs of the pupils while remaining committed to inclusivity.

Inclusive language, policies, developing understanding, training for staff and ongoing meetings with parents are critical approaches to ensure alignment and communication between home and school and across the school. Teaching pupils about gender diversity and the experiences of transgender and non-binary individuals should be both age-appropriate and dependent on the "pathway" the pupil is accessing. Pupils accessing the Formal pathway can access and process this learning. For example, challenging gender stereotypes through discussions, role-playing and storytelling is an excellent approach to the topic. Introducing stereotypical "gender-specific" toys, such as dolls and cars, and using these as a way-in for conversations around pupils can encourage them to explore interests and activities regardless of gender norms.

Addressing gender and orientation must be done with sensitivity. Inclusive education on this topic entails exploring what it means, accepting multiple forms of expression and exploring a range of family structures and identities.

3. Race

We have explored this quite thoroughly...!

4. Religion and belief systems

Similarly, regarding race and ethnicity, understanding different religions and beliefs in SEND settings can be planned, implemented and delivered through the three curriculum pathways: Formal, Semi-formal and Pre-formal.

All pupils could benefit from multicultural experiences and sensory, social stories with props, similar to the "Coming to England" story but focused on various religious stories. All pupils would benefit from trips and visits to local places of worship, with scaffolding teaching and learning opportunities. In doing this within cultures where there is less understanding, support or tolerance of SEND, it is an excellent opportunity for the SEND setting to demonstrate not just solidarity and support but to provide some information and education on how to best support families and parents of children with SEND, so that they are less isolated.

Visiting places of worship as curriculum enrichment activities are also useful, as they can be multi-sensory experiences with sounds of prayers, smells and tastes; for example, visiting a Mandir as part of learning about Hinduism can be quite a sensory experience for pupils.

For pupils accessing a more "Formal pathway", whether within the SEND setting or within mainstream schools, pupils can access further information about religions, beliefs and stories and understand the messages and morals of the stories. They may be able to discuss their unique perspectives on some of the content and ask questions, as well as learn about similarities and differences between religions.

Schools can network with religious leaders to attend specific coffee mornings for specific groups of parents and those interested so they can discuss their specific challenges and receive advice as they wish. It also provides the school with the platform to share information and develop an understanding of the religious leaders so that they are better positioned and equipped with the knowledge to support their communities who can remain isolated and unable to attend their places of worship.

5. Age

SEND settings should develop an understanding of different life stages by celebrating birthdays and milestones and creating opportunities to organise intergenerational activities such as "siblings' day" or "grandparents' day". Understanding different life stages is a crucial component of the curriculum. Incorporating lessons that support pupils in understanding these different life stages and the changes that occur as people age can be conducted through contextual experiences and appropriate resources.

For example, Formal and Semi-formal pathway pupils could visit older people's homes to build relationships, showcase their work, play games or perform songs/dances. They could also practice their writing skills and send letters and postcards to these homes, sharing content on what they have been doing in school. They could also be invited into school to celebrate key festivals and celebrations, such as D-Day, Remembrance, Diwali, Christmas, and so on. This would give pupils opportunities to hear and learn from older people and hear the stories from their lives.

In the Formal pathway, children and young people could practice their enterprise and self-help skills through activities such as "organising a tea party", working out the required ingredients, multiplying by how many people are attending, walking to the local shops to purchase the ingredients and asking for help if they are stuck or cannot find something. They can then learn to pay for the items and see if they have enough.

Pupils can learn about birth through experiences such as incubators for chick or duck eggs, watching them hatch and grow over a period, thus experiencing the early stages of the life cycle.

6. Marriage and civil partnerships

The concept can be introduced according to relevance and accessibility per pathway. Stories and examples that reflect the diversity of families in society can be helpful in initially introducing these concepts to pupils.

Role plays, drama, social stories and comic strip conversations can help pupils understand the diversity of families. Pupils accessing the Formal pathway can access conversations about types of relationships and the importance of commitment, love and mutual respect in marriages and civil partnerships. This also allows Formal pathway pupils to ask and answer questions, which can lead to more debate, discussion and sharing of their opinions and views. It also provides opportunities to discuss equality, equity, acceptance and tolerance.

7. Pregnancy and maternity

Implementing this topic to SEND pupils will again depend on the pathway that the pupils are in. Pupils in the Pre-formal and Semi-formal pathways may experience looking after a baby (doll), holding it, and stroking it with care, learning that the baby is fragile and that they must use a calm and soft touch. Lessons could be multi-sensory (I have known one teacher to bring in her baby granddaughter for this type of lesson!). This could include listening to a baby cry, as some children could be sensitive to this sound of noise sensitivities.

Pupils accessing the Formal curriculum may access lessons on human reproduction, pregnancy and childbirth, depending on their age and stage (whether the content is appropriate to their cognitive level of development). Interactive models, videos and discussions could be used to teach about pregnancy's biological and emotional aspects.

Schools could organise activities to celebrate parents, such as hosting "Mother's Day breakfast" or "Father's Day breakfast."

Embedding the nine characteristics in school policies: Moving beyond tokenism

Embedding the nine protected characteristics into school policies and practices is the most effective way to ensure the practice is not stand-alone or in response to a one-off movement towards inclusion. A strategic long-term action plan can be created as part of school statutory equality policies, and this is the most effective way to keep inclusion, diversity and equity at the forefront of all school practice.

Creating and embedding comprehensive anti-discrimination policies, with medium- to long-term plans, that explicitly protect all nine protected characteristics is vital, as well as ensuring these policies are communicated to all staff, pupils and parents. Establishing policies that mandate the inclusion of diverse perspectives and experiences in the curriculum ensures that teaching materials and resources reflect the diversity of the pupil population and support their sense of belonging. Implementing policies that provide equal opportunities for all pupils in curriculum access, assessment and accreditations should also ensure robust tracking and monitoring to identify the success and limitations of initiatives, identify any further potential gaps and action plans to close any identified gaps further.

Creating an Inclusive school culture: Training, language and participation

To embed policies, a supportive school environment with a progressive attitude is key. Providing ongoing training and professional development for staff on issues related to diversity, inclusion and the nine protected characteristics should include inclusive teaching and learning opportunities, attitudes and mindsets, which create inclusive classrooms, thus ensuring pupils are fully supported and inclusion is actively embedded and promoted in everyday school. The curriculum should be reflective of this commitment to advocating for the nine protected characteristics.

Using inclusive language in the school develops inclusive practice. Doing this, alongside celebrating diverse cultural traditions and accommodating individual needs, promotes a culture of respect and acceptance. Involving pupil and parent participation in discussions about diversity and inclusion and providing opportunities to provide input on school policies and practices is good practice.

Chapter summary

This chapter explores the importance of incorporating the nine protected characteristics outlined in the Equality Act 2010 within special schools. These characteristics – age, disability, gender reassignment, marriage and civil partnership, pregnancy and maternity, race, religion or belief, sex and sexual orientation – must be integrated into school policies and curriculum to create an inclusive environment. The chapter provides practical strategies to embed these values and foster empathy, respect and community across different pathways.

TIFFIN TAKE-AWAY

1. **Holistic integration of the nine protected characteristics into the curriculum**
   Schools must embed the nine protected characteristics into their daily teaching and learning practices. This includes incorporating diverse stories, role models and activities that reflect age, disability, race, gender, religion and more. Through inclusive materials and experiential learning, pupils can better understand diversity, empathy and social responsibility. This approach enriches the educational experience and prepares pupils for life in a diverse society.

   - How can your school ensure that the nine protected characteristics are consistently reflected in both the curriculum and school activities?

2. **Collaborative engagement with families and the community**
   Involving parents, carers and community members in the process of embedding these characteristics strengthens the connection between home and school. Engaging families in discussions around inclusion ensures that schools respect diverse cultural values while promoting equity and acceptance. Regular feedback from families can help schools better tailor their approaches to suit the needs of their specific communities.

   - How can your school better collaborate with families to ensure inclusive practices reflect the community's diverse needs?

3. **Create a supportive and inclusive school culture**
   Fostering an inclusive school environment involves more than just policy; it requires a collective commitment from all staff members to model and promote values of equality and respect. Ongoing staff training, inclusive language and the active celebration of diversity through events, assemblies and activities ensure the school's ethos is inclusive and welcoming. Establishing a supportive culture also means actively addressing any forms of discrimination that arise within the school community.

   - You could consider the steps your school can take to create an inclusive culture that acknowledges the nine protected characteristics and challenges discriminatory practices.

References

Lindsay, S. and Edwards, A. (2013) "A systematic review of disability awareness interventions for children and youth". *Disability Rehabilitation*, 35(8): 623-646.
Price, R. (2018) *Inclusive and special education approaches in developing countries*. Institute of Development Studies: Knowledge, evidence and learning for development.
Slee, R. (2008) "Beyond special and regular schooling? An inclusive education reform agenda". *International Studies in Sociology of Education*, 18(2): 99-116.
Young, R. (2020) *Representations of disability in literature and elementary education*. University of Mary Washington: Eagle Scholar.

12

How can young ethnic minority people with SEND be prepared for an intersectional life in modern Britain post-schooling?

"... yeah, but SEN schools are like a nest.

What happens when they leave?"

where's the car gone? Did you park it up the road? Why is there glass everywhere??!

The car, it turned out, had been stolen, and then urinated and defecated on inside. Car seats and seatbelts were ripped out. "Pakis go home!" had been spray painted in black across the bonnet of my dad's car.

I was 11 or 12 years old.

We had to find a different way to get to school that morning.

The condition of the car was so awful that the police told my parents it would be very upsetting to see it. Later, it was more upsetting to find out that my primary school friend, who lived up the road, did it and got away with it. This happened in a London borough in the early 1990s.

Ten years later, when our parents moved us to a leafy Berkshire village, my sister and I decided to go for a lunchtime walk in the snow. Chatting and laughing, we walked past a pub on the corner of the high street. A young man in his early twenties was standing outside smoking a cigarette. On any other day, we would not have even noticed him. As we walked past, he sneered, hocking back his phlegm and shot it towards us. I froze and looked back. Fight/flight mode firmly activated, to see a menacing look, as if to say, "Come on then".

He did not say anything.

I did not say anything.

But what was implied spoke volumes.

DOI: 10.4324/9781003416081-16

We did not belong.

And I am not 100% convinced that feeling has ever gone away.

Educational inequality: How bias limits ethnic minority pupils' potential

As they leave school, many ethnic minority pupils with SEND will experience a range of challenges rooted in systemic biases that will impact their transitions throughout their lives from education to employment or further education, health and housing.

As school leavers, ethnic minority young people have less access to professional networks and resources which could facilitate career development opportunities, including mentorship, work experience placements and internships. Many come from lower socio-economic backgrounds, which can limit their access to higher education and job opportunities, or whose families experience financial constraints that may force them to accept immediate employment.

Additional challenges may include affected mental health and wellbeing due to experiences of discrimination, racism, lack of opportunities and the impact of intuitional barriers. These biases include discrimination in the job market, recruitment or promotion biases and attainment gaps; for example, DfE data continues to show that Black Caribbean boys continue to perform less well academically behind other groups.

In a 2019 news report in The Guardian, Siddique identified that

> Black Britons and those of South Asian origin face shocking discrimination in the labour market at levels unchanged since the late 1960s... applicants from minority ethnic backgrounds had to send 60% more applications to get a positive response from an employer than a White person of British origin.

The Race Disparity Audit (2017) identifies that ethnic minority families, specifically Pakistani, Bangladeshi and Black groups, are more likely to live in poverty and live in areas of deprivation. These outline the possible experiences of the average ethnic minority school leaver, which may have a lasting effect on their career trajectories and socio-economic status.

Ethnic minority pupils with SEND will encounter unique and compounded challenges. Their intersection of race and SEND exposes them to multiple layers of societal and systematic barriers. They navigate a complex social landscape marked by discrimination and misunderstanding, affecting their intersection across various sectors, including law enforcement, healthcare and employment. For instance, young Black men with SEND are especially vulnerable to negative stereotypes, which can result in disproportionately adverse encounters with the police. Chouinard and Davis (2016) discuss how these individuals are frequently misinterpreted or mishandled by authorities due to racial and disability stereotypes, highlighting the need for better awareness and training within law enforcement.

The criminal justice system: SEND and racial profiling

"Is that your car, sir?"
Yes. My dad answered.
"Where are you going, and where have you come from?"
I took the kids to McDonald's. They are in the back of the car, and we are going home.
"Did you buy this car?"
Yes!
We waited for what felt like an hour.
Then, when the police decided, we were allowed to go home.

This was my experience of my dad being stopped during one of the first times he had taken his new car out for a drive. I was around nine years old.

White people are the least likely racial group to experience crime, as the risk of being a victim of crime is the highest for the ethnic minority community. Confidence in the police to provide support when needed is lowest in the Black community. Those from minority backgrounds are more than 1.5 times more likely to be stopped and searched" than White groups, with those from the Black community being over three times as likely to be arrested and six times as likely to be stopped and searched than White groups.

Data from "Statistics on Ethnicity and the Criminal Justice System" (2022) shows that more than half of young people cautioned or sentenced for an offence had been recorded as having SEND support or Education, Health and Care Plan (EHCP). More young people were from Black ethnic groups than from other groups. Additionally, data shows that of those cautioned or sentenced for an offence, a large proportion of the Black ethnic group had received suspensions or permanent exclusions from school.

Health disparities: The overlooked intersection of race, disability and healthcare

In terms of health, Black African and Caribbean were most likely to be overweight at 10/11 years of age, and Black Africans were also the most overweight ethnicity at 4/5 years of age. Black men were also most likely to use illegal drugs and show increased drug dependency over time. Black women are more likely to experience depression and anxiety; Black men are more than ten times more likely to suffer a psychotic disorder compared with White men.

In 2014, 4,800 in 100,000 British Black Caribbean adults were in contact with NHS mental health and learning disability services, compared with 3,600 in 100,000 adults overall.

Black Caribbean adults were most likely to be detained under the Mental Health Act. Additionally, for those referred to psychological therapies, White groups were the most likely to see a recovery, and Bangladeshi and Pakistani were least likely to see a recovery.

Race and educational attainment: Why do some ethnic minority groups struggle more than others?

Data shows that, over time, there has been a marked improvement in attainment in some ethnic minority groups. Some ethnic groups are performing better in school than in previous years. There are noticeable "intra-group differences" within ethnic groups; for example, Chinese and Indian pupils are the highest-achieving groups at GCSE, followed by Bangladeshi, Black African and White British.

In reviewing this data, Demie (2022) suggests that the improvement could be due to "new generations of minority families embedding themselves into British culture and appreciating the varied opportunities that are available in British education". Based on this assumption and data, all ethnic minority groups should demonstrate similar rates of progression and increased levels of attainment. However, this is not the case. Black Caribbean and Pakistani pupils remain the lowest achieving groups. GCSE results from 2023 show that pupils' attainment, both in receipt of Free School Meals and without, was the lowest in the Gypsy Roma, Irish Traveller, mixed White and Black Caribbean groups.

Additionally, average attainment 8 scores by ethnicity and SEND demonstrate that Black Caribbean pupils with an EHCP and on SEND support are also the lowest-attaining group of pupils.

Similar results are identified in the 2022/23 Early Years Foundation Stage Profile results, with Irish Traveller, Gypsy/Roma and Black Caribbean, and Pakistan groups being the lowest achieving groups from the ethnic minority groups. **Therefore, the underachievement of Black Caribbean pupils is observed throughout their entire educational experience, from their first days in their schooling through to GCSEs. They are also statistically more likely to experience a post-education life of crime and mental health difficulties. We must question why.**

Low educational attainment and progress are strongly associated with economic disadvantages. Black Caribbean pupils are more than three times more likely to be eligible for Free School Meals compared with Chinese pupils, one of the highest attainment groups. The underachievement of Black Caribbean pupils is not a new concept. Since Coard's work in 1971, there has been ongoing and repeated research indicating there are compounding factors causing low attainment and underachievement, including structural inequalities, systemic racism, unconscious and conscious bias, racial stereotyping, poverty and low expectations of Black Caribbean pupils.

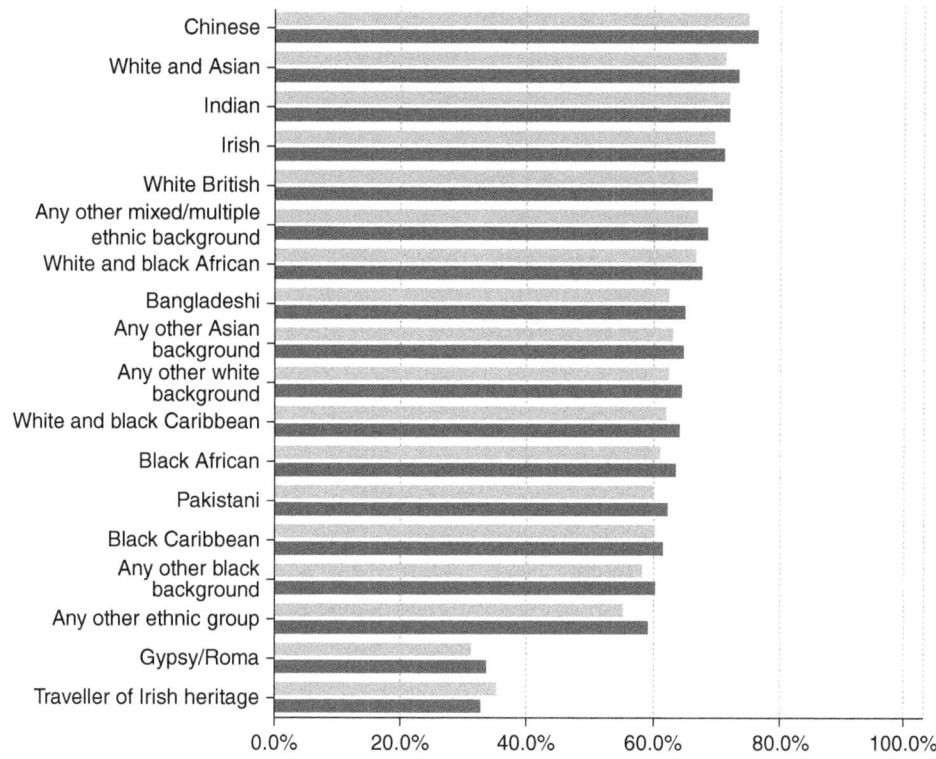

Figure 12.1 EYFS results per ethnic groups (2021/22 and 2022/23)

Source: Adapted from Department for Education (2023).

Research also indicates that as the teaching workforce is predominantly White, and due to racial stereotyping, Black Caribbean pupils receive less support, focus and attention and are placed in bottom sets because of teachers' low expectations. They are also likely to be disciplined more harshly for less serious behaviour and less likely to be praised by teachers compared to pupils from other ethnic groups. Research indicates that Black Caribbean pupils are also three times as likely to be permanently excluded from school compared with White British pupils and those of school-leaving age, mixed White and Black, and Black Caribbean are the least likely to stay in education, employment or training, compared with other ethnic groups.

Similar trends are observed in ethnic minority pupils with SEND, and the DfE data shows a similar pattern, in that average attainment 8 scores by ethnicity and SEND demonstrate that Black Caribbean pupils with an EHCP, as well as those with SEND support, are also the lowest-attaining group of pupils (Key Stage 4 performance: Ethnicity Facts and Figures, 2021-2022, DfE).

What the data does not account for or explain, however, is the "inter-group" differences in attainment, in that there are notable differences in attainment within the ethnic groups.

For example, in 2023, Black Caribbean average attainment 8 score was 41.7, compared with Black African at 50.9. Similar trends are observable in the Asian category, with the Indian average score at 61.3, compared with Pakistani at 49.1. Roberts and Bolton (2023), in educational outcomes of Black pupils and pupils identify that although progress 8 scores are reported as Black pupils making +0.22 progress when the group is sub-divided, "Black African pupils attained standard passes in both English and Maths GCSE at 69%... higher than the national average of 65%... Black Caribbean pupils had significantly lower pass rates at 52%. Black African pupils also made more progress, with an average progress 8 score of +0.37, while for Black Caribbean pupils, the average score was −0.24". Therefore, the same pattern of underachievement in Black Caribbean pupils is observed.

Progression to higher education for Black young people also shows a total of 71.2% for Black Africans but only 45.8% for Black Caribbean. Black Caribbean boys are also less likely to attend university at 34.4%, compared with Black Caribbean girls at 56.5%.

The effects of systemic racism, unconscious biases, and so on, could be questioned at this point as how can these apply to only specific subgroups within ethnicity groups when we see some subgroups performing well, demonstrating increased progress over time?

Demie (2022) argues that the difference in Black African and Black Caribbean attainment is due to parents of Black African pupils taking more of an active role in their child's education, "reinforcing the importance of education and supporting through their schooling". Mirza's work argues that "different migration patterns of Black African and Black Caribbean people may be a factor". Black African migration occurred later, and they tended to assume middle-class occupations "more akin to the ideals of university education". Meanwhile, the wave of migrants to the UK from the Caribbean in the 1940s and 1950s tended to fill working-class occupations in factories and building sites, living in inner-city areas, within White working-class areas. The achievement of the Black Caribbean group is similar to that of the White working-class group, whose attainment is the lowest among all ethnic categories.

Various research suggests that parents from African backgrounds value education and have high aspirations for academic success, similar to Indian and Chinese groups. African families may also invest in tuition, mentors and support for their children. There is less research on reviewing the intra-group disparity in the underachievement of Pakistani pupils. Strand (2021) illustrates that Pakistani and Bangladeshi groups have lower socio-economic status of all groups, with Pakistani being the lowest.

However, the study also showed that Black Caribbean, Black African and White others demonstrated similar levels of socio-economic status. Yet, Black African pupils go on to achieve better than the other sub-categories. The study also shows that "over 40% of Black African, Pakistani, and Bangladeshi parents were Long-Term Unemployed, or working in semi-routine or routine occupations".

Strand continues to present that all ethnic groups, apart from Black Caribbean, perform better than White British pupils. Strand presents a concept of the "immigrant paradigm" developed by Kao and Thompson (2003, in Strand, 2021). The theory is that recent immigrants place a stronger emphasis on education and achievements as a means of escaping the poverty and lack of opportunity they may have experienced themselves. Education serves as an opportunity to experience social mobility.

There is also an explanation of the underachievement of Black Caribbean pupils, which is similar attainment to White British, in that these pupils are "longer-standing migrant groups, with the largest waves of migration in the 1950s"; therefore, this group has assimilated with White British, and maybe "particularly disadvantaged... may be the least likely to be optimistic about the possibilities of education to transform their lives".

"Defiance – Fighting the Far Right", a recent Channel 4 documentary, shows that there was sometimes a semblance of unity between White working-class British and Black Caribbean, in that they spoke English and followed the same religion. Therefore, other ethnicities sometimes regarded the assimilation of Black Caribbean communities into the UK as smoother than their own.

Strand also identified the migration patterns and explained the differences in achievement between Indian and Pakistani pupils.

> Indian migrants were more likely to be of high socio-economic status in their host countries; many were professionals and managers and migrated to a more varied and diverse selection of geographical areas. Other groups, such as Pakistani migrants, while also tending to move to poor areas of inner cities where housing was cheap, tended to move to areas with higher levels of ethnic segregation, which meant they retained greater cultural homogeneity.

The Race Disparity Audit (2017) illustrates that Pakistani and Bangladeshi ethnic groups have the poorest proficiency in English. They are also the ethnic groups that are more likely to be unemployed, although their employment rates have increased by 10% since 2004. Of those who are employed, they are the most likely to be in low-skilled and low-paying occupations. Pakistani and Bangladeshi women are the least likely to be employed and the most likely to be economically inactive.

Pakistani and Bangladeshi groups also tend to live in privately rented accommodations, and overcrowding is widespread living in the most deprived areas: 31% of Pakistani and 27% of the Bangladeshi population live in the most deprived 10% areas, which is exceptionally high in comparison with the overall population of 10% living in these areas.

What the data and research do not explain, however, is that Pakistani and Bangladeshi experience similar levels of socio-economic challenges and experiences of deprivation, yet Bangladeshi pupils achieve higher GCSE scores at 54.4 than Pakistani pupils at 49.1. This disparity is ever widening and is reflected in the 2024 GCSE results. Historic GCSE data shows a significant upward trajectory in the attainment data for Bangladeshi pupils since 2014.

Abley, Jaffar and Gent (2004) found that distinct differences affect the Pakistani community, which affects the attainment and achievement of Pakistani children. "Pakistani children's pre-school experiences of play and language, as the acquisition of English language, was identified as one of the blocks to their learning".

Parents' lack of English or acquisition of English affects pupils' linguistic experiences, and parents' inability to communicate in English and parents' knowledge of the British school system may lead to disengagement. With the resurgence of racism against Muslims following September 11th, as well as the Iraq war, "Muslim identity became associated with negative images." Furthermore, these feelings are exacerbated in the Pakistani group of parents of children with SEND.

Hatton et al. (2004), in their work on South Asian parents supporting a child with severe learning disabilities, found that the highest rates of depression and anxiety were within the Pakistani community. Caring for a child with disabilities without support created serious mental health issues and emotional distress in this community group.

DfE data from 2021-22 demonstrates that after Gypsy Roma and Irish Traveller, the highest rates of persistent absence are mixed White and Black Caribbean at 31.4%, followed by Pakistani at 27.1%. Attendance data for SEND schools demonstrate the same pattern of non-attendance. Abley et al. (2004) research found that the Pakistani community would take a great deal of extended and term-time leave to visit their home country and seemed unaware of the importance of attendance and emphasis on school values. They understood the school might celebrate Eid, but they felt this was tokenistic and felt the time off school serves to maintain their cultural heritage, and they "need to know where they come from".

There is enough data and research to illustrate the underachievement of children from the Black Caribbean and Pakistani ethnic groups. Despite the lack of universal and consistent data on the achievement of pupils with more severe and complex needs, there is also enough data and research to suggest that the same trends and trajectories faced by these communities in mainstream schools prevail and apply to SEN schools.

Employment inequality: The future for ethnic minority pupils with SEND

Destination of school leavers data DfE (2021-22) shows that all school leavers with identified SEND are less likely to sustain a destination in education, apprenticeships or employment. Additionally, Bangladeshi and Pakistani students are the least likely to sustain a destination. Pupils from White and Black Caribbean, or Black Caribbean backgrounds, are less likely to continue in a sustained destination compared with any other ethnic group.

Longer-term data demonstrate the same trends in sustained destinations 1, 3 and 5 years after finishing key stage 4. Those with EHCP are the least likely groups to have a sustained destination, and this is the same for the Black pupils, with a significant reduction from 90% in Year 1 to 55.3% in Year 5. The Race Disparity Report (2017) found that unemployment rates in ethnic minority communities are 2.5 times higher than White British unemployment rates.

Powell (2024) shows that overall employment rates of people with disabilities have increased compared with the previous year; however, from that group, "less than a third of disabled people with… autism, severe/specific learning difficulties… were in employment". While there is no intersectional data available, we can review the data on SEND and ethnicity separately, which shows the same patterns in various areas, and conclude that those from minority backgrounds with SEND continue to experience multiple and significant barriers throughout their education, work experiences and opportunities of employment, compared with other ethnic groups.

The same trends prevail repeatedly.

Employment rates in ethnic minority groups, both disabled and non-disabled, are less than in White groups. Further analysis of this data shows us that there are more disabled men in employment than women. It also shows that employment rates for ethnic minority communities were lower than employment rates for people from a White background, and again, research also found that disabled people from Black, Pakistani and Bangladeshi ethnic groups had the lowest levels of employment every year from 2013 to 2023.

The government released a range of papers and initiatives to increase the number of people with disabilities into employment, for example, the "Transforming support" white paper stating that it was aimed at helping "more disabled people into work…". Other papers include "Shaping Future Support: The Health and disability Green Paper", "Disability Action Plan", "Improving Lives: The Future of Work, health and disability", the "National Disability Strategy", and also "Access to Work" and "Work and Health Programmes".

A press release by the Department for Work and Pensions, 2021 considered how to provide further support to those with disabilities, including a trial of 15 job centres becoming "autism-friendly" and an increase of 26,000 job coaches undergoing accessibility training to improve job centre services for disabled people. Work coaches will support individuals with tools that may support job searching, including magnifiers, immersive readers, automated captions and support with completing job applications and navigating the interview process.

The report also outlines a range of measures, including:

- Increasing the high-needs revenue funding for children and young people with complex needs;
- Further funding to improve accessibility and adaptations for children and young people to existing provisions;
- CPD for teachers on meeting the needs of children with SEND;
- Training more educational psychologists;
- Increasing pupil voice;
- Support improvements to internships;
- Increase the number of disabled people entering apprenticeships, and for those that do they go on to thrive.

Although measures have been identified to support people with disabilities at work, none of the initiatives and strategies, including the National Disability Strategy, have reviewed any intersectional data. There is no consideration at all on how disabled people from specific ethnic groups may experience compounded effects of being an ethnic minority, and also SEND, thus being further disadvantaged.

There is a notable lack of strategic effort to recognise this presented data, identify causal links to the DfE data and statistics or attempt to close these gaps to improve life outcomes for SEND school leavers.

It is concerning that the government has not tried to review the disparity between the Black Caribbean and Pakistani ethnic groups and the wider ethnic groups in any of the identified areas.

The role of schools in preparing ethnic minority pupils with SEND for life beyond education

The government must develop a comprehensive strategy that reviews intersectional data and outlines a coordinated plan across education, criminal justice, healthcare, and policy sectors. This strategy must address the systemic, ingrained and persistent racism evident in these areas, with an emphasis on tackling the root causes and disparities highlighted in the data.

However, we know that the government is slow-acting and continues to demonstrate racism and bias within itself. Therefore, in undertaking the creation of an anti-racist curriculum, there is a call to action to not only review and embed "anti-racist practice" but also go beyond, consider the next steps, consider and prepare our young people with SEND for life as an ethnic minority beyond the school gates, and in the wider world.

Responding to this data and addressing these huge disparities for our Black Caribbean and Pakistani communities should form the basis of our anti-racist curriculum for children with additional needs. It is the school's responsibility to know this data. To learn it. To respond to it, irrespective of whether ethnic minority staff are employed in the school or ethnic minority leaders will or will not lead the work because "it makes them feel too uncomfortable".

The true meaning of an "anti-racist curriculum" is taking responsibility and committing to collective action to make meaningful changes to these issues.

We need to go beyond the steel drums and samosas.

Past "Handa's Surprise" or "The Runaway Chapati".

The curriculum offered to our ethnic minority children with SEND requires a drastic review to consider how we can plant the seeds for change. What happens from the first day of school to the last day as school leavers? It is essential to deconstruct this data and review what strategies schools can implement to address some of these trends so that the EYFS to GCSE data looks more balanced. These actions would form stage 4 of creating an "anti-racist curriculum" by developing knowledge of, and a commitment to, embedding "anti-racist practice" in your organisation.

Career development: Teaching skills for the future

> Young people with special educational needs and/or disabilities are less likely than their peers to be in sustained education, employment, or training, meaning high-quality careers guidance may be particularly important for this group.
> *(Independent review of careers guidance in specialist settings, 2024)*

It is a statutory expectation that all educational settings provide a range of tools to support young people in their understanding of potential careers, including developing their self-awareness, career clarity and goal setting, using the 8 Gatsby Benchmarks.

Careers and accreditation plans, career guidance and 11-19 career plans focused on Preparation for Adulthood should be embedded, like a golden thread, throughout the young person's educational journey. Career guidance should be integrated into transitional planning and preparation for the next steps, identifying individual needs, ensuring planning equips learners with the knowledge needed to make informed decisions, identifying gaps or barriers to progress and forming the school's curriculum.

Individual career plans focusing on Preparation for Adulthood should be created from Year 7, and targets should be set in pupils' annual reviews in collaboration with the pupils, their families and school staff, reviewing what measures need to be taken by home and school to ensure there are aspirational opportunities for young people. Good practice includes augmentative and alternative communication (AAC) aids and symbol-supported text to ensure learners can contribute to their annual reviews. Some pupils used Makaton, keyword communication and AAC voice output to communicate their work experience and career expectations. Pupils should use these communication aids throughout their school experience to ensure they can use their "voice".

Careers can be embedded in the "Personal Development" curriculum, ensuring pupils' knowledge and skills are developed over time systematically and sequentially, for example, learning about the world of work in KS3 but developing understanding to include different career pathways and identifying their aspirations in KS4, to understanding the world of work, developing employability skills, job searching, CV writing, mock interviews and completing applications in KS4. A comprehensive careers curriculum would ensure pupils are ready for certain aspects of their careers, including communication, timekeeping, professional behaviour and appropriate language use. The curriculum that pupils access should also include travel training focused on learning to travel independently and extending independence skills in the wider community.

However, career support provided to pupils with SEND is inconsistent and not robust enough. Careers programmes can sometimes not meet the needs of pupils with higher levels of independence or academic abilities.

In an Independent review of "Careers guidance in specialist settings" by the DfE (2024), various work experience company providers identified that schools do not provide enough information on pupils, their needs, and what they should aim to get from the experiences.

> there does not appear to be a concern with what the student is actually doing. We ask the school how we can ensure they engage, and they just say "do anything you can"-it's fine... I know there is work being done on work experience to improve it, but that hasn't reached SEND schools yet. Not enough guidance for employers on what to do with work experience.

Therefore, despite the curriculum's focus on careers, there is a communication deficit in that schools sometimes do not provide enough information about the pupils' needs or work with the employer to ensure the work experience is successful and meaningful to the young person by identifying with the employer what they should be getting out of the experience.

The school's career programme should include a range of work experiences and "supported internships" thus giving young people with SEND access to a "high-quality, real-life working environment... to enhance their employability skills and independence and to improve their confidence." However, the school curriculum should also the following areas:

Job readiness

Preparing pupils for the workforce involves teaching them job-specific skills, workplace etiquette, searching for jobs, career coaching and guidance. Experiencing various work experience placements and internships can provide practical insights into various careers. "Minority ethnic youth employment outcome" (2022) found that many ethnic minority young people live in "deprived areas and have reduced employment opportunities, and there are cultural differences within their communities that may lead to reduced labour market aspirations".

Ethnic minority young people felt they needed to "assimilate to secure good quality work, which requires social capital, education, and experience of navigating institutions". This presents a significant challenge for ethnic minority young people with SEND, as any one of these strands is a colossal undertaking to unpick and address and requires a great deal of support. Careers leaders need to be aware of this and work through this to ensure a diverse range of work experience opportunities can be provided to young people.

CV building and interview skills

Pupils should receive lessons on writing and creating a CV, filling out job applications and preparing for interviews. Mock interviews and CV workshops can help pupils to build confidence.

Social interaction and communication

Skills such as initiating conversations, practising active listening and responding appropriately in conversations are crucial to social integration. Role-playing, social stories and comic strip conversations can be useful tools for supporting young people in developing these skills.

Additionally, not all settings use knowledgeable and experienced career advisors to provide advice and guidance. Best practice suggests that career planning should be undertaken with collaboration from the parents and carers. However, research indicates that parents and carers "can be anxious about their child's future"; thus, some families will disengage with the school's attempts to discuss the future. Parents of pupils attending specialist provision also tend to live further distances from the school and will find the school's geographical location challenging to get to.

It is also acknowledged that sometimes parents are from lower socio-economic status; they may be uneducated themselves and not place value on education or may have unmet additional needs themselves. Research suggests that schools can use various strategies to increase engagement with the school to improve parental knowledge, understanding and collaboration to support the young person's career development, including newsletters, careers fairs, parents' evenings, annual reviews and parent workshops.

A family liaison worker could support parents in visiting educational settings, building relationships first and then bringing them into schools. This person can provide regular calls and check-ins with parents and may help them with research, advice and support regarding the next steps. Parents can feel overwhelmed with navigating the transition out of school and onto further education after so many years of being within the "same system".

However, this research is focused on the experiences of ALL ethnic groups, which requires further review and strategic plans to address these issues and promote collaborative and joined-up working between home and school.

Preparing ethnic minority young people with SEND for careers

As educators considering how to implement an "anti-racist curriculum", we must recognise that even the "Independent review of careers guidance on specialist settings" (Ofsted, 2024) fails to consider any racial disparity in the access to careers, thus disregarding all data which indicates substantial differences in pupils with SEND accessing employment opportunities between the ethnic groups. There is little recognition of this intersectional group and even less recognition, guidance, support and planning to ensure that schools identify and remove barriers. Little is currently being implemented to address the sustained underachievement of these groups.

It is, therefore, our responsibility to consider this data and consider how to identify and remove barriers for ethnic minority young people with SEND, especially Black Caribbean and Pakistani groups. We must ensure school staff know this data and ensure that we close the gaps in providing accessible and equitable opportunities for these groups. Recognising this disparity, addressing it, and implementing measures to reduce it is meaningful and forms the basis of impactful anti-racist work.

An anti-racist framework in specialist settings should go beyond increasing multicultural opportunities and representations or decolonising the curriculum, recruitment, retention and career progression of ethnic minority staff. In the world of SEND, anti-racist work should include identification and measures to practically remove barriers and increase opportunities so that pupils have a real chance to engage and succeed through the practical application of skills.

Schools' career and accreditation policies, careers guidance and 11-19-year-old career plans should acknowledge and plan to reduce gaps and increase opportunities for ethnic minority pupils. Schools, including SEND provisions, should embrace anti-racist measures, such as understanding the pupil's community and giving the young person a voice through whichever means are relevant for the pupil. Schools should continue to understand the pupil, their needs, interests and aspirations where appropriate and applicable. Underachieving ethnic minority groups of young people and their families should be identified and included in School Improvement Planning processes, ensuring robust quality assurance measures are embedded to monitor pupils' progress.

Partnering with parents to increase engagement and promote success

Parental involvement is regarded as essential to ensure pupils have support with career guidance from their families. Supporting their child with transition planning or supporting their children organise themselves for their work experience placements or consulting with the work placements to ensure the experience was tailored for their child was key. Supporting children with accessing experience and transporting them to and from this was also crucial. However, the report showed that many schools find it difficult to engage effectively with parents and carers and label parents from ethnic minority backgrounds as "hard to reach". These parents tend to be viewed as disengaged and interpreted as "dismissive" or "angry" based on their ethnic backgrounds.

Research suggests that Pakistani and Bangladeshi parents are least able to speak English or, in some cases, demonstrate literacy levels in any language. Therefore, disengagement is not a choice, but could be because the schools are communicating with them in inaccessible ways, which may be insufficient. Parents of diverse community groups can be labelled as "angry" or "difficult"; however, schools can fail to recognise that these stereotypical labels are assigned without understanding that some groups experience ongoing and systemic racism. These parents must work hard as they navigate identification processes independently and without adequate support from the school or local authority. These parents are equally anxious and afraid for their child's future.

In "They will need time" (Abley, Jaffar and Gent, 2004), a project case study on raising the achievement of mainstream Pakistani pupils in London, Abely et al. found that a range of implemented strategies successfully increased engagement from Pakistani parents. A range of measures were taken by various schools, which led to successful engagement, including:

- Focus on increasing the engagement of parents from specific ethnic groups, including their lack of involvement in schools, high numbers of unauthorised absences due to term-time holidays and extended holidays and overall lack of engagement from home. These formed part of the school's improvement plans.
- Workshops for parents led by bilingual staff.
- Thorough induction and admissions processes for new children.
- Training for new staff, including supporting EAL (pupils with English as an additional language) children.
- Family literacy lessons.
- Informal meetings with parents.
- Links with local religious leaders to support building relationships.

These strategies are far more labour- and time-intensive for the school staff. The focus is on understanding the importance of attendance, basic school life principles, curriculum and improving English. It could be deemed that the paper is also 20 years old, and things have progressed in this time. Still, Pakistani groups remain underperforming in mainstream and special schools, as well as being one of the ethnic groups that are least likely to be employed and continue to be the ethnic group that speaks the least English. Schools could audit the needs of their parents and create stakeholder engagement plans based on this information. They could devise specific strategies and interventions for their school to improve engagement from the parents.

Demie and McLean (2017) identify a range of barriers for Black Caribbean pupils, including lack of parental aspiration and low expectations, low literacy and language barriers, absent fathers, single-parent families and socio-economic disadvantage, including poverty and poor housing. Research shows us that Black Caribbean pupils are almost three times more likely to be excluded from school than other racial groups, and, interestingly, children from this group were more likely to be excluded from school even when they were in the small minority of their racial group within the wider school population, rather than if there were a more significant number of children from the same ethnic group.

> Bias and parental response to historical bias or the current threat of bias could form a part of the explanation for the disparities experienced by ethnic groups that have taken the brunt of racial discrimination. Historically and before the mainstreaming of most children with SEND following the Warnock Review in 1978, Black Caribbean children were over-identified with SEND and segregated from other children in schools for the "educationally subnormal", to the clear detriment of their educational and broader life outcomes.
>
> *(Coard, 1971)*

Black pupils continue to experience a great deal of disadvantage through intersections of race, SEND, as well as poverty. They are likelier to experience systemic biases at school and are most likely to be identified with SEND. They continue to be over-represented in SEMH, more likely to receive Free School Meals, least likely to receive support for their identified need, including teachers having low expectations of them and more disciplinary interactions from teachers, and most likely to be excluded from school. Additionally, they are less likely to achieve GCSEs or a university education and less likely to gain paid, sustained employment.

Preparing pupils to identify and navigate discrimination in real-world challenges

Wheeler et al. (2024) identify that many Black boys entering Youth Offending Services tend to be boys who have experienced ongoing racism and discrimination, as well as have unmet Special Educational Needs.

Racial profiling, including stop and searches, disproportionately affects young Black males, and they are six times more likely to be stopped and searched compared with White groups.

The responsibility lies with the police to review and reform the systemic and structural racism which targets the Black community. There are reports of parents suggesting that, as much as it is a disgraceful and saddening concept, parents of Black children have "the talk" with their children to ensure they are equipped with the understanding and strategies to navigate these encounters should they be unfortunate enough to experience them. What happens to autistic Black boys or Black boys with other identified SEND, who may not have the cognitive capacity to fully understand these interactions with the police?

> Teachers need greater knowledge about students of Black Caribbean background. They need to know the history of Britain's involvement in the slave trade, the circumstances which led up to the arrival of people from the Caribbean to the UK and what challenges they faced, such as racism, difficulty in finding housing and employment and which many continue to face today.
>
> (Demie, 2022)

For structural and systematic racism to be addressed, schools must start becoming uncomfortable and reviewing their curriculum, not just to increase multicultural teaching or representation. They must also scrutinise what the data over the past 50 years is telling us, recognise that these trends have not changed, and actively make changes to break these barriers that are becoming firmly entrenched.

Building a curriculum for empowerment

Ethnic minority young people with SEND working within the "formal pathways" must access a curriculum that supports them in developing practical experiences in communication, advocating for themselves, travel training, navigating social transport, reading timetables, interacting with others to locate routes, making payments and coping with unexpected changes. These skills are vital in promoting independence and developing the "street smart" ability. These experiences can also provide opportunities to build resilience and self-advocacy, teaching pupils to communicate their thoughts and feelings and use their voices.

Through role-play scenarios, social stories, comic strip conversations, and videos, pupils can learn about their rights and how to manage and vocalise if they experience that these have been compromised. Pupils must be taught to read verbal and nonverbal communication skills, including expressing themselves clearly, interpreting body language and using social cues effectively, which can be tricky for some neurodiverse people.

Ethnic minority pupils, as part of the Preparation for Adulthood and the Personal Social and Emotional Development curriculum, should learn about structural racism and discrimination to feel empowered. They must develop the skills to recognise potential discrimination and bias. They should also learn how to identify and seek help if they think they have experienced any racism, including role-playing encounters with various community professionals, and where relevant and appropriate, understanding and communicating their legal rights, critical for their safety and wellbeing. Schools could be proactive in their education, for example, inviting the police into lessons to have these conversations about rights and responsibilities in the community, so our ethnic minority young people have interactions with the police in safe environments, supported to ask questions, to challenge and not be afraid.

As this chapter has repeatedly identified, parental collaboration is key to success. Parents play an essential role in supporting their children in developing their knowledge, understanding, and independence. Through this collaboration, home and school can work together to ensure consistent opportunities are offered to young people to demonstrate their increasing independence, which are aligned between the two settings.

Schools must complete an audit to determine how they can best support parents and carers and what further curriculum adaptations may be necessary. As we have seen, there seem to be some parallels within specific community groups. However, it is important not to generalise by community to perpetuate stereotypes but to audit and respond to the identified needs.

Some community groups experience a great deal of denial in accepting their child's diagnosed needs and spend many years searching for "fixes" due to SEND not being outwardly discussed, accepted or celebrated. These communities may place a heavy emphasis on education and, as such, do not always easily understand children with additional needs working below their chronological ages, questioning when this may "self-correct". These groups require cultural sensitivity and possible cultural assimilation through cultural days, including festivals and celebrations, language support and workshops to present and explain curriculum, assessment and career routes.

Other community groups are fully aware of the ongoing systemic and structural racism they face. Community groups, through community leaders and organisations, could provide workshops for parents and pupils, acting as role models and offering support to navigate their career paths.

It is also common for parents of children with SEND to sustain low expectations for their child, wishing for them to be "safe and happy", or stating that they do not really care about an academic curriculum. These comments are concerning; in knowing the underachievement of specific ethnic groups, we would hope for parents to try to understand the SEND curriculum offered and how their child is supported to gain the knowledge and skills they need to be as independent as possible.

Schools and families should work together to ensure that expectations are aligned. Teachers' low expectations of ethnic minority groups of pupils can significantly affect engagement, behaviour and attainment, and parents of these young people are aware of these issues. Building better relationships, having higher aspirations for pupils and working closely with families to set appropriate targets and review engagement strategies and barriers to learning will all contribute towards sustaining success for groups of pupils.

Preparing ethnic minority pupils with SEND as school leavers involves equipping them with essential skills to navigate a complex and potentially discriminatory society. From the ages of 14-16, these young people need focused support to develop their sense of self, advocacy skills, independence, social skills and resilience against biases they may experience through structural racism. They will encounter specific challenges and require comprehensive support through inclusive curriculum design, professional development for staff, and active parental involvement to fully support pupils' successful and progressive transitions to the subsequent phases of their lives - their adulthood experiences.

Schools must adopt a proactive, multifaceted approach to address the barriers faced by ethnic minority young people with SEND. Implementing a range of strategies based on research and best practice can support the school in delivering equitable outcomes, preparing young people with the skills and strategies needed to navigate a society where they often face multiple disadvantages.

Engaging in these efforts is not just beneficial; it is anti-racist practice at its core, enhancing the educational experience and environment for all pupils by establishing a culture of diversity, equity and inclusion. Employing a combined range of strategies, including those identified by the independence review, will allow schools to create bespoke interventions to increase engagement. Increased engagement can allow for a collaborative approach to promoting engagement with parents to create a secure and informed career plan and trajectory for our young people.

Race, SEND and healthcare

Independence should form a core thread of the tapestry of Preparing for Adulthood from pupils' first days in school. In "We Deserve Better: Ethnic minorities with a Learning Disability and Access to Healthcare" (NHS Race and Health Observatory, 2023), it is stated that those with disabilities from South Asian communities tend to have shorter lifespans compared to other groups. Access to healthcare services, such as dentists, is inequitable due to poverty and deprivation. The research also found that diabetes, cardiovascular disease and infant mortality are higher in diverse community groups compared with White British.

South Asian children have the lowest levels of physical fitness of all groups, and Black, Pakistani and Bangladeshi groups tend to be the most overweight and obese groups.

As educators, we should use research to inform our practice, review and audit where we are, amend our curriculum and set targets as part of our School Improvement Planning.

Preparing for adulthood: Life skills and independence

Pupils should access a comprehensive personal, social and emotional development (PSED) curriculum that promotes independence and self-care. Pupils should be taught essential self-care and personal hygiene skills, including brushing teeth, grooming and dressing appropriately. For example, in EYFS, some of our pupils might need to manage and build upon the sensation and experience of having their hair managed with brushes/combs as they grow. Over time, this could be adapted to look at different hairstyles, too, as a school leaver, looking at appropriate hairstyles for employment, interviews compared with party hairstyles. Schools should support pupils in developing their skills over time.

Domestic chores

Skills such as cooking, cleaning, laundry and organisation are essential for household management. Many young people with additional needs will benefit from practical lessons in these areas, and these can easily be incorporated into the school curriculum, using task schedules, timetables and now and next boards, and implementing at various points in the day, including setting the table for lunchtimes.

Opinions on whether children and young people should participate in chores can vary culturally and not just according to different ethnic groups. Targets should be set with parents, ensuring they understand that through developing these skills, they are preparing the young person for their adult lives.

Physical exercise

"Sport for all" (Sport England, 2020) found that people from Asian, Black and Chinese backgrounds are more likely to be physically inactive compared with those who are White. Teachers in SEND settings also need to be mindful, as children are often transported to school and home again, sitting in their transportation for an hour or so each way. Some pupils may go from a high-rise flat without garden access to their school transport, arrive at school and go home again with little daily exercise. Schools must account for this and ensure adequate levels of movement throughout the day, primarily as this movement also supports sensory and self-regulation, which affects their engagement in learning.

Healthy eating

Many pupils with additional needs can be fussy eaters and have limited diets, which can make it difficult for parents to ensure there is a varied diet. Sometimes, behaviour is controlled by food, as it is easier to give in. It is understandable that parents provide their children with whatever they will eat. However, sensory and food de-sensitisation programs and strategies can lead to considerable gains in children over time and when the consistency of approach is sustained. Making healthier food choices and understanding moderation through visual aids, including calendars/now and next boards, and so on, are successful strategies in supporting some pupils to make better food choices.

Travel training and safety in the community

Teaching pupils how to use public transportation, read schedules and navigate routes is essential for promoting independence. Pupils require practical experiences like guided trips and travel simulations.

Many diverse communities may consider encouraging this level of independence as neglectful instead of considering ways to encourage and facilitate independence. Consider the case study of Jay and the family's overenthusiastic support, which he felt was limiting and delayed his autonomy.

Schools should consider and collaborate with families to agree on ways forward for their young people. It is important to ensure alignment between home and school.

The final stretch: Ensuring post-school success for pupils from minority backgrounds with SEND

Preparing young people with SEND for life in modern Britain, particularly those from ethnic minority backgrounds, requires a comprehensive approach that addresses the layered challenges they face. This is creating an anti-racist curriculum. Schools and policymakers must commit to continuous improvement in policies and practices, ensuring that our pupils are equipped to thrive in a diverse and complex society. The journey involves comprehensive strategies that span education, law enforcement, healthcare and employment, all aimed at creating an equitable and inclusive future for every pupil.

Ethnic minority young people with SEND in modern Britain encounter a multifaceted array of barriers that span across race, disability and socio-economic status. Schools and educational settings play critical roles in preparing young people for life beyond the classroom by effectively addressing and mitigating these barriers as anti-racist practices.

For these young people, developing a positive sense of identity is crucial in preparing them for the wider world beyond school life. Integrating their cultural backgrounds into the curriculum to reinforce their self-esteem and develop their identity and resilience against discrimination is critical. By addressing the specific challenges they face and providing comprehensive support through inclusive curriculum design, professional development for staff and active parent involvement, schools can help these pupils transition successfully into adulthood.

Chapter summary

This chapter highlights the compounded challenges faced by ethnic minority pupils with SEND as they transition into adulthood. From systemic racism and bias in education and employment to disparities in healthcare and criminal justice, these students often face unique barriers that hinder their development and opportunities.

The chapter emphasises the need for schools to adopt anti-racist practices, develop inclusive curricula, and collaborate with families to prepare these young people for life beyond school. It calls for a shift from token multiculturalism to practical, meaningful actions that equip pupils with the skills, resilience and support needed to thrive in an unequal society.

TIFFIN TAKE-AWAY

1. **Building self-awareness and resilience through a culturally responsive curriculum**

   Schools must develop a curriculum that integrates the cultural backgrounds and lived experiences of ethnic minority pupil, reinforcing their self-esteem and building resilience against potential biases and discrimination. This includes representation in learning materials, discussions on identity and activities that foster positive self-concept and pride in their heritage. Ensuring pupils have a strong sense of self will empower them to navigate a society that may challenge their identities.

   - You could review how your school incorporates cultural diversity and self-identity into the curriculum to help ethnic minority pupils with SEND build resilience and confidence.

2. **Comprehensive preparation for independence and adulthood**

   Preparing ethnic minority pupils with SEND for adulthood requires focused instruction in practical life skills, such as financial literacy, travel training and job readiness. Schools need to integrate career guidance, real-world experiences and social skills development into their curriculum, ensuring students are equipped to manage the realities of work and independent living. Building independence through systematic, hands-on training is critical to fostering confidence and capability.

   - What strategies can your school implement to better prepare these pupils for independent living and employment?

3. **Engaging families as active partners in transition planning**

   Schools must collaborate closely with families to develop individualised transition plans that reflect the specific needs of ethnic minority pupils with SEND. Many families, particularly from minority backgrounds, may face language, socio-economic or systemic barriers that complicate their involvement. Schools should use culturally sensitive approaches to engage families in transition planning, ensuring that their input shapes a holistic and realistic plan for the pupil's future.

   - You could review how your school could create stronger partnerships with ethnic minority families to better understand and support successful transitions into adulthood.

References

Abley, J., Jaffar, S. and Gent, B. (2004) *They will need time*. Redbridge Education Service. The RAISE projects.

Chouinard, J. and Davis, J. (2016) "Theorising affordances: From request to refuse". *Bulletin of Science, Technology and Society*, 36(4): 241–248.

Coard, B. (1971) *How the West Indian child is made educationally sub-normal in the British school system*. McDermott Publishing.

Demie, F. and McLean, C. (2017) "Black Caribbean underachievement in schools in England". Lambeth Local Authority. https://pih.org.uk/wp-content/uploads/2021/05/black_caribbean_underachievement_in_schools_in_england_2017-1.pdf

DfE (2021-2022) 16-18 destination measures. https://explore-education-statistics.service.gov.uk/find-statistics/16-18-destination-measures

DfE (2022-2023) Early years foundation stage profile results. https://explore-education-statistics.service.gov.uk/find-statistics/early-years-foundation-stage-profile-results

Demie, F. (2022) "Tackling teachers' low expectations of Black Caribbean students in English schools". *Equity in Education and Society*, 1(1).

GOV.UK (2017) Race Disparity Audit. www.gov.uk/government/publications/race-disparity-audit

GOV.UK (2022) Statistics on ethnicity and the criminal justice system. Ministry of Justice. www.gov.uk/government/statistics/ethnicity-and-the-criminal-justice-system-2022/statistics-on-ethnicity-and-the-criminal-justice-system-2022-html

Hatton, C., Akram, Y., Shah, R., Robertson, J. and Emerson, E. (2004) *Supporting South Asian families with a child with severe learning disabilities*. Jessica Kingsley Publishers.

Ingstad, B. and Whyte, S. (1995) *Disability and culture*. University of California Press.

Learning and Work institute (2022) "Minority ethnic youth employment outcomes". Rapid evidence reviews. Investors in people.

Mirza, H. and Warwick, R. (2022) "Race and ethnicity". Institute for Fiscal Studies. Nuffield Foundation.

National Disability strategy (2022) www.gov.uk/government/publications/national-disability-strategy

NHS Race and Health Observatory (2023) "We deserve better: Ethnic minorities with learning disability and access to healthcare". www.nhsrho.org/research/review-into-factors-that-contribute-towards-inequalities-in-health-outcomes-faced-by-those-with-a-learning-disability-from-a-minority-ethnic-community/

Ofsted (2024) "Independence review of careers guidance in specialist settings". www.gov.uk/government/publications/independent-review-of-careers-guidance-in-specialist-settings

Powell, A. (2024) "Disabled people in employment". House of Commons Library. Research briefing.

Roberts, N. and Bolton, P. (2023) "Educational outcomes of Black pupils and students". Research briefing. UK Parliament. House of Commons.

Siddidque, H. (2019) "Minority ethnic Britons face 'shocking' job discrimination". *The Guardian*. www.theguardian.com/world/2019/jan/17/minority-ethnic-britons-face-shocking-job-discrimination

Sport England (2020) "Sport for all". www.sportengland.org/news/sport-for-all

Strand, S. (2021) "Ethnic, socio-economic and sex inequalities in educational achievement at age 16: An analysis of the Second Longitudinal study of young people in England". Report for the Commission on Race and Ethnic Disparities. University of Oxford.

Wheeler, R., Agyepong, A., Martin, M. and Peter, M. (2024) "Accessing special educational needs and disabilities (SEND) provision for Black and mixed heritage children: Lived experiences from parents and professionals living in South London". Global Black Maternal Health.

13
How to collaborate with stakeholders and the community to prepare for life beyond the school

"... but people out there just don't understand them..."

"Mummy, I need to scrub my skin to make it clean; it's dirty and brown. I need it like Princess Elsa."
It was devastating to see my then 3-year-old scrubbing her skin in the bath and observe her feelings, even at a young age, that her skin colour was somehow "bad".
Three generations.
Fighting to stop racism.
Staring into the face of racism.
Emerging seeds – an awareness brewing that you may not be quite "right".

Transitioning from school to adult life poses significant challenges for the average ethnic minority young person, let alone a young person with identified additional needs. The intersection of disability and race creates dual layers of challenges, amplifying the barriers these pupils face. It necessitates an educational approach that encompasses both understanding and support.

Preparing for adulthood in early school life

Effective preparation for adulthood should begin early and be embedded within school policy, processes and the curriculum. This preparation involves collaborating with pupils and parents to define clear, achievable end-of-key stage and end-of-school outcomes, such as developing communication, independence and participating in the wider community. The Department for Education's SEND code of practice (2014) emphasises the importance of preparing for adulthood from the earliest years of education, suggesting that the curriculum tailors life skills education to each pupil's aspirations and abilities. This ensures they acquire the necessary skills to navigate adult life successfully.

We can call for schools to provide a curriculum that matters, including supporting ethnic minority pupils with SEND and affirming their cultural and racial identity. Incorporating pupils' cultural heritage and experiences into the school curriculum, as well as reviewing and improving representation and anti-racist approaches, are crucial in forming secure "exosystems" and "macrosystems" in society (Akbar, 2019). We revisit where we started.

Reviewing the "exosystems": The role of diversity in school governance

The McKinsey Report (2019) found that the more diverse teams are in terms of gender, ethnicity and cultural diversity, the more likely these teams are to outperform less diverse peer teams. The greater the levels of diversity, the higher the likelihood of outperformance by between 30–40%. The likelihood of outperformance is higher in ethnicity than gender.

We know that having diverse boards leads to improved governance, and by having individuals from various backgrounds, we enrich our school community. Research from "Governors for Schools" suggests that diverse boards foster better governance and create inclusive environments that benefit the entire school community through challenging stereotypes, promoting inclusion and ensuring that all voices are heard in strategic decision-making. This is especially important when representing parents.

Why representation on school boards matters

A diverse board reflects the broader school community, making pupils, parents and staff from all backgrounds feel included. The Key (2018) found that diverse school governing boards "mean more robust debate, better decision-making, and improved educational outcomes for children", and the National Governance Association (2021) found that diverse boards are more likely to challenge and bring different perspectives to decision-making processes.

Diverse boards are also more likely to engage effectively with parents and the wider community, particularly in areas with higher ethnic diversity. This aligns with the idea that diverse boards better reflect the broader school community and make pupils, parents and staff from all backgrounds feel included. Research suggests that diverse school leadership teams were more likely to implement inclusive policies and practices, benefiting pupils from all backgrounds. Additionally, Worth et al. (2022) found that schools with more diverse governing boards were more likely to be rated as "Good" or "Outstanding" by Ofsted, suggesting a link between board diversity and overall school quality.

Tackling the leadership gap: Increasing ethnic minority headteachers and governors

The Department for Education's "School Governance in 2020" report highlights that only 10% of school governors in England were from minority backgrounds, compared with 34% of pupils. Headteachers from minority communities make up only around 4% of the population; therefore, tackling the underrepresentation at the governor and headteacher levels is critical. To address these challenges, organisations like "Governors for Schools" have launched initiatives to promote diversity in school governance; for example, their "Everyone on Board" campaign aims to increase the number of ethnic minority governors and raise awareness about the importance of diverse representation.

The Department for Education has also recognised the need for greater diversity in school leadership. In 2022, they launched "Diversity in School Leadership" to increase the number of headteachers from underrepresented groups.

The London Borough of Ealing will commence a "Diversity in Leadership" programme to support the career progression pathways for teachers from minority ethnic backgrounds. This is especially welcome, as over 70% of the pupil population in this borough is ethnic minority. The programme will consist of personal assessments, support from leadership coaches, presentation and public speaking training, application and interview workshops, a mock recruitment experience from application and interview and feedback. It will also include shadowing placements and networking, with opportunities to learn from one another.

However, with "77% of boards reporting difficulties in recruiting new governors and trustees" and "dangerous teacher shortages" in the UK, representation does not appear to be a solvable issue or a priority in the coming years as schools try desperately hard to remain afloat.

Despite this, existing school governors, who may be White, should consider how to become influential allies in anti-racist work, helping to create a more inclusive and equitable educational environment. They should positively leverage their privilege and positions to advocate for anti-racist policies and practices, that is, through the school's equality policy. Governors should ensure they access diversity and inclusion CPD including recruitment and retention of ethnic minority teachers and leaders, supporting the headteacher to develop a workforce plan to identify and meet any disparities. They should also familiarise themselves with national and school data and trends. They should be prepared to hold their leadership teams accountable regarding curriculum intents, family engagement and outcomes for young ethnic minority people with SEND.

Governors should ensure they are prepared to pose questions to the leadership team around curriculum intentions and implementation and if the curriculum offer represents the pupil population or if it suitably prepares young people for diverse communities and a larger, more diverse world. Governors should review pupil outcomes and identify any disparities in data, including requesting pupil outcomes data per ethnic group, which they should use to challenge leadership teams regarding any differences in progress, attainment, engagement levels, teaching and learning, as well as question the identified strategies to support the identified groups/areas of underachievement.

In SEND schools, governors must be educated and informed and demonstrate awareness of the intersections of race and SEND. They should question their leaders on pupil behaviour per ethnic groups, suspension and exclusion data and ensure a wide range of supportive, restorative and proactive strategies are used to support these pupils. Governors could review parental engagement rates per ethnicity group, how communities are supported in developing their knowledge and understanding of their child's diagnosis, and how they are supported in creating awareness of strategies to support their child.

MATs – Multi Academy Trust level practice

Academy Trusts can take a proactive and comprehensive approach to diversity and equity. They have immense potential to be more progressive in leading the way with diversity and equity in schools compared with local authorities due to greater autonomy and flexibility. We saw the example of the London Borough of Ealing leading the "Diversity in Leadership" programme, and the London Boroughs have made a commitment to offer a "London Leadership Programme". It is only in specific local authorities (LAs), determined by the LA commitment itself, that we focus on developing diverse ethnic minority leaders.

Academy boards could include anti-racist objectives as a part of their strategic aims and Trust's policies, thus communicating a commitment to promoting an anti-racist culture and values. The board could hold the CEO and headteacher accountable for creating and sustaining the development of a workforce strategy, addressing the issues around recruitment and retention of ethnic minority teachers to leaders, and the concerning data of ethnic minority ITT's negative career trajectory.

Further considerations could include reviewing the financial allocation of funds, for example, reviewing which schools within the Trust or LA have the most diverse needs regarding diverse ethnic groups, ability, efforts and resources required to engage minority groups' parents. For example, in more diverse areas, more translation services might be required in specific schools to create good engagement with parents and funding sessions for career guidance in different languages. Hence, parents can contribute and collaborate with school staff to identify suitable targets and plans for their children. These costs should be factored into the school's essential needs. Overall, there needs to be a commitment to diversity and equity, an assurance that every level of the organisation demonstrates commitment to equity, continual improvement and accountability.

Trust targets should embed the commitment to creating an equitable Trust and wider schools, and these targets should inform a part of headteacher appraisal targets. There should be an expectation for these to be included in the School Improvement Planning and disseminated to teacher appraisal targets. Through taking this approach, the anti-racist work becomes firmly placed on the map and communicated with strength and unwavering support from the top-down, in support and allyship for the diverse community.

> ### 🔍 CASE STUDY
>
> A MAT demonstrates a progressive commitment to diversity and inclusion through various initiatives, including staff networks and champions, enabling advocacy for equality within school settings, and a range of equality and recognition awards.
>
> Their "Break the Cycle Anti-Racism Network" was formed in response to data and research on systemic racism in education and wider society.
>
> They champion the "5 C's", including:
>
> - Conversations about the issues that need changing;
> - Communication "upwards" of staff views;
> - Commitment to hold Oasis (the Trust) to account for the changes;
> - Challenging to educate all staff about anti-oppressive practice;
> - Curriculum that properly emboldens and reflects our commitment to inclusion and diversity.
>
> Multi Academy Trusts can also collaborate with other trusts that are further along their journey in equity work, either with maintained schools or between MATs. The Key (2022) identifies that collaboration can be:
>
> a) With other Trusts as partnerships, a working party, a collaborative governing body, or a collaborative partnership;
> b) With maintained schools: through regular meetings, schools can work towards a collaborative project and trial various initiatives and feedback, e.g., introducing blind applications as a means of supporting anti-racist recruitment initiatives.
>
> The Key also identifies three ways in which they can support school improvement, including:
>
> 1. Top-down improvement – strategies built and dictated by the MAT. While this may not be effective in meeting the individual needs of the schools within the Trust, there is potential to demonstrate a whole MAT commitment to equality and ensure that the School Improvement Plan embodies a target towards equity work.
> 2. Bottom-up improvement: where the issues of each school feed into the improvement model; for example, one school may have more diversity within their school compared with the other schools in the Trust – how would the Trust ensure that they are responsive and able to support each school's individual needs, especially in this area?
> 3. Peer-to-peer improvement – account for where schools can share resources and knowledge – how is the MAT using the skills and expertise within each school to upskill the other schools in the Trust?

Building accountability: Long-term plans, School Improvement Plans and headteacher targets

Embedding a commitment to diversity and inclusion and addressing barriers faced by minority groups into the School Improvement Plan and headteacher appraisal targets ensures these priorities remain central to school development.

When leading anti-racist work in schools, governors and the senior leadership team should be familiar with school data and trends, for example, reviewing ethnic groups of the pupils and their families. They should also be aware of engagement levels within each group and barriers they may face in engaging, and they should review what measures the school has taken to support better engagement. Leaders and governors could undertake equity, diversity and inclusion (EDI) training together to further explore the individual school data and discuss possible ways forward, creating strategic plans over 3-5 years to promote better representation through the curriculum and anti-racist practice. These targets could form the annual School Improvement Plans but also feed into and build upon the school's equality policy.

The School Improvement Plan is also expected to link with the headteacher's appraisal targets. These are then further disseminated to the teacher targets, for example, "Medium Term Planning, activities and resources including books, pictures and props, will reflect the class and school diverse population" or "Increased engagement from all parental groups, through adapted and culturally responsive, communication including newsletters and videos". The headteacher and leadership would be expected to employ a comprehensive CPD and quality assurance plan to review implementation, progress and impact of the SIP actions, which they will report to governors and demonstrate high levels of impact and accountability.

Embedding this work within the School Improvement Plan also ensures ongoing opportunities throughout the year for the leadership team, including the headteacher, to have these conversations with the governors on implementation, successes and barriers the school continues to face in the area. The governor meetings would then allow governors to delve into these matters further and support and guide the team.

Therefore, these collective measures would ensure that the focus on diversity is not tokenistic or tick-boxing but progressive, sequential, meaningful and embedded in the school. It can encourage a whole-school commitment from all stakeholders and provide meaningful focus on the work.

Political influence: How "macrosystems" shape SEND education for ethnic minority pupils

In reviewing Bronfenbrenner's social ecological model, we now explore the "macrosystem" influence on individuals and their development. Macrosystems are concerned with broader and more societal influences, including political contexts and cultural values.

Local authorities

> please just take my daughter... I don't know what to do or where to go to get her into a school (in Punjabi)

This mother turned up at the gates of a school I was working in, buzzing on the intercom, insisting we immediately offer her daughter a place. She had limited English and no understanding of the county processes. She did not know her child's SEND officer or what she needed to do to navigate the SEND/EHCP process. Devastatingly, this is common.

In the 20 years I have been working in education, I have seen this scenario frequently, although in different forms. The EHCP processes are complicated and frustrating for ALL families. Additional barriers around language, being new to the country and a lack of support from the wider community due to family and friends telling you, "It'll be OK, there is nothing to worry about" can make parents desperate for information and support.

In Special Needs Jungle (2021), Haye states, "The response the SEND child receives could vary depending on the setting and the child's, and the teacher's, individual perceptions. Misunderstanding cultural differences can compound systemic racism, so having two protected characteristics (race and disability) rather than just one is a double-edged sword."

The silence on racism in the SEND policy

There is little research or awareness of the intersection between race and disability. The Sewell Report (2021), conducted in response to the murder of George Floyd and the global focus on institutional and systemic racism, states that "he does not believe Britain is institutionally racist", and the Sewell Report, "Commission on race and ethnic disparities" (2021), states:

> The commission has not had a focus on special educational needs in the report due to existing government activity. In September 2019, the Department for Education (DfE) launched a new review to improve support for children with additional needs. The review aims to improve the services available to families who need support and equip staff in schools and colleges to respond effectively to their needs and end the "postcode lottery" they often face.

Therefore, according to these reports, Britain is NOT racist, and it has not considered SEND support for SEND or any intersectional effects. Still, the government is trying to improve services around SEND.

When the "Special Educational Needs and Disabilities (SEND) and Alternative Provision (AP) Improvement Plan – Right Support, Right Place, Right Time" (2023) was published last year, it also failed to mention ethnicity or race. It was another publication that evaded any review or attempt to tackle this intersection of pupils in the community.

There is a persistent refusal to acknowledge overt racism, structural inequality and systemic racism experienced by ethnic minority pupils with SEND and their families.

Ofsted's role: Where anti-racism falls short

The Ofsted School Inspection Handbook updated (2024) and comprehensive, refers to "understanding and appreciation of the wide range of cultural influences that have shaped their heritage and that of others" and "interest in exploring, improving understanding of and showing respect for different faiths and cultural diversity and the extent to which they understand, accept, respect and celebrate diversity". Furthermore, "understanding and appreciation of the range of different cultures in the school and further afield as an essential element of their preparation for life in modern Britain".

Ofsted expects "pupils have sufficient age-appropriate awareness and understanding of protected characteristics". They also hope that "formed policy following consultation with parents".

We can, therefore, conclude that Ofsted is in support of and will review:

a) A curriculum which demonstrated cultural awareness and respect for diversity, including pupils' heritage and that of others, preparing pupils for life in modern Britain.
b) A curriculum and teaching and learning opportunities demonstrating an understanding of protected characteristics. An active promotion of inclusion and tackling discrimination.
c) Parental consultation and policy formation on diversity policies have been created through consultation with parents and meaningful conversations.

We can also assume that Ofsted promotes a level of "decolonising the curriculum" through "understanding and appreciation of the wide range of cultural influences that have shaped their heritage and that of others".

However, what is apparent is that we are entirely lacking recognition of, or commitment to, reviewing and insisting on the "anti-racist" practices we have explored so far.

Regarding schools' commitment to developing and embedding anti-racist measures, for example, countering the challenges posed by the lack of ethnic minority ITTs completing their training and achieving QTS, Ofsted states that "discrimination at the application and recruitment stage is out of scope during our inspections". Therefore, they do not consider if or how schools are committed to developing anti-racist practices or if they are making any efforts to support ethnic minority teachers into teaching positions. **It is simply not a part of their inspection process.**

A call for action: Prioritising anti-racist practices in SEND schools

So, where is the motivation and incentive for any school in the country to lead anti-racist work in their schools? Why would they care?

Additionally, with the vast majority of headteachers, leaders and teachers being White and lacking the lived experiences of marginalised groups, there can be a disconnect in understanding the urgency of this work. It is not just another "task" to tick off; it is about changing the fabric of our schools and making them truly inclusive and equitable for all pupils. Without personal experience driving that understanding, this vital work is all too easy to be side-lined.

We must inspire educators to see the profound impact of integrating anti-racism into their schools, not as an obligation but as a moral imperative to ensure that every child, regardless of background, feels seen, valued and supported.

A 2023 report by the UK Parliament suggests that "Ofsted plays a crucial role in inspecting schools and ensuring that the quality of education remains high" as well as "93% of schools said they were satisfied with the way the inspection was carried out and 85% agreed that the benefits of inspection outweighed any negative aspects".

Therefore, according to parliament (and not those working in schools!), staff feel inspections are helpful. If this is the case, why is the DfE not using the persistent and concerning disparities in attainment data between ethnic groups, the shocking statistics of ethnic minority ITT applications, and their abysmal lack of career progression to create strategies, workforce planning and measures to improve the attainment of specific ethnic groups? Why is this triangulation of analysis and improvement not being applied by the DfE?

Why are they not reviewing the barriers these ethnic groups face and ensuring that schools are supported, encouraged, recognised and celebrated for their efforts and strategies to close the attainment gaps between these groups? For example, looking at strategies schools employ to engage with their "hard to reach" families?

It should also be considered that when we know that Black and Asian groups with an EHCP make the least progress at GCSE levels, why are schools not being assessed against this national data, reviewing whether the trends are mirrored in individual schools, whether leaders know these trends and have planned pro-actively in their School Improvement Plans and taken preventative measures to reduce disparity, providing every possible opportunity for success?

Additionally, when we are aware that those from Black Caribbean, Pakistani and Bangladeshi backgrounds persistently have the least favourable life outcomes, what measures are the DfE, Ofsted, Local Authorities, or Multi Academy Trusts taking in recognition and support to counter these barriers for these groups of pupils? Why aren't we taking proactive stances on the data? Why do we not see all of the above references in any of this data regarding their strategic aims? These issues are persistent, with no solutions presented anywhere.

Chapter summary

This chapter delves into the compounded barriers faced by ethnic minority pupils with SEND. By reflecting on systemic racism and the intersection of race and disability, it calls for schools to adopt anti-racist practices, improve representation and tailor life skills education to empower pupils from diverse backgrounds.

The chapter emphasises the importance of early, individualised preparation for adulthood plans, engaging parents and creating a curriculum that affirms racial identity while equipping pupils with the skills to overcome societal barriers. The need for diversity in school governance and leadership is also highlighted as a crucial component in fostering inclusive practices and policies.

 TIFFIN TAKE-AWAY

1. **Early and individualised preparation for adulthood**
   Schools must begin preparing pupils for adulthood from their earliest education stages. Tailoring life skills education to each pupil's abilities and aspirations and ensuring that lessons cover critical areas such as communication, independence and navigating public services is key. This preparation should be integrated into school policies and aligned with the Department for Education's SEND Code of Practice to ensure that pupils are ready to transition smoothly into adult life.

   - You could think about how your school can embed early preparation for adulthood into the curriculum, ensuring it is both personalised and aligned with the needs of pupils, e.g., promoting independence and communication.

2. **Affirming racial and cultural identity in the curriculum**
   Schools must affirm the racial and cultural identities of ethnic minority pupils with SEND through the curriculum. By integrating their cultural heritage and lived experiences, schools can foster a sense of belonging and counter feelings of exclusion or inferiority. Representation in teaching materials, stories and role models can help pupils develop pride in their identities and equip them with the resilience needed to face societal biases.

   - How can your school ensure that the curriculum and learning materials reflect the cultural heritage and lived experiences of pupils with SEND from diverse backgrounds?

3. **Creating equitable opportunities for post-school success**
    Schools must ensure that ethnic minority pupils with SEND have equitable access to post-school opportunities, including employment, higher education or community integration. This includes offering tailored career guidance, work experience placements and connections to community resources. Schools must also advocate for these pupils in broader societal contexts where biases may limit their chances of success.

    - What steps can your school take to ensure ethnic minority pupils with SEND have access to the same opportunities as their peers when transitioning into adulthood?

References

Akbar, S. (2019) "The experiences of minority ethnic heritage parents having a child with SEND: a systematic literature review". *British Journal of Special Education*, 46(3).

Haye, M. (2021) "Finding the racial minority voices in SEND". Special Needs Jungle. www.specialneedsjungle.com/finding-racial-minority-voices-send/

HM Government (2023) Special Educational Needs and Disabilities (SEND) and Alternative Provision (AP) Improvement Plan Right Support, Right Place, Right Time.

McKinsey Global Institute (2019) MGI in 2019. www.mckinsey.com/~/media/McKinsey/Featured%20Insights/Innovation/Ten%20highlights%20from%20our%202019%20research/MGI-in-2019-A-compendium-of-our-research-this-year-vF.ashx

Ofsted (2024) School Inspection Handbook. www.gov.uk/government/publications/school-inspection-handbook-eif/school-inspection-handbook-for-september-2023

DfE SEND code of practice: 1 to 25 (2014) www.gov.uk/government/publications/send-code-of-practice-0-to-25

Sewell Report (2021) "Commission on race and ethnic disparities: The report". https://assets.publishing.service.gov.uk/media/6062ddb1d3bf7f5ce1060aa4/20210331_-_CRED_Report_-_FINAL_-_Web_Accessible.pdf

The Key (2018) "Governor stories – Encouraging diversity on school governing boards". https://thekeysupport.com/blog/gov-stories-encouraging-diversity-on-school-governing-boards

Worth, J. McLean, D. and Sharp, C. (2022) "Racial equality in the teacher workforce: An analysis of representation and progression opportunities from initial teacher training to headship". National Foundation for Educational Research. Teach First: Ambition Institute.

14
Conclusion

As a British Asian (but not a Tory supporter), I felt a strange mix of pride and anxiety as Rishi Sunak lit the diva lamps outside Number 10 with his family for Diwali in November 2023. Pride as it felt like "look at us – we made it". The collective "we" did not exist because we had nothing in common except our skin colour. That was enough to briefly unite us at that moment. It was the familiar, comforting scene of a diva light, which was only ever shared publicly as part of "Today We're Learning about Diwali", but it was now playing out in front of the country.

It also filled me with anxiety.

"Oh no – what are you doing? Why are you drawing attention to us? Just blend in!" I also simultaneously thought to myself and said aloud.

An instinctive response to forewarn and prevent the inevitable "we don't want this f***ing p*ki!" comments, which, very publicly, but inevitably, did come later in the year and during the election.

Ethnic minority staff are leading initiatives in schools to promote diversity and inclusion in the school community, leading to their own increased feelings of isolation, stress, and compromised wellbeing. They have led these projects, asking for "allyship" and aiming to promote top-down support to help promote equity against a political backdrop and government leadership team that continued to demonstrate prolonged and sustained racist attacks on the country's ethnic minority population. I will refresh your memory and share a few:

- Regarding a meeting with Diane Abbott, Tory donor Frank Hester in early 2024 stated that "she made him want to hate all Black women" and that she "should be shot".
- Boris Johnson, in his article in *The Telegraph* (2018) regarding Muslim women's veils, stated, "It was absolutely ridiculous women chose to go around looking like letter-boxes", previously also making a comparison to "bank robbers". Following this, the country saw a "rise in hate crime against Muslims by 375%" (*The Independent*, 2019), with many attacks on Muslim women who wore niqabs or veils being called "letter-boxes" and "ninjas".

- Boris Johnson's title of his 2002 column, "Africa is a mess, but we can't blame colonialism", and "The problem is not that we were once in charge, but that we are not in charge any more".
- In 2008, Boris Johnson allowed a piece to be printed in *The Spectator*, which stated that "Orientals… have larger brains and higher IQ scores… Blacks are at the other pole".
- In a 2002 column in *The Telegraph*, Boris Johnson described Black people as "piccaninnies" with "watermelon smiles".

Yet, an independent panel investigating the comments decided that he was "respectful and tolerant" and entitled to "use satire" in his articles. The panel found that his language could be regarded as "provocative", but they could not censor language to emphasise viewpoints.

Additionally, there are other huge political scandals to consider, including Hostile Environments and the Windrush Scandal, which was "decades of immigration legislation explicitly aimed at reducing non-White immigration from the Commonwealth".

This is the backdrop, the national landscape, in which we strive for equity.

As we review the data demonstrating sustained intra- and inter-group inequalities from EYFS attainment to GCSEs, employment opportunities, socio-economic, housing and health disparities, we see a history of systemic and institutionalised racism that has led to these ongoing disparities. Educators must consider the work of researchers and writers such as Akala, who provide insights into how these came to be, how and why they are sustained and how people of colour can retain their personal sense of agency to make sustained and meaningful changes in their lives.

We lead anti-racist work in schools, usually led by ethnic minority staff, to champion equity and, in efforts to recognise and reduce these disparities, to be met with intense racism and hatred from our political leaders. We review the attainment data and employment data, to be told: "We no longer see a Britain where the system is deliberately rigged against ethnic minorities" (Sewell Report, 2021).

Our country's leaders demonstrate overtly racist statements, which directly cause a rise in racist incidents.

"Move out of the way, you f***ing p*ki!!!"

I manoeuvred my car into a gap, allowing the car driving towards me to pass. Our windows were both open, as it was a sunny summer morning. I was on my way to school, and my husband was on the passenger side. A lady in her mid-30s or 40s shouted this through the open windows as she drove past me. I reported her to the police. And the case went to court.

She was let off.

Because they felt the radio, which was faintly on in the car at the time, cast "reasonable doubt" as to whether we heard her correctly. She was also alone, and I had a witness. There was still doubt. The road was a quiet, side road and narrow, and the cars passed each other extremely closely. There was still doubt. As we left, I was told by someone in the court, "She can't have her life ruined and a conviction on her records over a comment like that – they gave her another chance".

I knew that would be the outcome.

But I was glad I spoke up and fought back. And they were right – the experience may have been enough of a fright for her to consider not repeating her behaviour.

First-generation immigrants experienced a great deal of racism, with increased racial tensions and faced overt violence, discrimination and extreme hostility. I grew up knowing that I would always need to have a fight in me because "that's just the way it is for ethnic minorities in the UK".

When I had children, I knew I would need to instil some semblance of the same "fight" in them, but I did not know to what extent. Had things changed? Are things changing?

I am a British Asian, born and grew up in West London, with a heavy London accent.

I was horrified, shocked and affected by the Summer Race riots of 2024. It felt like we had come full circle – the same fight, generation after generation.

I watched mobs of angry White men, women and, sadly, children displaying all ranges of anger, rage and verbal and physical racist behaviour on Twitter videos. Videos of mobs stopping and circling cars, pulling out brown-skinned drivers by their hair, spitting at brown-skinned women and children, barricading hotels and setting buildings alight, with people trapped inside, to young girls skipping down the road singing "p*kis go home! No p*kis allowed!" being cheered on by her mother. It was deeply upsetting.

I knew what to expect and braced myself. But I was not ready for my young children to be exposed to this, not at their young ages. I did not want to explain all of this to them. I stayed indoors for almost two weeks, eagerly looking at updates on where the next racist rally was due to be held. My children asking every morning with eager anticipation, "what are we doing today?!".

It felt like a frightening and lonely place to be. I was worried for families, friends, parents of children who attend the school and ethnic minorities around the country.

One day, I plucked up enough courage to venture out to Hobbycraft to buy a range of activities so we could go back home and stay inside until things were calmer. On the drive home, I nervously stopped at the red traffic lights.

A white van pulled up alongside me. "Oh, here we go", I thought.

I stopped myself from looking over. Until I did.

To be met with a young, White boy, no older than 12, wearing black-rimmed glasses and a mop of black hair, who looked like Harry Potter. Sitting in the passenger seat.

He smiled a beaming smile.

And gave me a thumbs up.

And I found an ally for a moment. I sighed with relief.

What followed was an extensive, rapid and effective response to the hate crimes by the Labour government and the police.

"Wednesday is the day – it's going to be a bad one, stay inside everyone" were the messages circling on social media and in family and friends' WhatsApp groups. When Wednesday came, we were all inside the safety of our homes. I turned on the TV for an update to see mass anti-racist marches across the country.

There was an outpouring of solidarity, of allyship. And I felt a flood of relief and comfort wash over me.

It was beyond moving. It was a collective hug that said, "We've got you, don't worry".

I thought back to Blair Peach, who was exceptionally brave to be one of a much smaller group of protesters at the time. Who lost his life through demonstrating allyship with our community over 44 years ago. And I realised that, while we have some way to go, a lot has changed for the better in this time that has passed in between both events.

When I shared this story with White friends or colleagues, I was amazed by the lack of awareness or understanding of how wider ethnic minority communities, including me, would have been affected by the Summer Riots.

"Yeah, but you're not a migrant in a hotel!"

"You're fine, you speak just like a Londoner."

"They weren't targeting YOU though", or "I didn't even consider YOU would have felt like that, as they're not after YOU …"

No. I am not a migrant. But I am brown. And being "non-White" makes me a visible "other." This makes me, and my family and friends, targets.

So, the overt fight is not over.

And we know neither is the covert fight.

What does the published data of ethnic minority teacher training applicants tell us? Data illustrating the limited career progression of ethnic minority teachers, the attainment data of some ethnic minority community groups and the ongoing experiences of the ethnic minority parents of children with SEND tell us?

Racism and biases are still very much entrenched here, too.

This book is written through the lens of working with children and young people with SEND, with mild to severe learning disabilities across a range of settings, from early identification to school leavers at 16. The content of the book can also be applied to the intersection of ethnic minorities and "specific learning difficulties", which can often be "masked" in schools as pupils tend to struggle through their mainstream schooling; their experiences of their needs not being understood by their communities are very much congruent with the overall negative perception of SEND by ethnic minority communities:

> Mum told me from the start that she did not accept that I'm dyslexic – my culture didn't believe such a condition existed; they just believed you must study and work twice or three times as hard to catch up or to be better than your peers. There was a taboo in having a disability, even a 'hidden' one, and in Ghana, physically disabled people were shut away. They were always hidden, not integrated.
> (Brissett-Bailey, 2023)

The book also focuses on the experiences of recently arrived, working-class, ethnic minority parents and families who may be first-generation, living in densely populated areas, often in areas of deprivation. These were also my grandparents. Therefore, the experiences may be similar in that it is difficult to assimilate; they may live and socialise with ethnically separate groups to help and support one another. They may spend a great deal of time working and trying to survive while navigating a new culture with new systems.

There is debate over what constitutes second- or third-generation immigrants, as the lines are blurred. My husband, whose parents arrived in the UK from India in the 1970s, were in their 30s, and my husband was born in the UK; he is a second-generation immigrant. However, my parents immigrated to the UK in the 1960s when they were 1 and 9 years old, with their parents. They went to school in the UK and (attempted to) assimilate into UK culture; they were fluently bilingual and had less to do with their home countries than their parents.

After arriving in the UK, my dad did not return to India for a holiday until he was in his 40s. They are regarded as "1.5 generation immigrants". As my mother arrived in the UK at 1 year old, she will have had an experience closer to second-generation immigrants. I would then be regarded as a "second-generation immigrant".

> Second generation are often bilingual… through schooling, better language skills, more opportunities and higher levels of interaction with other British-born people… they pick up the same habit and beliefs… yet they are still heavily influenced by their parent's homeland and traditional values… Third-generation migrants are increasingly moving away from inner city London communities to more affluent suburbs… and are more driven by rising affluence and aspirations have better employment prospects, a choice of better schools… it is easier for the third generation of migrants to emerge as dynamic young professionals and… ambitious wealth creators
>
> (Gooden-Jones, 2024).

Aside from the case study on Jay, I have also not focused on the experiences of second- or third-generation responses to SEND and diagnosis of SEND. Through education and better-paid jobs, thus better socio-economic standing, these generations also tend to enter the middle-class categories. Middle-class parents often have the financial resources, language skills and contacts or have accessed some level of signposting to advocate for their child's needs effectively. Some are also more likely to invest in private tutoring, independent therapist reviews, extracurricular activities and interventions to enhance their child's learning experiences and "potential". They tend to display a better understanding of their child's diagnosis.

I write as a female, British-born, second-generation+ immigrant, headteacher. I write of four generations of experiences in the UK, of my grandparents, parents, my own and those of my 7-year-old and 5-year-old daughters – in the hope that there is a substantial and positive change.

I write to advocate for those most in need.

Research suggests that British-born ethnic minorities may distance themselves from new immigrants to align with the dominant culture and gain social acceptance. This can result in a reluctance to engage with or support new immigrants. Hatton (2004) suggests that some South Asian parents have identified these issues: "Sometimes I have spoken to Asian staff and doctors, and they have not spoken to me in Punjabi, even though they can see that I find it a problem to speak English. I cannot explain myself deeply in English… Even now, I feel angry at the Asian doctors as they have been very arrogant with me" and "I have problems with the Asian staff at the children's hospital. The doctor seemed to think very highly of herself and was very arrogant towards me. I have found Asians to be more arrogant and English staff to be more humble".

A term used to explain this behaviour is "pulling the ladder up", meaning "making it difficult for others like you to follow in your footsteps and achieve similar career or social success". Humza Yousaf, in The Times (2024), used this term to respond to the statement made by Suella Braverman that "Multiculturalism makes no demands of the incomer to integrate. It has failed because it allowed people to come to our society and live parallel lives. They could be in society but not of society. And, in extreme cases, they could pursue lives aimed at undermining the stability and threatening the security of society." In response, Yousef (2024) argued that "Too many Tory MPs of colour are happy 'to pull the ladder up' behind them and not help other ethnic minorities now they have been successful themselves".

I made it as a headteacher, and that has given me a platform to continue advocating for those in need, whether that is race, disability or any other barrier that limits one's potential to flourish. It has allowed me the opportunity to both apply what I know and seek out what I don't know to try to make a difference. It has enabled me to have the opportunity to not "pull the ladder up" others but look for ways to educate, inform and support families to better understand and support their children. I am also interested in reviewing ways in which second- and third-generation immigrants can support wider ethnic minority communities in promoting awareness, recognition and education of SEND.

As we conclude this exploration of SEND, disability and race in education, it is evident that a truly "anti-racist curriculum" moves beyond the "food and festivals" approaches to embrace a deep, meaningful commitment to embedding anti-racist practices throughout every aspect of school life, from governors, staff, pupils, curriculum and the wider community, including the political landscape.

The journey demands courage and self-reflection. A commitment to confront uncomfortable truths about our society, our education systems and our own biases. It requires us to actively dismantle the structures of institutional racism that have persisted for generations to challenge practices. We must look for alternatives, hold people and systems to account for stereotypes and create spaces where all our pupils, families and staff, regardless of their race, disability or background, can see themselves being represented and thrive.

Courage demands putting these topics on the table to discuss.

The path forwards involves continuous learning, open dialogue and a commitment to amplifying diverse voices and experiences. It means critically examining our curriculum, policies and practices to ensure they promote equity and inclusion. It requires us to actively seek out and value the perspectives of ethnic minority pupils, families and educators and to create genuine partnerships that inform and shape our educational approaches. It also requires us to feel confident to support but challenge ethnic minority parents' and families' ideas and interpretations of disability, providing education, proactive strategies and support accepting their child's disability – instead, instilling hope and developing an understanding of the potential of their child.

We have the power and responsibility to be agents of change. By embedding anti-racist practices into the very fabric of our schools, we can create lasting change which goes far beyond our classrooms.

References

Brissett-Bailey, Marcia (2023) *Black, brilliant and dyslexic: Neurodivergent heroes tell their stories.* Jessica Kingsley Publishers.

Gooden-Jones, M. (2024) "Third-generation diaspora: to be or not to be". *The Prisma - The multicultural newspaper.* https://theprisma.co.uk/2024/04/15/third-generation-diaspora-to-be-or-not-to-be/

Hatton, C., Akram, Y., Shah, R., Robertson, J. and Emerson, E. (2004) *Supporting South Asian families with a child with severe learning disabilities.* Jessica Kingsley Publishers.

The Independent (2019) "Islamophobic incidents rose 375% after Boris Johnson compared Muslim women to 'letterboxes', figures show". www.independent.co.uk/news/uk/home-news/boris-johnson-muslim-women-letterboxes-burqa-islamphobia-rise-a9088476.html

The Spectator (2016) "The Boris archive: Africa is a mess, but we can't blame colonialism". www.spectator.co.uk/article/the-boris-archive-africa-is-a-mess-but-we-can-t-blame-colonialism/

INDEX

Note: *Italic* page numbers refer to figures.

Abbott, D. 201
Abley, J. et al. 174, 181–2
accountability 43, 49–50, 195
admin and office staff 54–5
advocacy role 72–6, 155
Afghanistan 65
age *see* generational divide; life stages and intergenerational activities
Akbar, S. 7, 8, 11, 191
Akinde, F. 11
Allen, T. et al. 42
allyship: call for 100–1; creating 105–8
anti-racist framework: four pillars 29–33, *34*, 84–5, *114*
anti-racist practice 31–3
art 96; installation (McQueen) 28; project (Windrush Day) 91
Asian cultures 14–16; *see also* South Asian cultures
assemblies, cultural 120
assessment *see* identification, assessment and diagnosis
audits: curriculum 125–8; parent and community collaboration 184; Race Disparity Audit/Report 168, 173, 175; self-auditing 106
autism: Asian community under-representation 70; "curing" 15–16; National Autistic Society 11, 32, 64

Bangladeshi and Pakistani groups 16–17, 172–5, 181–2
Banks, J. 88–90, 93, 118, 136
beliefs *see* religion, and belief systems
belonging: identity and 118, 133, 137; sense of 45–6
Benjamin, F. 123–5
Bhopal, K.: and Myers, M. 122; and Pitkin, C. 102, 104, 106
bias: against Black Caribbean pupils 69, 72; implicit and explicit 93, 106; limiting potential 168–9; mandatory training 156; racial and gender 151; recognising and addressing disparity 54; self-auditing 106; unconscious 84, 101–2, 142
Black Africans and Black Caribbeans 169–70, 172

Black boys/young men 168–9; *see also* criminal justice system; police and racial injustice
Black children: cultural heritage and lack of cultural representation 119; educational attainment and employment/unemployment 175; educational attainment and intra-/inter-group differences 170–4; multicultural *vs* anti-racist education 145; and parents 69–70, 182; Social, Emotional and Mental Health (SEMH) needs 31–2, 54, 69, 72
Black History 28–9, 82; "Coming to England" (Benjamin) 123–5
Black History Month 28–9, 32
Black History University of Portsmouth 129
Black Lives Matter (BLM) 27–8, 46, 81–2, 96, 122
blame and past life beliefs 63, 64
blind applications 157
Braverman, S. 207
Brissett-Bailey, M. 205
British colonialism 5, 27, 82, 115
British Educational Research Association (BERA) 32, 42–3
Bronfenbrenner, U. 7, 8, 18–19, 89, 195

Cameron, D. 157
career development skills 177–8
career progression: limited 153–5; pathways 157–8
Chaggar, Gurdip Singh 26
Children's Commissioner 10
class *see* socioeconomic status
clothing, cultural 121
coaching 5; decolonising the curriculum 29, 122; job/work 175
Coard, B. 31, 69, 119, 182
Cockburn, L. 61–2
Cole, A. and Burke, C. 10–11
collaboration *see* community partnerships/collaboration; parent/family partnerships/collaboration
collaborative arts projects 121
collaborative planning 58–9
collective role of staff 53–4

colonialism: British 5, 27, 82, 115; *see also* decolonising the curriculum

communication with parents 47, 131-2; case study 71-2; *see also* language; *entries beginning* home-school

communication skills: social interaction and 179-80; verbal and nonverbal skills 183

community: breaking bias and embracing anti-racist curriculum 83-4; connections and real-world learning 89-92; injustice and legacy of resistance 81; invisible histories: exclusion of ethnic minority narratives 82-3; as mesosystem 12-14; roots of Black Lives Matter (BLM) 81-2; school improvement plans 55; *see also* parents and communities

community partnerships/collaboration 89, 120, 122, 184; *see also* stakeholders/community collaboration (preparing for life beyond school)

community support networks 75, 88, 92

conferences, networks and education festivals (case study) 94

contextual learning 117-18

conversations *vs* silence 55-8

Cooke, T. et al. 25

COVID-19 pandemic 24-5, 27, 36

CPD 36, 42, 50, 55, 84, 96, 192; decolonising the curriculum 122; governors 87, 192; *see also* professional development

creative expression 96

Crenshaw, K. 41, 74

criminal justice system: racial profiling 169, 182-3; *see also* police and racial injustice

"crisis management capabilities" 155

critical approach 146-7

Critical Race Theory 84

critical thinking and empathy 89

cultural calendar: authentic cultural representation 137; creating 137-8; and cultural connections 136; enriching educational experience through diversity 143; evaluating and updating 138; family involvement 139-40; "food and festivals" trap, avoiding 141-3; fostering inclusivity 136-7; implementing 139; promoting 138; technology, use of 140; White areas 140-1, 142-3

cultural competence 47; and cultural responsibility 84; developing 72-3; home-school liaison worker (case study) 48-9; in practice 69-72; role of cultural calendar 136-7; staff training 54-5, 92-3; training beyond classroom 54-5

cultural disconnect: White-dominated profession 153-4

cultural perceptions of disabilities 62-6, 70; generational divide 66-9

cultural representation *see* multicultural representation; representation

cultural tokens *see* tokenism

curriculum audits 125-8

curriculum resources 130

CV building and interview skills 179

decision-making: governors 85-6, 191; parents/families 74, 75; pupil 95; school vision and mission statement 41-2

decolonising the curriculum 31, 122-5; review 36; superficial gestures *vs* meaningful change 28-9; training and coaching 29

Demie, F. 152, 170, 172, 182; and McLean, C. 182

Department of Education (DfE) 28, 66, 120, 196; "Careers guidance in specialist settings" 178; ethnic minority teachers, leaders and governors 158, 191-2; SEND code of practice 190; statistics/data 32, 174, 176, 198

Department for Work and Pensions 175

diagnosis *see* identification, assessment and diagnosis

DiAngelo, R. 45, 46, 100, 101, 103

disabilities *see* cultural perceptions of disabilities

disability awareness and inclusion 161-2

distributed leadership models 156

diverse learning needs 93

diverse perspectives 119

diverse world, preparing pupils for 85

diversity group (case study) 56-8

Diwali: at Number 10 201; Indian families and problem of generalisation 113

domestic chores 186

dual burden: leading and advocating for change 155

dual stigma/"dual marginalization" 13-14, 72

Duggan, Mark, police killing of 81

ecological model, levels of influence on SEND development 7, 8, 18-19, 89, 195

Eddo-Lodge, R. 44

Education Health Care Plans (EHCP) 9-10, 12, 196, 198

educational attainment 170-4

educational inequality 168-9

embodied cognition 117-18

empathy, developing 93, 95, 141

employment inequality 174–6; *see also* labour market discrimination; socioeconomic status
empowerment: parents 72–6; pupils 94–6, 183–5; staff 149
Equality, Diversity and Inclusion (DEI), role of governor 49–50
Equality Act: nine protected characteristics 161–5; embedding in school policies 165; training, language and participation for inclusive school culture 165
equity: pupils 85; staff recruitment and retention 156
ethnic minority staff *see* allyship; leadership; recruitment and retention; staff; training; *entries beginning* White
exclusion 31, 32; of ethnic minority narratives 82–3
exosystem, professionals as 8–12

family, as microsystem 16–18; *see also* parent/family partnerships/collaboration; parents and communities
family liaison worker 179–80; case study 48–9
far-right politics 27; National Front 12, 81, 100
feedback: from families and members 132, 133; from leadership interviews 4, 151; from parents 88–9, 132
festivals 120–2, 164; education (case study) 94; *see also* cultural calendar; "food and festivals" trap, avoiding
Fitzgibbons, S. 12
Floyd, George, police murder of 25–6, 27, 81, 196
focus groups 88, 132
food: cooking classes 121; cultural differences 131; healthy eating 186; positive emotions and memories 119
"food and festivals" trap, avoiding 141–3
formal curriculum/learning pathways 115, 147, 149, 163, 164, 183
Franklin, A. 154
"functional skills" 115
funding: further education 158; Trust/local authority (LA) areas 193

gatekeepers of change 40
gender identity and sexual orientation 162–3
gender and racial bias, leadership recruitment 151
generational divide, perceptions of disabilities 66–9
girls/women with disabilities, South Asian cultures 66

"glass cliff phenomenon" 155
global school links 121
Gooden-Jones, M. 206
Google Translate 132
governors/governance: and accountability 49–50; diversity 191–3; and headteachers: leadership gap 191–3; National Governance Association 41–2, 49, 191; roles 49–50, 85–6; training/CPD 86–7, 192
guest speakers 120

"hard to reach" families 9, 49–50
Hatton, C. 63, 64, 66, 70, 119–20, 136, 206; et al. 15, 17, 174
Haye, M. 196
headteachers: appraisal targets 195; racial disparity 35–6, 44; *see also* leadership
healers/traditional medicine 65–6
health disparities 169–70
healthcare 185; exercise and diet 186
Hechinger Report 32, 47
higher education, Black African and Caribbean progression 172
hiring panels, diverse 156
home-school connection: neuroscience of skills transfer 116–17
home-school learning 132–3
home-school liaison worker (case study) 48–9
home-school values 87
Hope Not Hate (State of Hate) report 27, 35
housing 16–17

identification, assessment and diagnosis 9–12; racial bias and misdiagnosis 31–3, 54, 69–70, 72, 182; reluctance to seek 70–1
identity and belonging 118, 133, 137
"immigrant paradox" 173
immigrants, first-, second- and third-generation 205–6
"Inclusive Britain" strategy 28–9
inclusive environment 18–20, 107, 158; curriculum audits 125–8; curriculum design-mirrors and windows 118–19, 128–9; curriculum resources 130; *see also* school culture
Indian families and problem of generalisation 113
Indian physically disabled male (Jay) (case study) 67–8, 187
Ingstad, B. and White, S. 62, 65
Institute of Race Relations 17
institutional/structural/systemic racism 147; Black Lives Matter (BLM) movement

81-2; denial of 46; police 26-7; and White privilege 44; and White-dominated profession 153-4
international days 119, 121
"international evenings" 88
intersectional post-school life 167-8; career development skills 177-8; challenges 180; CV building and interview skills 179; educational attainment 170-4; educational inequality 168-9; employment inequality 174-6; empowerment through curriculum 183-5; healthcare 185; identifying and navigating discrimination 182-3; job readiness 178-9; life skills and independence 185-7; parent partnerships 181-2, 184; role of schools 176-7; social interaction and communication skills 179-80
intersectionality 40-1, 54, 66, 69, 74
interview skills 179
"invisibility syndrome" 154
invisible histories 82-3
isolation: ethnic minority leaders/teachers 104, 154; parents 63, 64, 68-9; to advocacy 72-6

job readiness 178-9
job/work coaches 175
Johnson, B. 201-2
Joseph Rowntree Foundation 16

Kalyanwala, S. et al. 66
karma beliefs 63, 64

labour market discrimination 168
Ladson-Billings, F. 72, 82, 86, 88, 95, 102, 108, 120
language: Google Translate 132; inclusive school culture 165; native 119, 120; parents/families 9-11, 70, 71, 174, 181, 196; support networks 88; translation services 76, 193
Lawrence, Stephen, murder of 26
leadership: and career progression struggles of ethnic minority teachers 4-7; for change 18-20, 35-7; ensuring purposeful work 40-50; gap: headteachers and governors 191-3; political 201-2, 207; pupil 95; shared 105-8; toxic 3-4; see also recruitment and retention; White fragility; White privilege
learning vs physical disabilities, perceptions across cultures 65
legal rights 183-4

libraries 120
life skills and independence 185-7
life stages and intergenerational activities 163-4
Lindsay, S. and Edwards, A. 68, 162
local authorities 196
local businesses 90
local sites, culturally significant 120
London Borough of Ealing 192, 193

McHayle, Z. et al. 32-3
McKinsey Report 191
Macpherson Report 26
McQueen, Steve: art installation 28
macrosystem, beliefs, values and religion as 14-16
Malik, N. 18
marriage and civil partnerships 164
MATs see Multi Academy Trust (MATs)
medical and social models of disability 62
Medium Term Planning 43, 195
mental health 168-70; parents 32-3, 64, 174
mentorship: support networks and career pathways 156, 157; see also coaching
mesosystem, community as 12-14
microsystem, family as 16-18
Miller, P. 7, 103, 152, 155; and Lashley, R. 4, 37
Mir, G. 10; et al. 17
mirrors and windows, inclusive curriculum 118-19, 128-9
Mirza, H. 151, 172
misconceptions about disabilities 63-4, 71
mission and values, alignment of 41-2
mistrust of professionals 70, 71
Moncrieffe, M. 29, 129
monitoring and evaluation of recruitment, retention and promotion 158
Multi Academy Trust (MATs) 193; case study 194
multicultural education provision 29-30
multicultural events 88
multicultural experiences vs anti-racist practice 145; beyond celebrations 147; combining 148-9; comparison 148; framework of anti-racist practice 146-7; legacy of multicultural education 145-6; professional development 149
multicultural representation: curriculum audits 125-8; curriculum resources 130; decolonising the curriculum 122-5; families and communities, engaging in curriculum development 130-3; neuroscience perspective 113-22; problem of generalisation 113

multiculturalism and surface solutions, limits of 55
multisensory teaching and learning 115-16, 117, 119, 121, 148-9; "Coming to England" (Benjamin) 123-5; religion and belief systems 163
music: art, drama and 96; curriculum 121; and dance workshops 120; positive emotions and memories 119

National Autistic Society 11, 32, 64
National Front 12, 81, 100
National Governance Association 41-2, 49, 191
National Housing Federation 16
neuroscience perspective 113-22

office and admin staff 54-5
Ofsted 50, 55, 180, 191; role of 197, 198
O'Hara, J. 15, 16, 74
older people's homes 164
ostracism by community 64
outreach services/programmes 75, 122

Pakistani and Bangladeshi groups 16-17, 172-5, 181-2
parent-teacher meetings 88
parent/family partnerships/collaboration 131-2; cultural calendar 139-40; and power 87-9; preparation for intersectional post-schooling life 181-2, 184; sex, gender identity and sexual orientation 162; stay-and-play sessions 119-20
parents see communication with parents; language; socioeconomic status; entries beginning home-school
parents and communities: audits 184; cultural competence in practice 69-72; empowering: from isolation to advocacy 72-6; engaging in curriculum development 130-3; mental health issues 32-3; multicultural representation 122; paradox of engagement 61; roots, branches, and representation 61-2; see also cultural perceptions of disabilities
Parks, Rosa 96
past life beliefs 63, 64
Peach, Blair, police killing of 99, 100, 204
peer discussion groups 106
peer learning and support 94
"Personal Development" curriculum (PSED) 178, 185-7
physical disabilities: Indian male (Jay) (case study) 67-8, 187; vs learning disabilities, perceptions across cultures 65

physical environment 117-18
physical exercise 186
physical and sexual abuse 66
police and racial injustice 25-7; and disability injustice 32, 168-9; murders 25-6, 27, 81, 99, 100; school invitations 184; stop and search rates 32, 169
political influence 195
political leaders 201-2, 207
positive sense of identity 187
post-school life see intersectional post-school life; stakeholders/community collaboration (preparing for life beyond school)
poverty see socioeconomic status
Powell, A. 175
"pre-formal curriculum" 115-16, 123-5
pregnancy and maternity 164
professional development 107-8, 149; tailored 157; training and 43-4, 44-5, 46; see also CPD
professionals: culturally competent services 75; as exosystem 8-12; mistrust of 70, 71

Race Disparity Audit/Report 168, 175
race riots 12, 13, 81-3, 203-5
racial bias see bias
racial injustice see police and racial injustice
racial profiling, criminal justice system 169, 182-3
racism: silence in SEND policy 196-7; see also institutional/structural/systemic racism
reading groups 106
recruitment and retention: diverse educational future 158-9; dual burden: leading and advocating for change 155; limited career growth 155; racial and gender bias 151; representation and challenges 151-2; responsibilities of governors 192; solutions for equity: overcoming barriers 156; strategies for enhancing 156-8; in White-dominated profession 153-4
reflective journals 106
religion: and belief systems 14-16, 62-6, 163; Muslim 174, 201; race and social class 173
religious festivals 121-2; see also Diwali
repetition and reinforcement 116, 117
representation: benefits of 73-4, 75; families 61-2; increasing 30, 123; recruitment and retention 151-2; under-representation 82, 84, 90, 119; see also multicultural representation

resistance: legacy of 81; to complacency 24
role models 121
Runnymede Trust 102

Scarman Report 27
scholarships 158
school boards 191; see also governors/governance
school culture 85, 100-1, 158, 165
school ethos 41, 42, 87, 95
school improvement plans 42-3, 50, 55, 195
school open days 122
school-community events/projects 90-1, 92
school-community relationship 102
school-family-community partnerships 139
self-auditing 106
"semi-formal curriculum" 115, 123-5, 164
sensory experiences see multisensory teaching and learning
Sewell Report 196, 202
sex, gender identity and sexual orientation 162-3
sexual and physical abuse 66
Shakespeare, T. 161
shame 63-5, 70
shared leadership strategies 105-8
Sharp, C. and Aston, K. 6-7
silence: on racism in SEND policy 196-7; stigma, superstition, and 62-3; toxic leadership and complicity 3-4; vs conversations 55-8
Sims, P. 32
Slade, G. 11
Social, Emotional and Mental Health (SEMH) needs 31-2, 54, 69, 72
social and emotional development (PSED) 178, 185-7
social interaction and communication skills 179-80
social media 30, 83, 90, 138, 140
social and medical models of disability 62
socioeconomic status 16-17, 40-1, 69, 168; Black Caribbean pupils 69, 182; inter-group differences 172-4; perceptions of disability 66; staff 104-5
Somalia 65-6
South Asian cultures 62-3, 65, 66, 69, 70, 168; beliefs about disability 15, 16; see also specific nationalities
Southall 99-100, 103
Southall Youth Movement 5, 13, 81
Sports England 186
staff: collaborative planning 58-9; collective role of 53-4; support networks 94, 156, 157; see also allyship; leadership; recruitment and retention; training; entries beginning White
stakeholders/community collaboration (preparing for life beyond school) 190; accountability: target and plans 195; early school life 190-1; local authorities 196; MATs (Multi Academy Trust) 193-4; Ofsted role 197, 198; political influence 195; prioritising anti-racist practices 198-9; silence on racism in SEND policy 196-7; see also governors/governance
stay-and-play sessions 119-20
STEM educational resources 90
stereotypes vs authentic cultural representation 137
stigma of disability 62-3, 70
stop and search rates 32, 169
Strand 172-3
Strand, S.: and Lindorff, A. 70, 72, 73; and Lindsay, G. 54, 69
"street smart ability" 183
structural racism see institutional/structural/systemic racism
Sunak, R. 201
support: parent/families 9, 19, 73, 75, 76; peer 94
support networks: community 75, 88, 92; staff 94, 156, 157
support staff roles 53
systemic racism see institutional/structural/systemic racism

taboos, cultural 63
targeted recruitment initiatives 157
targets and plans, accountability 195
teachers see allyship; leadership; recruitment and retention; staff; training; entries beginning White
technology: alternative formats/assistive 130, 177-8; careers 90; multisensory learning 119; school apps 131; see also social media
terminology 20
tokenism 74, 104; vs transformation 33, 40
toxic leadership 3-4
traditional healing/medicine 65-6
training (including workshops/interactive sessions): anti-racist themes 84-5; community 91, 102; cultural competence 54-5, 92-3; governors 86-7, 192; implicit and explicit bias 93, 106; inclusive school culture 165; parents 87-9, 131-2; and professional development 43-4, 44-5, 46; pupils 95;

self and others 105-6; *see also* coaching; CPD; mentorship
travel training and safety in community 186-7
Troyna, B. 30, 118, 141-2, 145-7
Turnbull, A. et al. 132

UK Parliament report (2023) 198
unconscious bias 84, 101-2, 142

values: home-school 87; and mission, alignment of 41-2; "values-based" responses 83; *see also* religion, and belief systems

Wheeler, R. et al. 182-3
White areas, cultural events in 140-1, 142-3
White fragility 45-6, 100-5
White privilege 44-5
White-dominated profession 153-4; *see also* allyship
whole school community, benefits for 73-4
Wilson, M. 117-18
Windrush Day art project (case study) 91
Worth, J. et al. 6, 7, 191

Yousaf, H. 207
Youth Offending Services 182-3

For Product Safety Concerns and Information please contact our EU representative GPSR@taylorandfrancis.com
Taylor & Francis Verlag GmbH, Kaufingerstraße 24, 80331 München, Germany

www.ingramcontent.com/pod-product-compliance
Lightning Source LLC
Chambersburg PA
CBHW082059230426
43670CB00017B/2897